Patronage at Work

In countries around the world, politicians distribute patronage jobs to supporters in exchange for a wide range of political services – such as helping with campaigns and electoral mobilization. Patronage employees (clients) engage in these political activities that support politicians (patrons) because their fates are tied to the political fate of their patrons. Although conventional wisdom holds that control of patronage significantly increases an incumbent's chance of staying in power, we actually know very little about how patronage works. Drawing on in-depth interviews, survey data, and survey experiments in Argentina, Virginia Oliveros details the specific mechanisms that explain the effect of patronage on political competition. This fascinating study is the first to provide a systematic analysis of the political activities of mid- and low-level public employees in Latin America. It provides a novel explanation of the enforcement of patronage contracts that has wider implications for understanding the functioning of clientelist exchanges.

Virginia Oliveros is Associate Professor of Political Science at Tulane University. She co-edited (with Noam Lupu and Luis Schiumerini) *Campaigns and Voters in Developing Democracies* (2019). Her research has appeared in *American Journal of Political Science*, *Comparative Political Studies*, and *Comparative Politics*.

Patronage at Work

Public Jobs and Political Services in Argentina

VIRGINIA OLIVEROS
Tulane University

CAMBRIDGE
UNIVERSITY PRESS

CAMBRIDGE
UNIVERSITY PRESS

Shaftesbury Road, Cambridge CB2 8EA, United Kingdom

One Liberty Plaza, 20th Floor, New York, NY 10006, USA

477 Williamstown Road, Port Melbourne, VIC 3207, Australia

314–321, 3rd Floor, Plot 3, Splendor Forum, Jasola District Centre, New Delhi – 110025, India

103 Penang Road, #05–06/07, Visioncrest Commercial, Singapore 238467

Cambridge University Press is part of Cambridge University Press & Assessment, a department of the University of Cambridge.

We share the University's mission to contribute to society through the pursuit of education, learning and research at the highest international levels of excellence.

www.cambridge.org
Information on this title: www.cambridge.org/9781009077354

DOI: 10.1017/9781009082525

First published 2021
First paperback edition 2023

A catalogue record for this publication is available from the British Library

Library of Congress Cataloging-in-Publication data
NAMES: Oliveros, Virginia, 1976– author.
TITLE: Patronage at work : public jobs and political services in Argentina / Virginia Oliveros.
DESCRIPTION: Cambridge, United Kingdom ; New York, NY : Cambridge University Press, 2021. | Includes bibliographical references and index.
IDENTIFIERS: LCCN 2021034122 (print) | LCCN 2021034123 (ebook) | ISBN 9781316514085 (hardback) | ISBN 9781009077354 (paperback) | ISBN 9781009082525 (ebook)
SUBJECTS: LCSH: Patronage, Political – Argentina. | Political culture – Argentina. | BISAC: POLITICAL SCIENCE / American Government / General
CLASSIFICATION: LCC JL2081 .O44 2021 (print) | LCC JL2081 (ebook) | DDC 306.20982–dc23
LC record available at https://lccn.loc.gov/2021034122
LC ebook record available at https://lccn.loc.gov/2021034123

ISBN   978-1-316-51408-5   Hardback
ISBN   978-1-009-07735-4   Paperback

To my parents

Contents

Tables

Figures

Acknowledgments

This book started as my dissertation project at Columbia University and has been almost ten years in the making, so the list of people and institutions to thank is long. At Columbia, the support of my dissertation committee was vital. Vicky Murillo, Isabela Mares, and Tim Frye made up a "dream team" of advisors who offered invaluable feedback and encouragement over the years. Vicky, the chair of the committee, was the best advisor one could ask for. She provided the perfect combination of high standards, constructive feedback, support, and sense of humor. Robert Kaufman and Ernesto Calvo generously served as external readers, and their suggestions during (and after) the dissertation defense were crucial in turning the dissertation into a book. Both Ernesto and Vicky have become friends over the years and have been continuous sources of support on this and other projects.

At various points during my years at Columbia, I also benefited from crucial advice and feedback from Andy Gelman, Lucy Goodhart, Shigeo Hirano, John Huber, Macartan Humphreys, Kimuli Kasara, Jeffrey Lax, Yotam Margalit, and, especially, from Pablo Pinto. I was fortunate to have an extremely smart, supportive, and friendly group of colleagues and friends at Columbia who made my years in graduate school both interesting and a lot of fun. I am in enormous debt to Narayani Lasala, María Paula Saffon, Milan Vaishnav, and especially Kelly Rader – all of whom have provided insightful comments about this project, support, and friendship throughout these years. Thanks are also due to Martín Ardañaz, Kate Baldwin, Guy Grossman, Kate Krimmel, Pierce O'Reilly, Laura Paler, Cyrus Samii, Thania Sanchez, Alex Scacco, Neelanjan Sircar, David Stevens, Pavi Suryanarayan, Rebecca Weitz-Shapiro, Peter Van der Windt, and Matt Winters.

In Argentina, many people contributed to making the fieldwork for this project both feasible and enjoyable. First and foremost, I want to thank all the public employees, political brokers, and politicians who generously gave me their time. Some were particularly essential to this project since they helped me to get mayoral permissions to conduct my research. They are not mentioned by name to preserve their anonymity, but I am tremendously grateful for their generosity. Miguel De Luca, María Soledad Delgado, and Gerardo Scherlis were also crucial to making this research possible. Anastasia Peralta Ramos, Ignacio Cesar, Ignacio Puente, and Nicolás Schujman (in Tigre); Leilen Lua Bouchet, Nahuel Avalos Theules, Alejandro Núñez Avendaño, and Leonardo Pez (in Santa Fe); and Sofía Checa, Marcela Godoy, Mariana Godoy, Mariana Macazaga, Gonzalo Rodríguez, and Ludovica Pian (in Salta) were fantastic research assistants. I am forever thankful for their excellent work, enthusiasm, and sense of humor along the way.

The field research for this project was made possible by the financial support that I received from various organizations and departments at Columbia University: the Center for International Business Education and Research, the Center for the Study of Development Strategies, the Institute of Latin American Studies (ILAS), the Department of Political Science, and the Graduate School of Arts and Science. A grant from Tulane University's School of Liberal Arts helped to cover costs associated with publication. The support of the Louisiana Board of Regents through the Board of Regents Support Fund (LEQSF(2016-17)-RD-ATL-08) allowed me to extend my third-year semester leave to an entire year and devote more time to writing.

Although this project started while in graduate school, I would have never made it that far without my years in the Political Science Department at Universidad de Buenos Aires. Those years were crucial in developing my understanding of politics as well as my interest in research. I would like to thank my colleagues and friends there for all the hours of endless conversations about politics, and Miguel De Luca and María Inés Tula in particular for introducing me to the (confusing but fascinating) world of empirical research.

The Political Science Department at Tulane University has provided a stimulating environment in which to complete this project. I was extremely fortunate to have many of my generous colleagues reading parts of this manuscript and providing detailed feedback. In particular, I would like to thank Geoffrey Dancy, Martin Dimitrov, Patrick Egan, Chris Fettweis, Mirya Holman, Christina Kiel, Celeste Lay, Casey Love, and Menaka Philips. I also want to thank Sally Kenney, Nora Lustig, Eduardo Silva, and David Smilde for their support and encouragement way beyond this project. As a Latin Americanist at Tulane, I have the pleasure and privilege of being part of both the Stone Center for Latin American Studies and the Center for Inter-American Policy and Research (CIPR). I want to especially thank Tom Reese, the director of the Stone Center, and Ludovico Feoli, the director of CIPR, for providing invaluable support during my years at Tulane. Ludovico also generously helped to organize a book conference around this book, where Ana De la O, Anna Grzymala-Busse, and Ken Roberts provided extremely thoughtful and insightful comments that significantly improved the manuscript. I am immensely thankful for the time they took to help me with this project.

Beyond Tulane, I have had many intellectual homes during the years I was working on the manuscript. I completed my dissertation while I was a visiting scholar at the Research Department at the Inter-American Development Bank. I owe a particular debt to Dan Gingerich, Ezequiel Molina, and Carlos Scartascini, who provided key support when I was in the final stages of writing the dissertation. I also thank the Yale Program on Democracy, as well as its director, Sue Stokes, for hosting me during my sabbatical, when I was completing revisions to the book. I am grateful for the intellectually stimulating and friendly environment I found at Yale, where along with Sue Stokes, Kate Baldwin, Ana De la O, Lucas Entel, Egor Lazarev, and Juan Masullo were key to making my stay productive and enjoyable. The final edits were completed while I was a visiting fellow at the Kellogg Institute for International Studies at the University of Notre Dame. Thanks are due to the fantastic academic community at the Kellogg Institute, and especially to its director, Paolo Carozza.

A great number of generous colleagues and friends have read all or parts of the manuscript and provided crucial feedback and suggestions when I needed them the most. Thanks are due to Santiago Anria, Tulia Falleti, Al Fang, Marcia Grimes, Ana María Ibáñez, Sebastian Karcher, Melis Laebens, Don Leonard, Noam Lupu, Jan Pierskalla, Luis Schiumerini, Christian Schuster, Sue Stokes, Milan Svolik, Mariela Szwarcberg, Guillermo Toral, Giancarlo Visconti, Matt Winters, Xiaonan Wang, Rodrigo Zarazaga, and especially to Ezequiel González-Ocantos and Rebecca Weitz-Shapiro for their insightful comments and suggestions. I also received thoughtful feedback at seminars at Brown University, University of Connecticut, CIDE, Duke University, University of North Carolina at Chapel Hill, University of Gothenburg, Harvard University, Inter-American Development Bank, University of Illinois at Urbana-Champaign, University of Pennsylvania, Maryland University, Michigan State University, Texas A&M University, University of Oxford, and Yale University, as well as at American Political Science Association, Midwest Political Science Association, and Latin American Studies Association conferences.

At Cambridge University Press, I am extremely grateful to Sara Doskow for her support and patience with this project. Sara also found two fantastic anonymous reviewers who provided insightful and detailed comments to improve the manuscript, for which I am very thankful. Tom Mowle and Elizabeth Rankin, at different stages of the project, provided excellent editing services. David Schwartz did the book's index. Parts of this book were originally published as "Making It Personal: Clientelism, Favors, and the Personalization of Public Administration in Argentina" and "Working for the Machine: Patronage Jobs and Political Services in Argentina" in the *Journal of Comparative Politics* and are reprinted here with the journal's permission. I thank the editors for that.

Finally, I would like to thank my parents, Rosita Wainer and Alejandro Oliveros, who shared with me their infinite curiosity and love for books and knowledge. Because of the endless conversations (and often heated discussions) with them and my brother, Santiago Oliveros, I learnt to love politics even before knowing that political science existed. This book is dedicated to them.

I

Introduction

During the Argentine winter of 2009, I was returning from a two-hour interview with Pablo and José,[1] sharing a taxi as we headed back to Buenos Aires from La Plata. As soon as we got into the car, both men started making phone calls. One of those conversations went as follows: "How many?" asked José; someone replied on the other end of the line. "Great! Thanks!" he responded in excitement and hung up. Then Pablo asked, "So? How many?" "Fifteen!" replied José, with obvious satisfaction. He continued, naming potential recipients, "María, Cecilia, Susana ..., " while counting on his fingers. Then, looking in my direction, he added, "You see? This is political activism – live! (¿Ves? Esto es militancia ¡En vivo y en directo!)."[2] In my most innocent voice, I asked, "How many *what*?" While Pablo seemed quite uncomfortable to disclose the information in my presence, José quickly replied, "Social welfare benefits! (¡Planes sociales!)."

Pablo and José are public sector employees, and both are also important Peronist political brokers (*punteros* or *referentes*).[3] Both obtained their jobs in the public sector through political networks. José became politically active in 1995, at age eighteen, when he "knocked on the door at a base unit" in his neighborhood.[4] He was an activist "for free, for a long time, out of vocation (*milité bastante tiempo gratis, por vocación*)." In 1999, he left his job in the private sector and lived on unemployment benefits for more than a year,

---

[1] To ensure anonymity, all interviewee names have been changed throughout the book. Author interview, La Plata, August 5, 2009.

[2] All translations from Spanish to English are mine.

[3] Brokers are local intermediaries between clients and patrons (usually elected officials or candidates) who "provide targeted benefits and solve problems for their followers" (Stokes et al. 2013, 75). They are also fundamental actors in political mobilization. See Chapter 2 for a detailed description of their activities. In Argentina, both *puntero* and *referente* mean political broker. The term *puntero*, however, has a relatively negative connotation, so brokers usually prefer *referente*.

[4] Base units (*unidades básicas*) are local party branches.

"waiting to be able to start having a salary, quote, unquote (*entre comillas*), from politics, from the administration." In 2000, he finally got a public sector job. Pablo, who "has always been a Peronist," became more involved in politics when he married in 1994. His mother-in-law ran a base unit. At the time, he was working in "nothing related to politics, no public employment, nothing (*nada que ver con la política, ni empleo público, ni nada*)." He eventually obtained a public sector job as well, through a politician his mother-in-law worked with.

Along with working their regular jobs in the public administration, José and Pablo are active participants in politics: they help with electoral campaigns, disseminate the party message, mobilize voters for elections and rallies, help their clients solve problems, distribute handouts and food, and, as the opening anecdote illustrates, participate in the discretionary distribution of welfare benefits to the poor. They are, in other words, paid political workers. They occupy public sector positions that they would not have received had they not been politically connected in the first place. In return, they work for the machine.[5] In José's words: "The activists (*militantes*), we get a salary. We work the hours we are supposed to work, we are not *ñoquis*, but I still feel that I owe my salary to politics."[6] Of course, not all (or even most) public employees are political brokers, but many other public employees are also involved in the provision of political services – they too obtained their public sector jobs with the understanding that they would provide political support in return. While not all public employees are involved in providing these services, the use of public employment to fund the salaries of political workers is certainly not unusual. The goal of this book is to shed light on this issue: patronage, or the exchange of public sector jobs for political support.[7] In the following pages, I provide a detailed description of what patronage employees do in exchange for their jobs, as well as a novel explanation of why they do it. In sum, this book aims to understand the specific mechanisms behind the electoral returns to patronage politics.

[5] "Machine" refers to a political organization that practices machine politics: "the manipulation of *certain* incentives to partisan political participation" (Wolfinger 1972, 374, italics in the original). The term refers both to the way public sector jobs are distributed and to the political services that those who get the jobs are supposed to provide in exchange.

[6] In Argentina, *ñoquis* (gnocchi, a potato-based Italian pasta) refers to workers who have no-show jobs, those who get paid without actually working. It is an Argentinean tradition to eat gnocchi at the end of the month, and the name implies that these "fake" employees only show up at the end of the month to collect their paychecks.

[7] Throughout this book I define "patronage" as the discretionary and personalized exchange of public sector jobs for political support. I use the term "patronage contract" in an informal way to denote that patrons and clients (public employees) engage in a *contract-like* exchange relationship in which politicians provide public sector jobs in exchange for political support. "Patronage contracts" are implicit or explicit agreements between those who get (or expect to get) a patronage job – the client/employee – and those who get (or expect to get) political support in return – the patron. I discuss this definition and the more general definition of clientelism in the next section.

1.1   PATRONAGE, ELECTORAL COMPETITION, AND THE QUALITY OF DEMOCRACY

The story of Pablo and José, two public sector employees who engage in political work in exchange for their jobs, illustrates some of the challenges facing new democracies. As a consequence of the "third wave" of democratization (Huntington 1991), more people have the right to vote today than at any other time in history. However, even across democracies, the extent to which elections are free and fair varies enormously.[8] In Latin America and elsewhere, it is not unusual to find democratic countries where the electoral playing field is skewed in favor of the incumbent party. The mechanisms supporting this imbalance are diverse, ranging from openly illegal practices such as government-sponsored election violence (Hafner-Burton, Hyde, and Jablonski 2014) and voter intimidation by state employees (Mares and Young 2018, 2019a) to more subtle ones, such as the use of government advertising to reward and punish the media (Brown 2011), the manipulation of the electoral calendar (Oliveros and Scherlis 2004), electoral reforms (Calvo and Micozzi 2005), and party finance regulations (Grzymala-Busse 2003, 2007) that benefit the incumbent party. When such mechanisms exist, elections might still be competitive, but they are less fair for the opposition and less free for voters.

One of the mechanisms that undermine the quality of democratic politics in many young democracies is the political use of public employment, or patronage.[9] In general, the use of any state resource for electoral benefit gives the incumbent party an unfair advantage at the polls. But patronage is particularly troubling for two other reasons. First, patronage appointments create opportunities for other illegal uses of state resources, such as political corruption, pork-barrel spending, and other forms of clientelism. Appointing friends to jobs in the public administration makes it easier for politicians to access resources and distribute them according to political criteria. Second, patronage has the potential to affect both the quality of electoral competition and the quality of democracy more broadly. Like other forms of clientelism, patronage arrangements are intended to generate political support. When successful, they affect the quality of political competition, generating the same negative consequences as other forms of clientelism in terms of accountability and representation. But the fact that patronage exchanges necessarily involve the use of state resources makes them

---

[8] Guillermo O'Donnell (1993, 1996), as well as many others after him, has also called attention to the variation in the quality of democracy within countries. Although it is beyond the scope of this book, an interesting literature has emerged that explores and explains this variation. See, for example, Behrend (2011), Gervasoni (2010), Gibson (2005, 2013), and Giraudy (2010, 2013, 2015).

[9] While probably more prevalent in new democracies, patronage is by no means exclusive to them.

fundamentally different.[10] Political bias in the distribution of public sector jobs affects the independence of public administration and raises serious concerns about unequal treatment by the state. Patronage can thus have a more damaging effect than other forms of clientelism on the quality of democracy, which suffers because of the effect of patronage on both political competition and on access to the state.[11]

This book describes *what* public employees do that affects both electoral competition and the quality of democracy, and also establishes *why* they do it. I argue that patronage jobs are distributed to supporters in exchange for a wide range of political services – such as helping with campaigns and electoral mobilization – that are essential for attracting and maintaining electoral support. Yet those who receive public sector jobs with the understanding that they will provide political services in return can easily renege on their side of the agreement *after* getting the job. Why would public sector employees comply with their side of the patronage contract once the job is in hand? Existing explanations are based either on fear of punishment (clients comply with their side of the agreement because they are afraid the patron will cut off the benefit if they fail to do so) or feelings of reciprocity (clients comply with the agreement because they want to help the person who has helped them).

By treating both patrons and clients – in this case, politicians and public employees – as equally sophisticated and self-interested individuals, my argument departs from existing accounts that tend to portray clients as passive, nonstrategic, or myopic actors.[12] What makes patronage contracts self-sustaining without punishment or reciprocity is that patronage jobs are distributed to supporters whose fates are tied to the political fate of the politician who has hired them. An incumbent politician (the patron) will maintain patronage jobs held by supporters (and protect their working conditions) while a competing politician will not, because supporters of the incumbent cannot credibly commit to provide political services for the opposition. Because their jobs and/or working conditions are on the line, supporters have a big incentive to help the incumbent stay in power by providing political services, which makes their original commitment to provide such services credible. This alignment of interests between patrons and clients (or politicians and patronage employees) makes patronage contracts incentive compatible and therefore self-sustaining.

I test the empirical implications of this theory using individual-level data from Argentina. By combining in-depth interviews with public sector employees, political brokers, and politicians with list and survey experiments

---

[10] Vote buying can, of course, also be financed with public resources, and this is often the case in Argentina, but it is possible to use private resources available to the opposition as well. Patronage, in contrast, is a resource *only* available to those in power.

[11] See Chapter 8 for a longer discussion.

[12] I discuss this point at length in the conclusion (Chapter 8).

embedded in a survey of 1,200 local public sector employees, I provide a detailed picture of how patronage works. I describe *what* public employees do in exchange for their jobs and explain *why* they do it. I find that a large proportion of public sector employees – particularly those who support the incumbent – are involved in political activities because they believe their jobs and working conditions are tied to the political success of the incumbent who hired them.

1.2 DEFINING CLIENTELISM AND PATRONAGE

Throughout this book, I define clientelism as the *personalized and discretionary exchange of goods or favors for political support.*[13] I refer to patronage as a subtype of clientelism, in which the good that is exchanged is a public sector job. In a clientelistic exchange, either the patron promises to deliver the benefit after the client provides political support or the patron provides the benefit with the expectation that the client will provide support in the future. The actual exchange only needs to be expected for the clientelistic arrangement to exist. It is always possible for clients to take advantage of the benefit and then renege on the clientelistic agreement by not providing the promised support. In turn, patrons can also fail to comply with their side of the bargain by requesting political support in advance and then failing to deliver the promised benefit.

Political support involves a number of different political activities (or services), ranging from the simple act of voting to participating in political meetings, attending rallies, or helping with electoral campaigns. In return, patrons provide different types of goods, ranging from handouts, favors, and money to unemployment benefits, housing subsidies, and public sector jobs.[14] The type of good or favor itself does not determine the existence of a clientelistic

---

[13] This definition is similar to those provided by Kitschelt and Wilkinson (2007b), Piattoni (2001), and Stokes (2007), among others. For a distinction between clientelism and other forms of electoral strategies (including programmatic ones) see Stokes et al. (2013, 6–18).

[14] The existing literature provides a wide variety of examples of the types of goods and favors that can be distributed through clientelistic exchanges: administrative favors provided by state employees (Oliveros 2016), access to workfare programs (Giraudy 2007; Lodola 2005; Ronconi and Zarazaga 2019; Weitz-Shapiro 2006), clothing, mattresses, medicine, milk, corrugated metal, construction materials, blankets, hangers, utility bill payments, money, eyeglasses, chickens, trees, and magnets (Brusco, Nazareno, and Stokes 2004), and even alcohol and drugs (Szwarcberg 2015) in Argentina; medicine, health exams, dentures, wheelchairs, orthopedic boots, and female sterilization in Brazil (Nichter 2011); property titles, subsidized housing and food, work opportunities, licenses to sell merchandise in flea markets (Magaloni, Díaz-Cayeros, and Estévez 2007), access to water (Herrera 2017), and supermarket gift cards (Cantú 2019) in Mexico; flour, cooking oil, and meals in Romania (Mares, Muntean, and Petrova 2017); furniture, animals, food, tools, and construction materials in Nicaragua (González-Ocantos et al. 2012); access to free healthcare in Turkey (Kemahlıoğlu and Bayer 2020); access to informal and illegal credit in Hungary (Mares and Young 2018); and money in the Philippines (Cruz 2019), Taiwan (Wang and Kurzman 2007), Indonesia (Pradhanawati, Tawakkal, and Garner 2019), and Kenya (Kramon 2016b).

exchange.[15] Although all the examples here are private goods, it is of course possible to distribute private goods through programmatic politics rather than through clientelism. In fact, as Stokes (2009) notes, in advanced democracies most welfare-state policies are targeted yet programmatic.[16] In programmatic politics, a set of rules stipulates the conditions under which citizens should receive certain benefits; all citizens who satisfy those requirements actually receive the benefit, without any bias or discretion. The group of people is defined in abstract terms – for instance, the poor or the unemployed – and all people thus defined receive the benefit. No member of that abstractly defined group of beneficiaries is excluded.

The characterization of the clientelistic exchange as personalized or individualized (and often face-to-face) helps distinguish clientelism from other forms of distributive politics, such as pork-barreling, in which the exchange involves a group of voters. In contrast to pork-barrel politics, where everyone who lives in a certain area would receive the benefit (e.g., electricity, access to water, or a road repair), in a clientelistic exchange, specific individuals can be targeted for benefits, and those who are not part of the exchange can be excluded. To be clear, politicians often target benefits to particular segments of the population with the hope or expectation that members of the benefiting groups will be more likely to vote for them. Such targeting is not personal, however, but rather focuses on a group that can be defined in abstract terms (as in programmatic politics) or by geography (as in the case of pork-barrel politics). In a clientelistic exchange, the benefit is not merely targeted, but targeted at the individual level.

At the same time, patrons know who receives the benefit. In the modern version of clientelism, clients usually have little or no personal contact with the patron. Rather, the personal connection is sustained by political brokers or some other type of middlemen "who provide targeted benefits and solve problems for their followers" (Stokes et al. 2013, 75). These intermediaries make sure to emphasize the personal nature of the connection. They routinely and publicly emphasize their "service to the people" and stress "their particular efforts to obtain the goods ... thus creating the appearance that were they not there, the benefits would not be delivered" (Auyero, Lapegna, and Poma

---

[15] Of course, pure public goods (such as clean air or national defense) are, by definition, impossible to distribute in a clientelistic way because no one can be excluded from their benefits. See Lizzeri and Persico (2004) for a conceptualization of clientelism based on the distinction between public and private goods. Similarly, Shefter (1977, 403) distinguishes collective benefits from divisible ones or "patronage of various sorts."

[16] See Weitz-Shapiro (2012, 2014) for an example of how the same program (a targeted food-distribution program in Argentina) can be distributed in a clientelistic or non-clientelistic way. Recent studies of conditional cash transfer programs in Mexico (De La O 2013, 2015; Díaz-Cayeros, Estévez, and Magaloni 2016) and Brazil (Zucco 2013), which show that distribution in these cases was in fact programmatic, provide further evidence that the type of good in itself (in this case a welfare benefit) does not necessarily imply clientelism.

2009, 5). The fact that the goods distributed through clientelism are often private, rather than public, goods makes credit claiming comparatively easier (Desposato 2007; Mayhew 1974; Müller 2007). However, credit claiming might be harder in certain cases, such as in the distribution of targeted government programs (Weitz-Shapiro 2014). In those cases, patrons and brokers have to make an additional effort to convince the clients of the personalized and discretionary character of the benefit.[17] This personal dimension of the exchange implies that clientelistic relations are ongoing, usually sustained over long periods of time.[18]

The clientelistic exchange is discretionary because patrons (or brokers) enjoy considerable discretion about who receives the benefit – or at least they can make clients believe they have such discretion. Most of the contemporary literature chooses to characterize the clientelistic exchange as contingent on clients' behavior rather than simply discretionary. Indeed, most definitions of clientelism emphasize the quid-pro-quo nature of the exchange in a very specific way: the provision of the goods and services is *contingent* upon the actions of clients. For instance, for Stokes et al. (2013, 13), "the party offers material benefits only on the condition that the recipient returns the favor with a vote or other form of political support."[19] From this perspective, two more conditions are necessary before an exchange can be classified as clientelistic. First, the patron can know, infer, or, at the very least, be able to make clients believe that it is possible to monitor political behavior. In the case of electoral support, this might involve some mechanism that violates the secret ballot or makes clients believe that such a violation is a real possibility. Second, clients should believe that they could be punished if they renege on their side of the agreement.[20] For a clientelistic exchange to take

---

[17] For a description of the strategies that politicians can use to create or increase voters' perception of discretion in the allocation of state resources and policy benefits, see Weitz-Shapiro (2014, Chapter 2), Mares and Young (2019a, 76–84), and Chapter 5 in this book.

[18] See, among others, Auyero (2000, 2001), Calvo and Murillo (2019), Díaz-Cayeros, Estévez, and Magaloni (2016), Kitschelt and Wilkinson (2007b), Szwarcberg (2015), and Zarazaga (2014). To distinguish these long-term relations from short-term ones, Nichter (2014) proposes distinguishing "electoral clientelism," in which the clientelistic exchange takes place in the short period around elections, from "relational clientelism," in which the exchange is not restricted to the electoral period. For her part, Muñoz (2014, 2018) proposes a subtype of "electoral clientelism" – "campaign clientelism" – that also takes place around elections for the purpose of getting voters to turn out at campaign events, rather than the polls. For a discussion on the duration of clientelistic relations, see González-Ocantos and Muñoz (2018, 752).

[19] For a similar perspective, see, among others, Frye, Reuter, and Szakonyi (2014, 2019), Grzymala-Busse (2007, 2008), Hicken (2011), Kitschelt and Altamirano (2015), Kitschelt and Wilkinson (2007b), Magaloni, Díaz-Cayeros, and Estévez (2007), Medina and Stokes (2007), Nichter (2008, 2014), Stokes (2007, 2009), and Weitz- Shapiro (2012, 2014).

[20] Others have argued that clientelistic exchanges are based on the collective monitoring of small groups (e.g., Cooperman 2019; Cruz 2019; Gingerich and Medina 2013; Rueda 2015, 2017).

place, the patron or the broker should be able to identify non-compliers and credibly commit to punish them.[21]

My understanding of clientelism is different. I do not assume that clientelistic exchanges require monitoring of specific voting decisions or political behavior, or that clients' fear of punishment is their main reason for fulfilling their side of the agreement. Whether monitoring and punishment (or the threat thereof) actually occur are both questions subject to empirical research and not an intrinsic part of the definition of the concept. In a clientelistic agreement both sides expect to obtain something from the other, but *whether* and *why* the agreement is in fact respected and patrons and clients actually obtain what they want are empirical questions.

To be sure, I am not arguing that monitoring of political behavior and fear of punishment are never present in clientelistic exchanges. In my definition of clientelism, the term "discretionary" includes such cases. These are not, however, *necessary* characteristics of these types of arrangements and therefore should not be considered intrinsic parts of the concept's definition.[22] As I argue, there is another explanation for why clients comply with their side of the agreement. Without being pressured to do so, clients can make an active and conscious decision to support their patron because they think it is in their best interest to do so. If clients believe that their political support is important to maintaining the status of the patron or broker from whom the discretionary benefits flow, clients have strong incentives to provide such support.

1.2.1   Patronage

Patronage is a subtype of clientelism in which the good received in exchange for political support is a public sector job.[23] I use the term "patronage contract"

---

[21] However, even authors who claim that some form of monitoring and the threat of punishment are intrinsic components of clientelistic exchanges often find themselves making exceptions in order to accommodate their definition to real examples. For instance, according to Kitschelt (2007, 303): "In established postindustrial democracies monitoring clientelistic exchanges, let alone enforcement, are not based on heavy-handed violations of the secrecy of the vote. It is rather indirectly based on social pressure, mediated by membership and activism in political parties, unions, business, professional associations, and churches." Kitschelt and Wilkinson (2007a) also take a step back and talk about "indirect monitoring and enforcement" (325) and "'soft' monitoring and incentives" (326). In contrast, the evidence of monitoring and punishment in non-democratic regimes appears to be stronger (e.g., Frye, Reuter, and Szakonyi 2014, 2019).

[22] There is another school of thought in the literature on clientelism that claims that feelings of reciprocity, rather than monitoring and punishment, are at the core of clientelistic exchanges (e.g., Finan and Schechter 2012; Lawson and Greene 2014). I discuss this perspective in Chapter 2.

[23] There is no consensus in the literature about the term "patronage." For instance, for Kitschelt and Wilkinson (2007c) and Chandra (2007), clientelism and patronage are interchangeable. The different uses of the two terms are in part linguistic – patronage is more commonly used in English-speaking countries while clientelism is more common in countries that predominately

informally to denote that patrons and clients engage in contract-like exchange relationships in which politicians provide public sector jobs in exchange for political support. Patronage contracts are implicit or explicit agreements between those who get (or expect to get) a patronage job – the client or employee – and those who get (or expect to get) political support in return – the patron. The term refers to the provision of political support both in the expectation of obtaining a job and in the aftermath of obtaining it; this is, of course, a type of clientelistic exchange only available to those in government. Furthermore, because "a steady and secure income" is a very valuable reward, patronage jobs are exchanged "not for a single vote but for broader electoral support" (Stokes 2009, 15). In fact, Argentinean patronage employees, for instance, engage in political services that go far beyond the mere act of voting, such as helping with campaigns, attending rallies, monitoring elections, and granting favors to voters (see Chapters 4 and 5).

This definition of patronage does not imply anything about the characteristics of the client (the employee or job recipient). The general understanding in the literature is that patronage jobs are distributed to supporters – which is consistent with the findings of this book – but it is not necessary to be a supporter to be involved in a patronage exchange.[24] Compared to people outside the partisan network, supporters are good candidates for patronage positions because they are more likely to be willing to provide political services (see Chapter 2). But an appointee who gets a patronage job through purely personal (nonpartisan) connections is also likely to be willing to provide such services (Kopecký, Scherlis, and Spirova 2008; Kopecký, Mair, and Spirova 2012; Kopecký et al. 2016; Scherlis 2010, 2013). In other words, the only characteristic of clients that matters for this definition is that, in exchange for a job, they implicitly or explicitly agree to provide political services for the patron.

It is also important to note that the types of political services that employees provide for their patrons are very diverse.[25] The services studied in this book are

---

use Romance languages (Piattoni 2001, 4). Some scholars use these terms differently than I use them in this book. For Schaffer (2007, 5), for example, patronage refers to a distributional strategy consisting of providing material support "within the context of enduring asymmetric, but reciprocal relationships," as opposed to vote-buying, which (for him) happens only at election time. Shefter (1977), Stokes (2009), and Weitz-Shapiro (2014), among others, define patronage in the same way as I do.

[24] This understanding is so common that Stokes et al. (2013) define patronage simply as clientelism directed at party members, while noting that the benefit offer is *typically* public employment (emphasis added). See Kopecký et al. (2016) for a different perspective.

[25] Chapters 2 and 3 describe these services in detail. Other scholars have proposed a definition of patronage irrespective of what clients give in return for the job appointment (Kopecký, Scherlis, and Spirova 2008; Kopecký, Mair, and Spirova 2012; Kopecký et al. 2016). For them, patronage refers simply to the discretionary power to make administrative appointments, without any detailing of what the patron receives in return. In the definition used in this book, what the patron gets (or expects to get) are in fact political services (or political support).

some of the most common among mid- and low-level positions in the bureaucracy, and as such, are quite different from those provided by political appointees in high-level positions, which generally involve control over public policy. Politicians usually wish to appoint people whom they trust to areas they consider important to their administration, ensuring that the bureaucrat will both implement the policies preferred by the politician and make the implementation easier. Moreover, high-level patronage appointments make it easier for parties and politicians to get public employees to do them favors, make exceptions, or look the other way. Such appointments may also facilitate political corruption (related to the financing of politics), clientelism (especially in the form of manipulation of targeted public programs), and pork-barreling.

1.3   WHY STUDY PATRONAGE?

Why focus on public employment? Why focus on the exchange of public sector jobs for political support as opposed to some other form of clientelism? Over the past two decades, political clientelism in developing countries has become one of the most-studied topics in political science.[26] Most research on clientelism, however, has focused on the exchange of goods for votes (vote buying) rather than on understanding how the exchange of jobs for political support (patronage) works. As a consequence, we still know very little about the specific mechanisms that explain the relationship between patronage contracts and political competition. We know even less about what sustains these contracts.

Patronage jobs are generally assumed to be distributed to an incumbent's supporters in exchange for political support. Thus, conventional wisdom posits that patronage significantly increases a party's chances of winning elections and staying in power. Yet we have surprisingly little systematic evidence about the type of political support or political services that patronage employees provide in exchange for their jobs. We lack any precise assessment of the kind of support that employees provide, which employees provide this support, or the extent of this practice in public administration. Moreover, we still do not have a sound explanation for why public employees provide such political support.

The limited attention that the comparative politics literature has given in recent years to patronage politics is particularly surprising considering that patronage is widespread and has been found in Western and Eastern Europe (Chubb 1981, 1982; Golden 2003; Grzymala-Busse 2003; Kopecký, Mair, and Spirova 2012; Pasotti 2010), the United States (Banfield and Wilson 1963; Johnston 1979; Wilson 1961; Wolfinger 1972), Asia (Callen et al. 2016; Iyer and Mani 2012; Pierskalla and Sacks 2020), Africa (Brierley 2021; Driscoll

---

[26] See González-Ocantos and Muñoz (2018), Hicken (2011), and Mares and Young (2016) for a review of the literature on clientelism, and González-Ocantos and Oliveros (2019) for the literature on clientelism in Latin America.

2018; Kopecký 2011), and Latin America (Brollo, Forquesato, and Gozzi 2017; Colonnelli, Prem, and Teso 2018; Grindle 2012). Not only is patronage a widespread phenomenon about which we know very little, but it is one that has significant economic and political consequences.

It is easy to see how the politically motivated distribution of public sector jobs could affect the quality of public administration and generate economic inefficiencies. Given that the criterion for selecting new employees for patronage contracts is their willingness or capacity to deliver political services rather than their skills, education, or ability to do the job, there is no formal mechanism to prevent unqualified individuals from getting hired, leading to poor public administration. The effect of hiring potentially unqualified workers, however, is limited by the fact that many jobs in the public sector do not require very sophisticated skills. Indeed, in today's polities, "most clientelistic intercessions operate above the fulfillment of minimal capacity requirements for entry into the administration" (Roniger 2004, 366). Moreover, political appointments can be restricted to low-ranking positions, while top positions that are more consequential to the functioning of the administration are filled using meritocratic criteria (Brierley 2021).

However, when partisan bias – even if limited – in hiring does affect the quality of the administration, economic resources end up being wasted. If the employees hired are unqualified for the job, public sector productivity drops, perhaps as a product of lack of proper qualifications or, if political appointees devote some of their working hours to the provision of political services, as a product of devoting less time to ordinary on-the-job tasks. Patronage may also reduce the incentives for discretionarily hired employees to perform on the job (Xu 2018). Additionally, high rates of administrative turnover, which often occur when hiring and firing decisions are politicized, can result in less-experienced public servants who have shorter time horizons and are often unwilling to engage in projects left over from previous administrations (Cornell 2014). Bureaucratic turnover can also disrupt the process of public service delivery, reducing the quality of services (Akhtari, Moreira, and Trucco 2017; Toral 2020). Additionally, if the purpose of hiring is to obtain political support, the size of the public administration may expand beyond its objective needs to instead reflect the political needs of the patron (Kemahlioğlu 2012). Spending on patronage, in turn, leads to the under-provision of public goods. When public money is used for political gain, less is available for public goods (Lizzeri and Persico 2001; Magaloni, Díaz-Cayeros, and Estévez 2007; Persson and Tabellini 1999).[27]

At the same time, following Weber's (1978) foundational ideas on how bureaucratic structures shape bureaucratic behavior, empirical studies have

---

[27] In some cases, however, the level of public employment is "not chosen only from the point of view of 'productive efficiency,'" but rather as a redistributive device to transfer income from the middle class to more disadvantaged citizens (Alesina, Baqir, and Easterly 2000, 219).

found a number of positive outcomes associated with professional bureaucracies in which hiring, promotions, and dismissals are insulated from electoral politics. Indeed, Weberian bureaucracies have been associated with economic growth (Evans and Rauch 1999), poverty reduction (Henderson et al. 2007), lower corruption (Bersch, Praça, and Taylor 2017; Charron et al. 2017; Dahlström, Lapuente, and Teorell 2012; Meyer-Sahling and Mikkelsen 2016; Oliveros and Schuster 2018; Rauch and Evans 2000), less disruptive protests (Cornell and Grimes 2015), more investment in infrastructure (Rauch 1995), improvements in health outcomes (Cingolani, Thomsson, and de Crombrugghe 2015), and more generous welfare systems (Rothstein, Samanni, and Teorell 2012).[28]

Despite all the negative outcomes linked to patronage politics, some scholars have argued that completely insulating the bureaucracy from politicians is not necessarily desirable. For instance, Müller (2007, 258) argues that, far from generating inefficiencies, patronage can be used to increase policy-making capacity, writing: "(b)y planting their trustees in the administration and the public sector more generally, political parties can make their policies better informed and smooth their implementation." From the principal–agent perspective dominant in the study of bureaucracies in the developed world (Pepinsky, Pierskalla, and Sacks 2017), one of the main problems in the relationship between politicians (principals) and bureaucrats (agents) is how to make sure that politicians can delegate responsibility to bureaucrats and still obtain their preferred outcome.[29] Patronage appointments are a possible solution to this problem; with full freedom to appoint supporters, the likelihood that the interests of the bureaucrat mirror those of the politician increases considerably. In this vein, Grindle (2012, 154) argues that in some Latin American countries "patronage systems encouraged the responsiveness of bureaucratic actors to executive policy leadership." Although these arguments have traditionally been applied to the study of the behavior of high-level public officials who determine policy implementation and not the middle- and low-level public employees who are the focus of this book, political appointees at any level may be more enthusiastic, responsive, and loyal workers when they share the preferences of politicians. For instance, Toral (2019) argues that, under certain conditions, political appointments at mid-levels of an administration (i.e., school directors) can improve public

---

[28] Ultimately, the more general argument behind many of these specific results is that elected officials behave differently than nonelected officials (because they face different incentives, have different time horizons, or have different expertise or information). The literature on this issue, especially in American Politics, is extensive and beyond the scope of this book. See Iaryczower, Lewis, and Shum (2013) for a review.

[29] The literature on this topic is vast (especially the formal one). See Gailmard and Patty (2012) for a review.

service delivery by ensuring social and political connections between politicians and bureaucrats.[30]

The distribution of patronage jobs also has a number of serious political consequences that can reduce political competition and the quality of democracy. Control of patronage jobs increases an incumbent's likelihood of re-election, reducing the level of electoral competition (e.g., Calvo and Murillo 2004; Folke, Hirano, and Snyder 2011).[31] Beyond the principled reasons – discussed below – for opposing this unfair advantage, a decrease in political competition is also costly because competitive elections are associated with a number of positive outcomes. Empirical studies show that increased political competition improves government performance by making politicians more accountable and responsive to their constituencies. Competitiveness has been associated with greater spending for primary education in Mexico (Hecock 2006) and in Africa (Stasavage 2005), higher economic growth in US states (Besley, Persson, and Sturm 2010), stronger rule of law in Argentina (Chávez 2003, 2007), better access to local public goods in Tanzania (Rosenzweig 2015) and in Mexico (Hiskey 2003), less politicization of the state in Eastern Europe (Grzymala-Busse 2003, 2007), and bureaucratic reforms involving meritocratic recruitment in Latin America (Geddes 1994) and the United States (Ting et al. 2013).

Crucially, in countries with "widespread institutional weakness" (Levitsky and Murillo 2005, 2009), such as Argentina and many other young democracies, political competition is an even more important mechanism of accountability and responsiveness. Politicians in democracies characterized by weak institutions are subject to low levels of horizontal accountability and enjoy ample opportunities to break and change the rules, but they still need to win elections to stay in power. In fact, institutional strength is the fundamental difference between young democracies with low levels of competition, and what Pempel (1990) has called "uncommon democracies," advanced democracies dominated by one party. According to Pempel (1990, 7), one undesirable consequence of single-party dominance is that "the longer a party is in power, the greater the opportunity it has to use state resources to shape and reshape its following." Such opportunities are considerably more numerous when institutions are weak, so low levels of electoral competition have more serious consequences in such contexts.[32]

Moreover, the use of any state resource for electoral competition provides an unfair advantage to the incumbent party. In this sense, patronage has much in

---

[30] Using data from schools in Brazil, Toral shows that when the incumbent mayor is defeated, schools managed by school directors who were politically appointed by the previous administration experience a drop in quality because the connection with the local government is lost.

[31] See Chapter 2 for an overview of the literature on the electoral returns to patronage politics.

[32] See Grzymala-Busse (2007) for a similar argument about the importance of political competition in the absence of "institutional safeguards" in postcommunist democracies.

common with the targeted manipulation of public programs and pork-barrel spending. In all these cases the electoral playing field is skewed in favor of the incumbent party. Elections may still be competitive, but they are less fair for the opposition because of the political use of state resources by the incumbent party. Furthermore, the use of state resources to finance political workers generates perverse incentives among politicians. If their success at the polls strongly depends on the political services provided by public employees, politicians have "little reason to care about the formulation of policies, the construction of programmatic parties, and practices of accountability" (Schaffer 2007, 11).

As a consequence of this unfair incumbency advantage, democratic accountability also suffers. When competition is fair, elections provide information about voters' preferred policies, which makes it easier for these preferences to be represented and translated into public policy. If incumbents have an unfair advantage in electoral competition, elections tend to provide less information about the distribution of voters' preferences. An uneven playing field can also affect levels of satisfaction with the functioning of democracy and decrease the legitimacy of elected leaders. In a study of party competition in Latin America, Kitschelt, Luna, and Zechmeister (2010) show that citizens express the least confidence in democratic practices in countries where programmatic party competition is weak. Similarly, empirical studies have shown that higher levels of (perceived) corruption (e.g., Anderson and Tverdova 2003; Rose-Ackerman 1999; Seligson 2002; Weitz-Shapiro 2008) and clientelism (Kitschelt 2007) reduce confidence and trust in democratic institutions.

It is also important to understand how patronage works because it directly affects opportunities for other forms of clientelism as well as pork-barrel spending and corruption. Bureaucrats have control over a wealth of resources that can be used and abused for political and personal gain. When politicians appoint "friends" to certain positions, they will often find it easier to get such patronage employees to do them favors, make exceptions, and provide the resources required for clientelistic exchanges and political corruption. Without patronage – without the possibility of discretionarily appointing "loyal" public employees – misuse of state resources for partisan or personal gain becomes more difficult.[33] Put differently, public sector employment is

---

[33] In the words of Piattoni (2001, 7): "In order to bend the administrative decision-making process to particularistic criteria, in view of the electoral return that this would yield, the elected officials need to be able to put pressure on career officials, hence to control (albeit informally) their hiring, firing, and advancement." See also Bozçağa and Holland (2018), Dahlström and Lapuente (2017), Díaz-Cayeros, Estévez, and Magaloni (2016), Dahlström and Lapuente (2017), Figueroa (2021), Fisman and Golden (2017), Geddes (1994), Gingerich (2013b), Grzymala-Busse (2007), Holland (2017), Kitschelt and Wilkinson (2007b, 36–40), Kopecký et al. (2008, 7), Kopecký and Mair (2012, 9), and Müller (2007).

"both a source of rents and a mechanism of rent distribution" (Grzymala-Busse 2008, 659).

Public sector jobs are also often the main resource used to pay for the work of brokers and activists. Although this is hardly ever the main focus of analysis, most studies of clientelism refer to public jobs as one of the principal ways of financing political work (Mares and Young 2016). The machine politics literature in the United States has long explicitly recognized and studied the importance of "jobs for the boys" to the sustenance of political machines. In the words of Key (1956, 382): "The operation of a party organization requires the services of many men and women ... Indirectly, a considerable part of party expense is met by the public treasury, and the chief means of channeling public funds to party support is through the appointment of party workers to public office." Although there are few studies of machine politics outside the United States that focus specifically on public employment, there is considerable agreement that public sector jobs are an important component of electoral machines.[34]

In addition to the economic inefficiencies associated with patronage, its erosion of political competition and accountability, and its likely enabling of other forms of clientelism and corruption, patronage has yet another serious effect on the quality of democracy. The biased distribution of public sector jobs raises serious questions about the independence of the public administration and the possibility of equal access to the state. Without clear rules for hiring and promotion, public employees owe their jobs to the patron who makes hiring decisions. The bureaucracy thus lacks independence, leading to a possible lack of impartiality vis-à-vis citizens. In patronage democracies, "proximity to a state official increases a voter's chances of obtaining valued state resources and services" (Chandra 2007, 87). What happens to the many citizens who lack connections to a state official?

At the same time, as Chubb (1981, 120) points out, "an able administrator can ... transform a routine bureaucratic procedure into a personal favor." In settings with widespread patronage, public positions that channel those favors are filled with partisan workers who provide political support to their patrons. Would a citizen who is clearly identified with the opposition get equal treatment? Would a citizen with no personal connections to anyone on the public sector payroll be discouraged from even asking for help? When the public administration is filled with patronage employees, ordinary citizens may feel excluded. Whether this impression of uneven access to the state is accurate or not, it could be enough to keep citizens without connections away.[35] When

---

[34] See, among others, Larreguy, Montiel Olea, and Querubín (2017), Levitsky (2003), Mares and Young (2019a), Stokes et al. (2013), Szwarcberg (2015), and Zarazaga (2014). Chapter 2 discusses this literature in detail.

[35] As Cox and McCubbins (1986, 385) put it: "Insofar as politicians can design the rules by which bureaucratic decisions are made, they can also (at least indirectly) influence the set of citizens that bring demands or complaints before the bureaucracy for redress."

those without personal connections are the poor – as is often the case – patronage is linked not only to uneven access to the state and therefore weak rule of law, but also to the reproduction of existing inequalities.

1.4 CHALLENGES TO THE STUDY OF PATRONAGE

Although patronage is often perfectly legal, it is particularly difficult to study because it constitutes a "gray area" of acceptable practice (Van de Walle 2007, 52). The challenges are sufficiently serious that, according to Geddes (1994, 105): "In the real world, there is no way to measure amounts of patronage or how much influence on the vote it has." Long before Geddes, Wilson (1961, 372) wrote: "So much secrecy is maintained in city politics that no exact data on patronage may ever be obtained in cities of any size." Since then, contemporary researchers have used different strategies in an attempt to generate more systematic data for the study of patronage politics.

Taking advantage of the fact that civil service rules are weak or nonexistent in some contexts, such as Argentina and many young democracies (e.g., Grindle 2012; Iacoviello 2006), a number of studies have tried to get around the problem of measuring patronage by using proxies such as the number of public sector employees (Calvo and Murillo 2004; Grzymala-Busse 2003; O'Dwyer 2004), the number of temporary employees (Brollo and Troiano 2016; Ferraro 2006; Kemahlioğlu 2012), the number of low-level employees (Driscoll 2018), or spending on personnel (Gordin 2002; Nazareno, Stokes, and Brusco 2006; Remmer 2007; Schiumerini 2018). However, cross-national analysis finds similar levels of meritocracy in actual hiring procedures among countries with and without legal merit requirements (Schuster 2017). While strict and clear civil service rules might be a good indicator of low levels of patronage, the absence of such rules does not necessarily mean that public sector jobs are distributed through patronage contracts. Neither a large number of public sector jobs nor high spending on personnel is a necessary or sufficient condition for patronage; those figures could easily hide (or not) patronage appointments. Both of those measures, for instance, would remain stable in a context in which new incumbents fire employees hired by the previous administration and replace them with their own supporters without increasing the number of employees or spending on salaries (Kopecký, Scherlis, and Spirova 2008; Meyer-Sahling 2006).[36]

A few recent studies in developing countries have managed to obtain unique public employee-level administrative data. In Ghana, for instance, Brierley (2021) combines subnational bureaucrat-level data on time of hiring with bureaucrats' ethnicity and home regions (to proxy for partisanship) to study

---

[36] For a longer discussion about the problems associated with these types of measures in general and the case of Argentina in particular, see Scherlis (2010, 39–42). For a similar discussion based on the Hungarian case, see Meyer-Sahling (2006, 277–81).

variation in patronage hiring across administrative ranks. In Brazil, scholars have combined an unprecedented dataset on the universe of the Brazilian public sector with a dataset on party membership (Brollo, Forquesato, and Gozzi 2017) and, in another study, with candidates and campaign donors (Colonnelli, Prem, and Teso 2018) to show partisan bias in hiring decisions.[37] In cases where it even exists, this type of fine-grained data is very hard to obtain in most developing countries (Brierley 2021), and Argentina, where data like this is simply not available, is no exception.[38]

The challenge, moreover, is not only to be able to assess whether public sector jobs are distributed with partisan bias or which jobs are distributed this way but to study the type of political support that patronage employees provide to their bosses in exchange for those jobs as well as the reasons behind this support. Because both politicians and public sector employees have incentives to misreport clientelistic exchanges, asking either of them directly about these political services is also problematic.[39] Employees could be reluctant to admit that they hold a patronage job because that could imply that they did not really "earn" it. From the point of view of the patron, admitting the existence of patronage jobs is even more problematic because it implies the use of state resources for political purposes. Even when patronage is often not illegal, politicians may view inquiries about it "as valence questions on which they suspect most citizens and observers to be on one side of the issue (against)" (Kitschelt and Wilkinson 2007a, 326).[40]

To measure the types and extent of the political services that employees hired through patronage contracts provide to their patrons,[41] I avoid the use of proxies and mitigate the problems associated with asking sensitive questions directly to the actors involved. Here, I test the empirical implications of my theory of self-enforcing patronage with a face-to-face survey of 1,200 local

[37] Other recent examples of studies that have managed to obtain unprecedented bureaucrat-level administrative data in developing countries include Pierskalla and Sacks (2020) for Indonesia and Hassan (2017) for Kenya.

[38] Chapter 3 describes the daunting process of obtaining the data necessary for the implementation of the survey that informs this study.

[39] On the problems of data collection for the study of clientelism, see Kitschelt and Wilkinson (2007a, 323–27).

[40] To get around this problem, some scholars have opted to implement expert surveys. For instance, Herbert Kitschelt directs the Democratic Accountability and Linkages Survey Project at Duke University, which aims to obtain information on leadership accountability from every country with multiparty elections (see https://sites.duke.edu/democracylinkage/). Peter Mair and Petr Kopecký directed another expert survey in fifteen European countries and five new democracies that focuses on party patronage (see Kopecký, Mair, and Spirova 2012). The Quality of Government Expert Survey (run by scholars at Gothenburg University) also surveys experts in public administration in 135 countries (Dahlberg et al. 2013). See Kitschelt and Wilkinson (2007a, 327–29) for an argument in favor of expert surveys.

[41] For a similar approach, see Gingerich (2013b). In his book, *Political Institutions and Party-directed Corruption in South America*, Gingerich also uses survey data, but he focuses on political corruption among high- and mid-level bureaucrats.

public sector employees (see Chapter 3). To minimize social response bias, I use a specific survey methodology, the list experiment, to guarantee respondents full anonymity. Another research tool, the survey experiment, allows me to assess why public sector employees comply with their side of the patronage contract. I complement the analysis of the survey results with in-depth interviews of public sector employees, political brokers, and politicians.

1.5 WHY ARGENTINA?

While the theory developed and tested in this book applies to many countries without strict civil service rules, Argentina offers an excellent setting in which to test it. Once infamous for its political instability,[42] Argentina is today infamous for its clientelistic politics. Fairly or unfairly, clientelism has received more scholarly attention in Argentina than in any other single country.[43] Besides its well-documented and widespread clientelism, Argentina provides an especially good setting for studying the mechanisms of patronage for several reasons. The country lacks stable civil service rules and has a large public sector with "well-developed patronage systems" (Calvo and Ujhelyi 2012). It has an extensive level of decentralization that results in significant variation in the size and characteristics of public employment across provinces and municipalities.[44] In addition, although some provincial regulations apply to municipal public employment, control over local personnel is the exclusive responsibility of local governments, which increases the variation in the distribution of patronage even more.

The Argentine Constitution has guaranteed job stability for public employees since 1949.[45] National, provincial, and local public sector employees often gain job security after a year and cannot be fired once they have attained permanent positions. Job security rules, however, are systematically bypassed through the increasing use of temporary contracts. According to estimates by Pomares,

[42] Argentina has been a stable democracy with free and fair elections since the return of democracy in 1983. Since then, the Peronist party (PJ) has won the presidential election five times (1989, 1995, 2003, 2007 and 2011), while the Radical party (UCR) has won it twice (1983 and 1999). In 2015 (after the fieldwork for this book was completed), a new party, Propuesta Republicana (PRO), won the presidential election and the key districts of the City of Buenos Aires and Buenos Aires province. In 2019, the PJ won the presidential election again.

[43] See, among others, Auyero (2000), Calvo and Murillo (2004, 2013, 2019), Calvo and Ujhelyi (2012), Camp (2017), Kemahlioğlu (2012), Levitsky (2003), Lodola (2005), Nichter (2008), Remmer (2007), Ronconi and Zarazaga (2019), Stokes and her coauthors (Brusco, Nazareno, and Stokes 2004; Nazareno, Stokes, and Brusco 2006; Stokes 2005; Stokes et al. 2013), Szwarcberg (2012, 2015), Weitz-Shapiro (2006, 2012, 2014), and Zarazaga (2014).

[44] Argentina is a federal republic with a presidential system, extensive decentralization, and significant regional variation. It has twenty-three provinces divided into more than 2,000 local governments (around 1,200 municipalities and 800 *comunas*), and a capital city (Buenos Aires) that is semi-autonomous.

[45] Article 14bis.

Gasparin, and Deleersnyder (2013), from 2003 to 2012 the proportion of federal public employees on temporary contracts increased from 15 percent to 30 percent. At the local level, temporary contracts are even more common (e.g., Scherlis 2010). Furthermore, even though there have been attempts to create a meritocratic system of recruitment, most appointments at all levels of the administration are still discretionary (e.g., Ferraro 2011; Grindle 2012; Iacoviello and Zuvanic 2006a). The government can appoint supporters to public jobs either by enlarging the public sector or by replacing temporary employees. As long as permanent personnel are not touched, every new president, governor, and mayor enjoys considerable discretion to appoint new personnel. This discretion is used (and abused) extensively to distribute patronage contracts, especially at the local level.[46]

Despite all the attention given it in the literature, Argentina is not an outlier among Latin American countries for the specific type of clientelistic exchange that is the focus of this book. An Inter-American Development Bank (IDB) evaluation of bureaucracy and civil service systems across Latin America classifies Argentina as a country with intermediate civil service development, a designation also given to Colombia, Mexico, and Uruguay (Echebarría 2006; see also Zuvanic, Iacoviello, and Gusta 2010). Even though all Latin American countries have established professional civil services, the extent to which merit is the only criterion used for hiring, firing, and promotion varies enormously across countries. Across Latin America, civil service systems exist parallel to political criteria (Grindle 2012; Iacoviello 2006; Zuvanic, Iacoviello, and Gusta 2010).[47]

All in all, the combination of well-documented and widespread patronage and high levels of decentralization – leading to significant variation in the economic and political settings in which patronage contracts arise – makes Argentina a particularly useful laboratory for studying patronage politics. Because the purpose of this book is to study *how* patronage works and not to establish whether patronage exists or how it varies, the choice of a country well known for its patronage politics seems appropriate. At the same time, Argentina's non-outlier status in terms of patronage appointments, at least by Latin American standards, makes the findings of this book relevant for other Latin American cases and other young democracies. Finally, Argentina's substantial subnational variation allows me to test the theory of self-enforcing patronage in very different settings without losing the advantages of conducting research in a single country.[48] Subnational variation also makes the portability of the results to other settings more plausible.

---

[46] See Chapter 7 for more details.

[47] See Chapter 7 for a longer discussion on how Argentina compares to other Latin American countries.

[48] Testing the theory in only one country can raise some concerns about the generalizability of the argument. Chapter 7 addresses this issue. See Snyder (2001) and Giraudy, Moncada, and Snyder (2019) on the advantages of the subnational comparative method.

1.6 THE ARGUMENT IN BRIEF

Why does the control of patronage increase an incumbent's chances of staying in power? What are the specific mechanisms behind the electoral returns to patronage politics? What do patronage employees do? What motivates them to do it? In line with other scholars, I argue that public sector jobs are disproportionally distributed to political supporters, i.e., those who are more closely connected to party networks. Since such government jobs are extremely valuable, the type of political support that is expected in exchange for public sector employment goes far beyond the simple act of voting. In fact, politicians distribute many low- and mid-level positions in the bureaucracy with the intent of maintaining a network of political workers on the ground to perform various political activities – such as helping with electoral campaigns or organizing and attending political rallies – that are essential for attracting and maintaining electoral support. Patronage jobs provide politicians in power with a "free" supply of political workers.

Patronage contracts, however, are difficult to enforce and both politicians and employees face a commitment problem. Politicians risk "wasting" jobs on employees who, once hired, may not comply with their side of the contract. For their part, potential employees (clients) promised a future job risk providing services for candidates who, once in office, might renege on their side of the agreement, withholding the job offer. This book focuses on the first type of commitment problem.

Why would public employees uphold the agreement and provide political services even *after* receiving the benefit of the job? How can the patron make sure not to "waste" jobs on citizens who will not fulfill their side of the contract?[49] Existing explanations are based on either feelings of reciprocity or fear of punishment. According to the first set of theories, clients (patronage employees) comply with their side of the agreement and provide the promised political services because they want to help the patron who helped them (e.g., Finan and Schechter 2012; Lawson and Greene 2014). According to the second set of theories, clients comply because they are afraid that the patron will cut off the benefit (fire them, in this case) if they fail to do so (e.g., Brusco, Nazareno, and Stokes 2004; Robinson and Verdier 2013; Stokes 2005, 2007).[50] Departing from these accounts, I argue that there is a third explanation for why public employees uphold the patronage contract. Patronage employees (clients) engage in political activities that support politicians (patrons) because their fates are tied to the political fate of their patrons.

Politicians use personal and partisan connections to screen potential patronage employees and separate perceived supporters from non-supporters.

---

[49] Throughout this book, I use the terms "voter" and "citizen" interchangeably. Voting is mandatory in Argentina from ages eighteen to sixty-five (although sanctions for not voting are rare) and elections usually have about 70 or 80 percent turnout.

[50] Chapter 2 discusses these two alternative explanations in more detail.

Perceived supporters may support the politician for ideological or personal reasons or because of past or expected benefits; they may have real connections with the party, or they may just wish to be perceived as supporters in order to obtain benefits. Indeed, perceived support is not about ideological affinity but rather about proximity to the party's network (Calvo and Murillo 2019). All things being equal, perceived supporters are more likely to comply with the agreement and provide political services because they are more likely than non-supporters to truly support the party or politician. This makes the provision of political services less costly for them.

Perceptions, however, can be misleading. In fact, once voters expect partisan bias in hiring decisions, they have an incentive – the prospect of a job – to move closer to the partisan networks and to pretend to have certain political preferences. Once hired, patronage employees may also change their minds about their political preferences or simply reduce the effort they are willing to devote to political services. Patronage employees still have the option of going back on their agreement after getting the job. Hiring supporters – or, more accurately, *perceived* supporters – is not in itself enough to solve the commitment problem.

Why, then, are patronage agreements respected? Patronage contracts are respected because patronage employees believe that their jobs and working conditions are tied to the political success of their patron. Public employees under patronage contracts believe that if the incumbent loses the election, their own jobs could be in jeopardy. Knowing that they are branded as supporters of the incumbent, patronage employees worry about keeping their jobs and/or working conditions if the opposition were to win. Just as the ousted incumbent did previously, a newly elected official will want to distribute patronage jobs to new employees who will be likely to provide political services for him or her. Because only *his or her* supporters can credibly commit to do that in the future, old employees who are known or perceived to be supporters of the incumbent will be replaced or demoted. Supporters of the incumbent thus have an enormous incentive to engage in political services aimed at keeping the incumbent in power. Patronage contracts are thus incentive compatible, and the commitment problem associated with the sequenced nature of the job-for-services exchange disappears.[51]

By providing a direct assessment of the specific mechanisms that explain the effect of patronage on political competition, this book makes two main contributions. First, it is the first systematic attempt to measure the types and

---

[51] As with other public goods (in this case, the incumbent's reelection) that depend on collective contributions (political services), patronage employees may be tempted to free ride on the political work of others. However, the specific (low) costs and (high) benefits involved in patronage agreements, the non-trivial contribution of each political service to the desired outcome (the reelection of the incumbent and thus the continuation of desirable working conditions) as well as the fact that at least some patronage employees are "committed" supporters make cooperation more likely in this case. Chapter 2 discusses this issue in more detail.

extent of the political services that employees hired through patronage contracts provide for their patrons. Importantly, as highlighted in this book, political brokers are not the only ones involved in these activities. Most of the literature has focused on brokers as central actors in machine politics, but many public employees who are not political brokers are nevertheless involved in the provision of political services. We know very little about the activities and motivations of these less studied and less influential but still critical political actors.

Second, I provide a novel explanation of the enforcement of these patronage contracts that has implications for understanding the functioning of clientelistic exchanges more broadly. By treating both patrons and clients – in this case, patronage employees – as equally sophisticated and self-interested individuals, my argument departs from existing accounts that emphasize either feelings of reciprocity or fear of punishment. Public sector employees comply with the patronage contract because their interests are aligned with those of their patrons. Clientelistic contracts need not imply passive clients behaving against their interests out of fear of being punished, nor need they imply particularly noble clients who always reciprocate favors. Clients can make sophisticated calculations when deciding whether to comply with the agreement or renege. At the same time, if patronage contracts, and clientelistic arrangements more broadly, are self-sustaining without punishment, clientelism becomes cheaper, harder to detect, and even harder to curb. If costly political machines are not needed to identify and punish non-compliers, clientelism becomes cheaper; if illegal threats, coercion, and monitoring devices are not necessary to convince clients to provide political support, clientelism becomes a lot more difficult to uncover and eliminate.[52]

1.7 PLAN OF THE BOOK

The rest of the book is organized as follows. Chapter 2 introduces my theory of self-enforcing patronage and its empirical implications. Following a discussion of the relationship between patronage jobs and political competition and a description of the types of political services that different types of public employees provide for their bosses, I lay out a new theory that seeks to understand the reasons behind the provision of these political services. Chapters 3 through 6 offer the main empirical tests of the theory. After describing the empirical strategy, the case selection, the interviews, and the survey, Chapter 3 shows that patronage jobs are disproportionally distributed to those more closely connected to the partisan network (supporters). Chapter 4 uses list experiments embedded in an original survey of 1,200 public employees to measure the types and extent of the political services that patronage employees provide for their patrons during elections – namely, attending

---

[52] I discuss the implications of the theory at length in Chapter 8.

rallies, helping with electoral campaigns, and monitoring elections. Chapter 5 focuses on one political service that employees perform in between elections: providing favors. Both Chapters 4 and 5 show that, as predicted by the theory, supporters are more involved than non-supporters in the provision of political services. Chapter 6 tests the theory's central implication, that public sector employees fulfill their side of the patronage contract by providing political services in pursuit of their own personal interests. Using survey experiments, this chapter shows that patronage employees believe that their fates are tied to the political fate of their patron, providing a strong incentive for them to help the patron remain in power. Chapter 7 presents evidence from other Latin American countries as an out-of-sample test of the theory in order to build more confidence about the external validity of the argument. Beginning with a general discussion of the characteristics of civil service systems in Latin America, I then discuss the cases of Argentina, Bolivia, and Chile. The final chapter reviews the major findings and discusses their implications for our understanding of the dynamics of clientelism and the possibilities for curbing it. The research findings draw particular attention to the interests and strategic behavior of clients, to what these interests and behavior mean for the eradication of patronage and clientelism, and to the particularly damaging effects of patronage for the quality of democracy and equal access to the state.

2

A Theory of Self-Enforcing Patronage

Although conventional wisdom holds that control of patronage significantly increases an incumbent's chance of staying in power, we actually know very little about the specific mechanisms that explain the relationship between patronage contracts and political competition. We know even less about what sustains these contracts. While the literature on clientelism has grown spectacularly in the past two decades, most of it has focused on vote buying – the exchange of goods or favors for electoral support – rather than on understanding the workings of patronage – the exchange of public sector jobs for political support.[1]

This chapter develops the theory of what I call "self-enforcing patronage" that explains *what* public sector employees do in exchange for their jobs and *why* they do it. Besides doing their regular work, patronage employees are expected to engage in a range of political services for their patron, the politician who hired them. However, those who receive public sector jobs with the implicit or explicit understanding that they will provide political services in return can easily renege on their side of the agreement *after* getting the job. Why would public sector employees comply with their side of the patronage contract after receiving the job? What is their incentive to comply?

Most of the literature argues that patronage employees do not renege on the agreement because they believe their patron would fire them if they did.[2] From this perspective, the continuation of patronage jobs is contingent on the

---

[1] As discussed at length in Chapter 1, I define patronage as the personalized and discretionary exchange of public sector jobs for political support. Patronage contracts are implicit or explicit agreements between those who get (or expect to get) a patronage job (the client) and those who get (or expect to get) political support in return (the patron).

[2] Some scholars have argued that clientelism is based on feelings of reciprocity rather than on fear of punishment (e.g., Finan and Schechter 2012; Lawson and Greene 2014). I discuss both alternative explanations in Section 2.5.

employee behavior: jobs are kept as long as the agreed-upon political services are provided. But this is not the only plausible explanation. I propose a different explanation, one that takes the incentives and agency of the clients (i.e., patronage employees) seriously. Departing from existing accounts, I argue that patronage contracts are self-sustaining without the threat of punishment because patronage jobs are distributed to supporters whose fates are tied to the political fate of the politician who hired them. Patronage jobs held by supporters (and their working conditions) will be maintained by the incumbent but not by the opposition, since the incumbent's supporters cannot credibly commit to providing political services for the opposition. It is thus in the best interest of patronage workers to provide political services to help the incumbent remain in power, making their original commitment to do so credible. It is precisely this alignment of interests between patrons and clients (incumbent politicians and patronage employees) that makes patronage contracts incentive compatible and therefore self-sustaining over time.

The remainder of this chapter is organized as follows. After discussing the relationship between patronage jobs and political competition, I describe the types of political services that public employees under patronage contracts provide for their patrons – services that are at the heart of the electoral returns to patronage politics. I then focus on the commitment issues associated with clientelistic agreements in general and investigate the case of patronage agreements in particular. Next, I introduce my theory of self-enforcing patronage, which explains what sustains these patronage agreements and how the commitment problem is solved. The chapter concludes with a discussion of potential collective action problems and the empirical implications and scope conditions of the theory.

2.1   PATRONAGE JOBS AND POLITICAL COMPETITION

The conventional wisdom, both in the traditional literature on machine politics in American cities and in more recent studies, is that control of patronage significantly increases an incumbent's chances of staying in power. Despite this widespread perception, there is little systematic evidence on the electoral benefits of patronage jobs. Part of the reason we know so little about this issue is because it is extremely difficult to collect systematic and reliable data on patronage.[3] Even in the American politics literature, which has studied machine politics for more than fifty years, the effect of patronage on elections has only recently been convincingly established (Folke, Hirano, and Snyder 2011). Taking advantage of the sequenced adoption of civil service reforms

---

[3] In her iconic book on bureaucratic reform, Geddes (1994, 105) argues that "there is no way to measure amounts of patronage," so her analysis explicitly relies on the following assumption: "All else being equal, the distribution of jobs and favors increases the probability of being elected."

across American states, Folke et al. use a difference-in-difference design to show that having access to state-level patronage increased the probability (by about 25 percentage points) of winning state elections.

In the case of Argentina, Levitsky (2003) has argued that one of the factors that explains the survival of the Peronist party in spite of the weakening of its linkages to labor unions in the 1980s and 1990s was its access to a politicized bureaucracy that allowed the party to distribute patronage jobs. Using provincial-level data (1987–2000) on the number of public employees, Calvo and Murillo (2004) show that public employment boosts incumbent electoral support when the Peronist party is in power. Similarly, Schiumerini (2018) uses provincial-level data from 1995 to 2011, finding that the Peronist party obtains a higher electoral return on spending on personnel than the Radical party. He also shows that provinces with more public employees had larger incumbency effects. Using data from 1987 to 2005, Scherlis (2005) argues that Argentinean provinces with higher levels of patronage have lower levels of political alternation and more "closed" and stable party systems. Gervasoni (2010), building on rentier theories of the state, finds a similar negative relationship between the size of the provincial payroll and levels of subnational political contestation. Calvo and Murillo (2019), in turn, use an innovative survey technique to measure the size of party networks and estimate their effect on voters' expectations and behavior. They show that the expectation of receiving a public sector job has a significant effect on the voting intentions of respondents, especially for voters who are more closely connected to party networks.[4]

Beyond Argentina, scholars have called attention to the role of public sector employees in helping the incumbent stay in power in a variety of contexts. Chubb (1981; 1982) shows the importance of patronage jobs in the Christian Democrats' construction of a monopolistic system of power in Palermo, Italy, that lasted for more than thirty years (see also Golden 2003). McMann (2006) attributes the persistence of hybrid regimes at the subnational level in Russia and Kyrgyzstan to the lack of "economic autonomy," the ability to make a living independent of the state. For him, in areas where the state dominates economic opportunities and thus there are very few job options outside public employment, incumbents have nothing to fear. Indeed, Frye, Reuter, and Szakonyi (2014) show that employees in government offices and state-owned firms in Russia are pressured by employers to engage in political

---

[4] Nazareno, Stokes, and Brusco (2006), in contrast, find no positive electoral returns to patronage at the municipal level in Argentina. Their results, however, are hard to evaluate because of the possibility of important selection bias in the data. Their sample includes only six provinces (out of twenty-four), which were – as they admit – selected by data availability. Provinces with higher levels of patronage might have larger incentives to withhold employment information. It is also possible that their measure of patronage, spending on personnel, is – as discussed in the introduction – not a good proxy for patronage. Neither high spending nor increases in spending is a necessary or sufficient condition for the existence of patronage appointments.

activities.[5] Greene (2010) uses a time-series cross-sectional dataset and examples from Mexico and Botswana to argue that patronage jobs (and other state resources) are key to explaining the survival of authoritarian dominant-party regimes. Magaloni (2006) also refers to public sector jobs as one of the resources used by the PRI (Partido Revolucionario Institucional) to sustain its hegemony in Mexico. Hassan (2017) shows that, in Kenya, a high presence of aligned (i.e., coethnic) security officers in regional executive branches of the internal security apparatus is associated with an increase in vote share for the incumbent president.

All in all, there is widespread agreement that the control of patronage increases the incumbent's probability of winning elections, even if this consensus is not always based on systematic evidence. Less clear in many of these studies are the specific mechanisms that explain the relationship between the distribution of patronage jobs and electoral outcomes. With the possible exception of some post-Soviet states, it is highly unlikely that the votes of public employees are enough to win a general election.[6] Patronage jobs are in fact exchanged for a kind of political support that goes far beyond mere votes. The traditional literature on US machine politics has long recognized the central role of "jobs for the boys" in funding the salary of party workers and electoral mobilization (e.g., Banfield and Wilson 1963; Pollock 1937; Wilson 1961; Wolfinger 1972). Wilson (1961, 371) put it simply: "Patronage is used to induce ... work for the machine by getting out the vote and dispensing favors to voters." More recently, public employment in new democracies, where weak civil service systems allow ample opportunities for patronage, has received some scholarly attention. Most of the research on clientelism, however, has focused on vote buying; relatively little work has been done to understand how patronage works. Furthermore, many studies of patronage focus on explaining variation in its use or existence (e.g., Brierley 2021; Callen et al. 2016; Driscoll 2018; Kemahlioğlu 2012; Pierskalla and Sacks 2020; Remmer 2007) and not on how it works. As a result, most of what we know today about public sector employees as political workers is based on studies in which the main focus of interest is not public administration, but clientelism.

Contemporary studies of clientelism recognize the importance of public sector jobs as a crucial component of electoral machines, especially as a way of financing the work of political brokers (Mares and Young 2016).[7] At the beginning of his well-known ethnography about clientelism in Argentina, Auyero (2001) includes a list of eleven actors (plus four elected officials) who

[5] In the Russian non-democratic regime, this is also true for some private employees, especially those employed in large firms and firms with immobile assets (Frye, Reuter, and Szakonyi 2014).

[6] This is not necessarily true for primaries; see subsequent text.

[7] Recall that brokers are local intermediaries between clients and patrons who are fundamental for political mobilization and who "provide targeted benefits and solve problems for their followers" (Stokes et al. 2013, 75).

are key participants in a local clientelistic network. Of those eleven, four are public employees and a fifth works part time for the municipality on a temporary contract. In what is probably one of the biggest surveys of brokers conducted to date (800 interviews in four Argentinean provinces), 30 percent of the brokers interviewed (excluding those who held elected office) reported being public sector employees. In fact, public employment was the largest single occupation mentioned (Stokes et al. 2013, 99). Zarazaga (2014) also conducted a survey of brokers (120 cases, using a snowball technique) in Greater Buenos Aires; in his sample, 50 percent of the brokers were public sector employees. Similarly, in a 1997 survey of 112 Peronist grassroots offices in La Matanza and Quilmes (Greater Buenos Aires), and in the City of Buenos Aires, Levitsky (2003, 195–97) found that two-thirds of those offices were run by brokers who had jobs in the public administration.[8]

Beyond the Argentinean case, Mares and Young (2018, 2019a, 2019b) report that during the 2014 Hungarian and Romanian elections, public employees or "state brokers" were in charge of implementing both positive (e.g., offering goods and favors) and negative inducements (e.g., threat of exclusion from policy benefits) in exchange for votes. Public school teachers serve as political brokers who mobilize voters in Mexico (Chambers-Ju 2017, 2021; Larreguy, Montiel Olea, and Querubín 2017), Colombia (Eaton and Chambers-Ju 2014), Thailand (Chattharakul 2010), and Indonesia (Pierskalla and Sacks 2020). In Pakistan, patronage jobs are distributed to doctors in public clinics who act as "local-level political interlocutors" during elections (Callen, Gulzar, and Rezaee 2020, 613). In Ghana, local governments distribute menial jobs to "party boys" who help with electoral mobilization (Brierley 2021; Driscoll 2018).[9]

Patronage jobs thus are often described in the clientelism literature as key components of electoral machines and as perhaps the most important way of financing the work of political brokers.[10] Although this research provides much insight into the political activities of *some* public employees, not all patronage employees are brokers – not even most of them – and brokers are not the only ones in the public administration who are involved in political activities. This book will show that, crucially, employees other than brokers engage in political

---

[8] On the use of public employment to finance the work of brokers and activists in Argentina, see also Auyero (2000, 2001), Calvo and Murillo (2019), and Scherlis (2010, 2013).

[9] Even in India, where the use of patronage jobs to sustain the work of brokers seems less common, slum brokers are more than three times more likely to hold government jobs than ordinary slum residents (6.68 percent vs. 1.77 percent) (Auerbach and Thachil 2018).

[10] Note that brokers with public sector jobs tend to be party brokers, those who are committed to one party and have no ties with any other organization, or "hybrid brokers," with "loyalties to both a single political party and to an organization" (Holland and Palmer-Rubin 2015, 1202). The loyalty, of course, goes to the party that hires them. For a description of other types of brokers, see Holland and Palmer-Rubin (2015) and Mares and Young (2016). For a typology of brokers' strategies, see Gottlieb (2017).

activities that are fundamental to attracting and maintaining electoral support. Most scholars focus on brokers because they are central actors in a variety of electoral and political activities; however, many public sector employees under patronage contracts are not political brokers, but they are nonetheless involved in the provision of political services. We know very little about the activities of these less studied and less influential but still key political workers.[11]

2.2   POLITICAL SERVICES

Even in contexts with widespread patronage, public sector employees are primarily concerned with the delivery of public services and the administration of state resources. Politicians who want to stay in power cannot distribute too many public sector jobs in exchange for political services without reducing their capacity to administrate efficiently and, as a consequence, harming their chances of reelection. Both the potential electoral returns of political appointees and the "on-the-job productivity" of public sector employees are essential for a politician's survival (Calvo and Murillo 2019). Indeed, the potential electoral gains from the distribution of patronage jobs can be counterproductive, since an inefficient bureaucracy leads to dissatisfied voters (Geddes 1994). Still, where civil service rules are weak or nonexistent, as is the case in most Latin American countries (e.g., Grindle 2012; Iacoviello 2006), politicians' discretionary power to appoint public sector workers can be used for political gain.

Politicians face a trade-off between hiring supporters chosen for their reliability and skills in providing political services and hiring workers selected for their qualifications and competence for the actual job. When politicians are particularly worried about their short-term political survival, they might prioritize political appointments; when they feel more secure in their positions, they might focus more on "effective governance" (Geddes 1994). This trade-off, however, is less relevant for the mid- and low-level positions studied in this book. First, as Geddes (1994, 143) points out, patronage appointments can be concentrated among jobs that are "inessential to implementation" (e.g., janitors, drivers, and regular office workers).[12] Second, it is possible as well that the supply of skilled supporters who are technically competent and loyal is sufficient to fill professional

---

[11] The difference between brokers and other, less influential, patronage employees is not always clear. Brokers are more involved in politics and provide political services more often than other patronage employees. They often have access to resources that regular patronage employees do not have. Their main focus is politics, even if they regularly perform their formal duties as public employees, and they often have political career ambitions. Put differently, their public sector jobs are a way to finance their political work. The opposite is true for regular patronage employees who, as this book shows, provide political work in order to keep their public sector jobs.

[12] Brierley (2021) and Driscoll (2018) argue this is the strategy used in Ghana.

positions.[13] Although the question is beyond the scope of this book, contextual factors such as the education level among the population (or among base supporters of the party) might condition the trade-off.

This book focuses on the jobs that are distributed with the expectation of receiving political support in return. Patronage employees are, of course, expected to vote for the patron who appointed them, but the type of support that is expected in exchange for a position in the public administration goes far beyond that. Indeed, it is unlikely that the number of votes cast by public employees could be enough to substantively change electoral outcomes in a general election, so using public sector jobs to simply buy votes is expensive and inefficient. The high cost of distributing public jobs does not mean that politicians do not use them for political gain; it simply means that politicians expect more than just a vote in return (e.g., Calvo and Murillo 2019; Calvo and Ujhelyi 2012; Kemahlioğlu 2012; Stokes 2009).

The type of political support that patronage employees provide to their bosses in exchange for their positions in the administration varies considerably according to rank. This book focuses on the political services that are most commonly performed by those who hold low- and mid-level government positions. Low-level positions refer to menial jobs such as street sweepers, janitors, drivers, maintenance workers, and security officers; mid-level positions include secretarial and administrative positions, as well as posts for professionals such as architects, doctors, engineers, lawyers, and accountants. While there is of course still variation within this group in terms of the types of services provided, they are fundamentally different from the services typically performed by high-level political appointees, who enjoy more power and often have access to significantly more resources. All countries accept some discretionary appointments at the top level of government: "Personal appointments that are expected to provide them [incumbents] with loyal advisers and others who are committed to their political agenda or vision" (Grindle 2012, 18). The political support provided by those appointed at the top of the administration is often related to maintaining control over public policy.

Naturally, politicians want to appoint someone they trust to areas that they consider important for their administration, someone who will implement politician-preferred policies or as Müller (2006, 191) puts it, "smooth the implementation of policies." Müller refers to this type of patronage, the allocation of important positions, as "power patronage," distinguishing it from "service patronage," which refers to the distribution of public sector

---

[13] A recent paper that combines individual-level data on party membership with data on the universe of formal workers in Brazil shows that supporters hired by the municipal government after their party is elected tend to be of similar (or even higher) quality than members of the runner-up party (Brollo, Forquesato, and Gozzi 2017).

jobs in exchange for the client's political support "outside" the job.[14] From the principal-agent perspective that predominates in the study of bureaucracies in advanced democracies (Pepinsky, Pierskalla, and Sacks 2017), one of the main problems in the relationship between politicians (principals) and bureaucrats (agents) is how to make sure that the politician can delegate responsibility to the bureaucrat and still obtain the preferred outcome.[15] Patronage appointments solve this problem by considerably increasing the likelihood that the interests of the bureaucrat mirror those of the politician. In addition to guaranteeing control over decision-making processes, political appointments at high and medium levels of an administration can also be motivated by other goals, including maintaining the party leadership, reinforcing or enlarging the governmental coalition, and bargaining with elective officials (e.g., Geddes 1994; Kopecký and Mair 2006; Wilson 1961).

However, "power patronage" can also be used for less noble purposes than solving problems of delegation and control. Having supporters appointed to relevant positions makes it easier for parties and politicians to get public employees to do favors, make exceptions, and look the other way while giving politicians access to state resources – which creates more opportunities for abusing those resources.[16] High-level patronage appointees can be enablers for political corruption and particularistic distribution, such as vote buying and pork barreling. The manipulation of targeted public programs for political gain – such as the allocation of welfare benefits, targeted food distribution, or conditional cash transfer programs – is also facilitated when the public employees involved in their implementation are supporters of the politician expected to benefit from the clientelistic exchange.[17] Many other government activities, such as business, housing, and market regulations and subsidies, loans, and procurement contracts for government infrastructure, permit considerable discretion and case-by-case targeting.[18] In all of these situations, appointing supporters to key positions gives politicians ample opportunities for corruption.[19] Finally, the diversion of state funds – or

---

[14] Similarly, Kopecký and Mair (2012) propose a distinction between patronage as an electoral resource (equivalent to Müller's service patronage) and patronage as an organizational resource (equivalent to power patronage).

[15] See Gailmard and Patty (2012) for a review.

[16] See, among others, Bozçağa and Holland (2018), Dahlström and Lapuente (2017), Fisman and Golden (2017), Geddes (1994), Gingerich (2013b), Grzymala-Busse (2007, 2008), Holland (2016, 2017), Kitschelt and Wilkinson (2007b), Kopecký, Scherlis, and Spirova (2008), Müller (2006, 2007), and Piattoni (2001).

[17] See Weitz-Shapiro (2012, 2014) for a study of the implementation of a targeted food distribution program in Argentina that shows the central role of the head of the social welfare office in cases of manipulation.

[18] See Kitschelt and Wilkinson (2007b) for more of these examples and Holland (2017) for examples of regulatory manipulation.

[19] See Hopkin (2004) for a discussion of the growing illicit party fundraising associated with the decline of the mass party model of funding.

bribes – for political activities or the use of public property for such activities also requires supporters in key administrative positions who are willing to collaborate with the politician (Figueroa 2021; Gingerich 2013b).

The political services studied in this book are of a different kind. I focus on the type of services usually provided by patronage employees in low- and mid-level positions, from janitors, maintenance workers, drivers, and administrative assistants or secretaries, to nurses, lawyers, and accountants. These employees are often involved in campaigning, organizing and attending rallies, voting in primaries, mobilizing voters for elections, organizing and attending political meetings, providing favors to citizens, distributing material incentives, and serving as partisan monitors at the polls on Election Day. All of these political services are particularly relevant in a relatively young democracy like Argentina, where attachment to party labels is weaker than in advanced democracies (Baker and Dorr 2019), parties hold inconsistent policy commitments (Lupu 2015), and the ideological placement of parties is often unclear (Calvo and Murillo 2013, 2019). In this context, particularly at the local level, electoral campaigns (Greene 2019) and "non-policy benefits" such as competence and clientelistic offers (Calvo and Murillo 2019) may play a larger role in determining electoral outcomes (Lupu, Oliveros, and Schiumerini 2019). As Chapters 4 and 5 show, many public employees in Argentina act as intermediaries between the government and voters by providing political services before, during, and after Election Day.

Public employees with patronage jobs owe their appointments to their patron: they have jobs that they would not have received were it not for the patron or patron's party. Most of them, however, combine their regular jobs in the public administration with their duties "outside" the job (political services). Only the most important brokers have true "no show" jobs.[20] As described by Banfield and Wilson (1963, 119) long ago:

---

[20] There is anecdotal evidence in Argentina that some discretionary appointments are occasionally (although rarely) made as a mode of fundraising: appointing someone who provides a name for a contract (usually in exchange for a percentage of the salary) but who is not expected to do anything in return; the salary is used to finance the party. This is illegal, of course, so it is hard to collect systematic data to test this use of public job contracts, but journalistic accounts sometimes refer to such a scenario (see also Scherlis 2010, 218). Moreover, appointments are occasionally (but also rarely) made to help someone in particular or return a favor. In Argentina, this seems to be more common among legislative employees than those appointed to the executive, but, once again, the evidence on this issue is only anecdotal (Scherlis 2010 and personal interviews). During my fieldwork, I encountered two such situations: in one, the appointment was made to help the widow of a former public employee; in the other, it was made to help an employee's sick relative. I also encountered a few cases of nepotism in which the appointees were relatives of the politician, collecting salaries without any expectation that they would be working. Influential brokers appearing on the payroll sometimes have "no show" jobs too but, in all three municipalities I studied, other employees could clearly distinguish employees who were doing full-time political work from the ones who collected their checks and did nothing in return.

To get the services of men with the ability and energy that the jobs require, the machine must offer precinct captains and ward leaders [brokers] substantial inducements. Captains are often "payrollers," that is, they have appointive public jobs they could not get or keep if were not for the party. Some have "no show" jobs: they are carried on the public payroll without being required to show up for work. A larger number have "show" jobs and work like other employees – some more conscientiously than most – but their absence on election day and on other special occasions when the party needs them are overlooked.

Public employees with patronage contracts provide political services during primary and general elections, and also between elections. Their role is crucial during the campaign and on Election Day, especially since the availability of volunteer activists in Argentina has decreased over the years (Levitsky 2003; Scherlis 2010; Waisbord 1996).[21] Local politicians usually do not have enough resources to afford professional campaigns with extensive media use (Kemahlioğlu 2012). Particularly at the local level, labor-intensive activities such as canvassing, conducting political meetings, painting graffiti, putting up posters, transporting voters to polling places, and organizing and attending rallies are still essential parts of campaigning (e.g., Calvo and Murillo 2019; Kemahlioğlu 2012; Scherlis 2010; Zarazaga 2014). The most influential patronage employees on the payroll – brokers – are also key actors in vote-buying strategies (e.g., Remmer 2007; Stokes 2005; Stokes et al. 2013; Zarazaga 2014). On the day of the election, patronage employees also help by bringing voters to the polls and by serving as partisan poll watchers.[22] This book focuses on three activities that are essential during elections: helping with the campaign, attending rallies, and monitoring elections.

Public sector employees, brokers, and activists in general are also critical in Argentinean primary races. In contrast to general elections – in which voting is mandatory and turnout is usually around 80 percent – very few people participate in intra-party elections. In primaries, patronage employees play active and important roles as voters, in addition to getting voters to the polls and monitoring the polls on Election Day. The key role of the "machine" in these low-turnout elections in Argentina has been emphasized by a number of scholars (e.g., De Luca, Jones, and Tula 2006; Jones and Hwang 2005; Scherlis

---

[21] In the case of the labor-based Peronist party, this decline was partly a consequence of the weakening of its linkages to unions in the 1980s and 1990s (Levitsky 2003). Indeed, for Levitsky (2003), one of the main factors that explains the successful transition of the Peronist party from "labor-based populism" was its access to a politicized bureaucracy that allowed the party to distribute (and take advantage of) patronage jobs.

[22] In Argentina, each party competing in an election has the right to assign a partisan monitor (poll watcher, or *fiscal*) in each precinct and a head monitor (*fiscal general*) in each polling place (typically a school). In addition, Argentine electoral law requires at least one and up to three citizens selected by the government to monitor the election and count the votes. Although the citizens selected by the government are the only ones with authority to make decisions on electoral issues, political parties consider it crucial to have their own people present to ensure that votes are fairly counted. See Chapter 3 for more details.

2010; Zarazaga 2014).[23] Since 2011, when the voting laws changed, primary elections have been mandatory for both parties and voters for presidential and legislative positions. With mandatory voting and high turnout, primary elections for national candidacies have become similar to general elections.[24] For local elections, however, electoral laws present significant variation; some provinces have mandatory primaries, while others preserve the old system of voluntary voting in primaries (Domínguez 2017). In the latter case, the central role for patronage employees, brokers, and activists remains unchanged.

Patronage jobs are also important in day-to-day public administration. One of the most important activities that patronage employees perform between elections is providing favors. In places with weak institutions, like Argentina and many other young democracies, public officials have considerable discretion about how and when to enforce rules. In this situation, for many people – especially the poor – it is crucial to have regular access to someone in government or to someone with access to government officials who can provide solutions to their problems, especially at the local level. The most politically influential and active patronage employees – brokers – do significantly more than just providing specific favors to those who approach the public administration seeking help. Brokers are usually in charge of facilitating the access of poor people to the state as well as helping the state reach poor populations.[25] Often patronage employees themselves, brokers act as intermediaries between people in need of favors and other patronage employees who are in a position to help. Their intermediary status allows brokers to provide a wide range of favors that would be impossible without these various connections to other patronage employees.[26]

In sum, public employees under patronage contracts constitute an invaluable supply of free political workers who provide numerous services to their patrons.

---

[23] According to De Luca, Jones, and Tula (2006, 11), for instance, primary election results "indicate which party machine has the most resources (and makes the most efficient use of its resources), not which candidate (or list of candidates) is most popular among, or ideologically compatible with, the primary electorate." See also Kemahlioğlu (2012) for an analysis of the effect of internal party politics on the distribution of patronage jobs in Argentina (and Turkey).

[24] Turnout was above 70 percent in the first primary election held under this law, in August 2011. For an analysis of this election, see Pomares, Page, and Scherlis (2011).

[25] As in many other low- and middle-income countries, poor areas in Argentina are usually isolated from the centers of power, because of real geographical distance, transportation, or security. Brokers thus are crucial intermediaries between the poor and the distant state. Brokers usually live in the same neighborhood as the people they help, and they are essential at providing information about poor people's needs to politicians and finding solutions to their problems. They are often also in charge of organizations that provide various services to citizens, such as sport clubs, soup kitchens, or health-care centers (e.g., Auyero 2001; Levitsky 2003; Szwarcberg 2015; Vommaro and Quirós 2011; Zarazaga 2014). In Argentina, brokers can also be crucial in preventing or instigating social unrest (Auyero 2007; Zarazaga 2014).

[26] Chapter 5 looks at the provision of favors by both brokers and other less influential patronage employees. It focuses both on direct demands for favors (from voters to patronage employees) and on indirect ones (through brokers).

Of course, the level of involvement of each individual varies considerably. While some, for instance, are in charge of organizing rallies, others merely attend those rallies; other employees do not provide any political service at all. Establishing the extent to which public sector employees are involved in these political activities is one of the goals of this book. What we do know from the existing literature is that public sector jobs are one of the main ways of financing political work. The control of patronage jobs, allowing the incumbent to finance political services, provides incumbents with an important electoral advantage over their competitors and increases their probability of being reelected. In this book, I unpack the specific mechanisms behind the electoral gains from patronage appointments, offering a detailed examination of the political services that low- and mid-level patronage employees provide and the logic behind this provision.

2.3   THE COMMITMENT PROBLEM

Patronage jobs provide politicians in power with an invaluable resource: "free" political workers. Patronage contracts, however, are far from ideal because they are not easy to enforce. One difficulty is that the exchange is sequenced, posing risks to both parties. The risk for clients who provide political services with the expectation of getting a public sector job is that the politician may decide not to hire them after all. The risk for the politician is that clients who receive public sector jobs with the implicit or explicit understanding that they will provide political services in the future can easily decide not to comply with their side of the agreement after getting the job. Another difficulty is that the law cannot be used to force either the politician or employees (or potential employees) to deliver on their promises (Piattoni 2001; Robinson and Verdier 2013). It is thus reasonable to expect clientelistic relations to be full of opportunities for defection and betrayal (Stokes 2007).

In the first type of exchange – in which political support is provided *before* the benefit is received – patrons need to be able to make credible promises to clients in order for the patronage agreement to be successful. If the patron cannot credibly commit to distribute public sector jobs after the election, clients have no incentive to provide political services during the campaign. This type of commitment problem – in which politicians' credibility affects the actions of clients in what Nichter (2009) calls "prospective clientelism" – is ameliorated when the benefit being exchanged is a public sector job. The distribution of public sector jobs has an advantage over other types of excludable goods in that the distribution is contingent on the politician winning the election (Robinson and Verdier 2013).[27] When the benefit is

---

[27] Although we agree on distribution being contingent on the politician's electoral success, the argument in Robinson and Verdier (2013) about why a public sector job is a credible way for politicians to redistribute is different from mine. They argue that patronage jobs are a credible

outcome-contingent, clients have a strong incentive to provide political services to make sure the politician actually wins the election. Politicians have a credible incentive to comply with their side of the agreement afterwards, not only because employees will be needed in the administration anyway, but also because political services will continue to be needed after the election. From the point of view of the patron, citizens who showed commitment by providing political services before the election are more likely to be willing to provide political services after the election, as we see below, so there is an incentive for the politician to give them jobs.

More generally, clientelistic exchanges are based on long-term interactions.[28] In these ongoing relationships, politicians care about reputation. Those who systematically break their promises to supporters will be unable to sustain their electoral base over time (e.g., Calvo and Murillo 2019; Díaz-Cayeros, Estévez, and Magaloni 2016; Zarazaga 2014, 2015). Clients, of course, prefer dealing with brokers and politicians who have a "reputation for delivering" on their promises, and brokers and politicians understand that keeping their promises is "crucial for maintaining clients' loyalty" (Zarazaga 2014, 24). This concern about reputation raises the cost of noncompliance for patrons and brokers. They can still opt to renege on their promises, but over time the strategy may not be sustainable. For all these reasons, opportunistic defection in "prospective clientelism" – particularly when the benefit exchanged is a public sector job that is contingent on the patron getting into power – seems less likely than defection when the job is distributed in exchange for future political support.

The rest of this chapter (and this book) focuses on this second and more problematic type of exchange – in which political support is provided *after* the benefit is received. In such a situation, politicians risk "wasting" jobs on clients who, once hired, might not comply with their side of the agreement. Patronage employees who receive public sector jobs with the understanding that they will provide political services in return can easily renege on their side of the agreement *after* getting the job. Why would patronage employees comply with their side of the patronage agreement after receiving the benefit of the

---

way of redistribution (in contrast, for example, to pure transfer of income) because patronage jobs distributed to members of the patron's group generate rents for the patron. The reason for limiting the effect to members of the patron's group is because, in their view, close links between patrons and clients help ameliorate the moral hazard problem: "Because the incumbent patron is in the same social network as these agents, this patron can observe their effort with relatively high probability, which reduces the moral-hazard problem sufficiently that the patron can make them credible employment offers" (Robinson and Verdier 2013, 267). So, from the point of view of the politician, the argument goes back to monitoring and punishment; with members of the group this is simply easier (cheaper) to achieve.

[28] See Auyero (2000, 2001), Calvo and Murillo (2019), Díaz-Cayeros, Estévez, and Magaloni (2016), Hicken (2011), Kitschelt and Wilkinson (2007b), Mares and Young (2018), Szwarcberg (2015), and Zarazaga (2014, 2015), among others.

job? How can politicians make sure not to "waste" jobs on employees who will not fulfill their side of the deal?

2.4   MAKING PATRONAGE WORK: A THEORY OF SELF-ENFORCING PATRONAGE

What makes patronage contracts self-enforcing is that patronage jobs are distributed to supporters whose fates are tied to the political survival of their patron. Patronage employees believe that patronage jobs (and associated working conditions) will be maintained by the incumbent after reelection but not by the opposition, since supporters of the incumbent cannot credibly commit to provide political services for the opposition.[29] Patronage employees therefore engage in political activities that support their patron because they believe that the benefit of the job (and its associated working conditions) is contingent on the politician remaining in power. Put simply: their incentives are aligned.

Politicians want to distribute patronage jobs to people who are most likely to comply with the patronage agreement and provide political services. Finding such employees, however, is not easy. Potential employees can promise future compliance, but for this promise to be credible in the absence of a threat of punishment for non-compliers or feelings of reciprocity, it has to be incentive compatible. Only when potential employees can credibly commit to providing political support in the future are patronage contracts self-sustaining. The need to make the contracts incentive compatible leads to the distribution of these jobs to supporters – or, at least, to those *perceived* as such. All potential employees can promise to provide political services in the future, but only supporters can make these promises credible,[30] believing as they do that the incumbent – but not a competing politician – will maintain their jobs and working conditions. Supporters therefore have important incentives to provide political services to help their patron stay in power, which makes their original commitment credible.

If politicians could somehow know *ex ante* how potential employees would behave once hired, then the problem of commitment associated with the sequenced nature of the patronage agreement would of course disappear. Full information about the intentions of potential patronage employees would minimize strategic defection and solve the commitment problem for politicians. As Calvo and Ujhelyi (2012) argue, there is heterogeneity in the willingness of potential public employees to provide political services; with complete information, politicians would just simply hire the "right type" – those who

---

[29] As explained below, depending on the context, the incumbent patron could be a politician or a political party; the opposition could be an individual politician or a party.

[30] As explained in the following paragraphs, being a "true" supporter or not does not change the predictions of the theory. What matters is whether or not potential employees are *perceived* (or branded) as supporters.

would be more willing to provide political services in the future. While the intentions of potential patronage employees to provide political services once hired is private information, their declared (or perceived) political preferences regarding the politician at the time of hiring are not.[31] When hiring is mainly conducted through informal channels – as is the case in many young democracies with weak civil service systems – it is possible for politicians to access that information and use it for their own benefit.

Politicians thus use referrals as well as partisan and personal connections to screen potential patronage employees and to separate perceived supporters from non-supporters.[32] Supporters might like the politician or the politician's party for ideological or personal reasons; because of past or expected benefits, they might have connections with the party; or they might just want to be perceived as supporters in order to obtain benefits. Perceived support is not about ideological affinity but rather about proximity to the politician's network, which may or may not be due to ideology. In line with Calvo and Murillo (2013, 2019), who show that voters' perception of the likelihood of being offered a public sector job increases among Argentineans who are more connected to partisan networks,[33] I argue that citizens who are closer to these networks, those whom I call *supporters* for simplicity, will be the ones that the politician chooses to hire.

Voters can make efforts to be visible to the patron (or broker) by inserting themselves further into the partisan network and making sure they are identified as supporters. They can, for example, campaign on behalf of their patron before the election or attend political meetings and rallies (e.g., Auyero 2001; Nichter 2009; Szwarcberg 2015; Vommaro and Quirós 2011). Supporters and non-supporters differ in their likelihood of providing political services in the future. All things being equal, those who demonstrate support are less likely to renege

---

[31] See Calvo and Ujhelyi (2012) for the design of optimal patronage contracts with no information about individual political preferences.

[32] Scholars who conceptualize clientelism as a long-lasting relationship and not as a one-shot interaction emphasize that patrons (or, more often, their brokers) know their clients well (e.g., Auyero 2001; Ronconi and Zarazaga 2019; Szwarcberg 2015; Zarazaga 2014, 2016). Moreover, an important part of the literature on clientelism has focused on discussing who gets targeted in the clientelistic exchanges, with the assumption (usually not directly problematized) that patrons and brokers can screen core and swing voters (e.g., Nichter 2008; Stokes 2005; Stokes et al. 2013). Finan and Schechter (2012) and Stokes et al. (2013) provide systematic evidence that brokers do know the political preferences of their clients. Schneider (2019) and Brierley and Nathan (2019), however, show that this is not the case in rural India and Ghana, respectively.

[33] According to Calvo and Murillo (2013, 2019), this is true for the Peronist party and the Radical party (the two parties that governed the municipalities included in this book and the two main Argentine parties at the time) and for the PRO (but not for ARI). To measure linkages between voters and parties, they use a measure of proximity to the network of activists for each party. They calculate this distance using questions such as: "how many people do you know, and they know you, who are activists of party x?"

on the agreement and are more likely to provide the promised political services. This is partly because they are more likely than non-supporters to truly support the party or the politician, making the provision of political services less costly for them. Politicians then use *perceived* preferences at the time of hiring as a proxy for citizens' future likelihood of providing political services. At the same time, politicians have a reputation to protect: politicians who systematically ignore supporters for patronage positions will be unable to maintain their electoral coalition over the long term (e.g., Calvo and Murillo 2019; Díaz-Cayeros, Estévez, and Magaloni 2016; Zarazaga 2014, 2015).

Other studies on clientelism and patronage in Argentina, as well as my own research, provide evidence of this pattern. Indeed, recent studies argue that politicians allocate resources based on preexisting linkages with the beneficiaries of those resources – especially in the case of patronage jobs (e.g., Calvo and Murillo 2004, 2013, 2019; Kemahlioğlu 2012; Stokes et al. 2013). Data from my own survey of public employees (described in Chapter 3) shows considerable discretion and political bias in hiring decisions in Argentina's public administration. Around 64 percent of respondents reported having found their job through an acquaintance, a friend, or a relative, and the majority of respondents (59 percent) considered personal connections to be "important" or "very important" for getting a job (see Chapter 3). Proximity to a political network, however, does not necessarily mean ideological affinity. In their survey of Argentinean voters, Calvo and Murillo (2019) show that voters' ideological self-placement (on a left-right scale) is not associated with their connections to specific partisan networks; i.e., regardless of their ideology, voters reported knowing similar numbers of activists from the two main parties. They also find no correlation between voters' ideological placement and their perceived likelihood of receiving public sector jobs if one of the parties were to win the election.[34] Regardless of the ideology of their survey respondents, distributive expectations about public jobs increase among those who are more connected to partisan networks. Data from my public employees' survey shows a similar pattern. Employees reported that personal connections were more important than partisan affiliation and political ideology as hiring criteria.

Still, the fact that public jobs are disproportionally distributed to perceived supporters does not solve the commitment problem. Perceptions could be misleading. In the case of "true" ideological supporters, those absolutely committed to the goals of the party or the politician, it might be possible to believe that their commitment is so strong that they will provide sustained political support for as long as it is needed. All things being equal, the higher their commitment, the less likely they are to defect. On the other hand, once citizens expect the distribution of patronage jobs on the basis of perceived political preferences, they have an incentive both to get closer to the partisan

---

[34] Interestingly, this is also true for handouts (Calvo and Murillo 2019).

network and to misrepresent their preferences in order to get a job. As Sofía, an employee from Salta, bluntly explains: "I've told you that I got this job through politics, but the thing is that I was politically active *in order to* get a job."[35]

Supporters, however, are often not completely partisan, i.e., solely motivated by the welfare of the party or the politician they support, and they are also not completely opportunistic, i.e., only motivated by their own welfare. Rather, they often act from some combination of the two.[36] At the same time, loyalty to the party or the politician may be endogenous to the patronage exchange itself (Calvo and Murillo 2019; Díaz-Cayeros, Estévez, and Magaloni 2016). Potential patronage employees could then have certain political preferences because they expect to get a job or, more strategically, they may pretend to have those preferences to get a job. Once hired, patronage employees may still change their minds about their political preferences or simply reduce the effort they are willing to devote to political work. Because the exchange is sequenced, employees with patronage jobs – even perceived supporters – can still renege on their side of the agreement after being hired. Being a supporter – or, more accurately, being *perceived* as one – is not in itself enough to guarantee compliance with the patronage contract.

What, then, explains the fact that patronage agreements are nevertheless respected? Why do public employees under patronage contracts keep providing political services after getting the job? Even when politicians are able to appoint perceived supporters who are more likely to provide political services in the first place – because they might truly care about the future of the party or the politician – this is not enough to guarantee compliance.

The fact that patronage employees believe that their jobs are tied to the political success of their patron is what makes patronage contracts self-enforcing. In the absence of civil service rules, the incentive structure of the patronage agreement is such that employees believe that the benefit of the job is contingent on the politician's reelection. Public employees under patronage contracts believe that if the incumbent loses the election, their own jobs (or working conditions) could be in jeopardy, which gives them a strong incentive to help the incumbent remain in power. Because the interests of patronage employees are then perfectly aligned with those of the incumbent – they both want the politician to stay in office – and providing political services could help achieve their common goal, the commitment problem associated with the sequenced nature of the clientelistic exchange disappears, and patronage contracts become self-enforcing.

But why do patronage employees believe that they could lose their jobs or suffer negative changes in their working conditions under a new

---

[35] Author interview, Salta, June 8, 2011.

[36] This terminology is adapted from Persson and Tabellini's (2000) characterization of politicians as both *partisan* (those who care about the well-being of particular groups of society) and *opportunistic* (those who want to maximize their own well-being).

administration? Perceived political preferences at the time of hiring have the same effect as do the public pledges discussed by Kitschelt and Wilkinson (2007b, 15): those whose support for the incumbent is publicly known "are effectively then cut off from any expectation of rewards if the opposition should win."[37] Because the distribution of patronage jobs is based on perceived political preferences (or proximity to the partisan network), once clients are hired as supporters for a patronage job their "true" political preferences do not matter anymore. Their *perceived* political preferences dictate the treatment they will receive from the opposition. Whether patronage workers are purely ideological and committed supporters, purely opportunistic ones, or – more frequently – something in between, they will be branded and treated as supporters of the incumbent by the opposition. Using the same logic that the incumbent applied to hire her supporters in the first place, a new incumbent will replace old employees with her own supporters. A new politician will want to distribute patronage jobs to people who are more likely to provide political services for her, and only *her* own supporters could credibly commit to do that in the future. Consequently, current employees will be replaced, demoted, or sidelined. As a result, supporters of the incumbent (or those branded or perceived as such) have a great incentive to provide political services to try to keep the incumbent who hired them in power.

The argument advanced in this book is related to the model of Robinson and Verdier (2013), who note that in prospective clientelism, *promises* of public sector employment tie "the continuation utility of a voter to the political success of a particular politician" (285). If the patron does not win the election, there are no jobs to distribute.[38] My theory of self-enforcing patronage, however, departs from their formal model in fundamental ways. Most importantly, the continuation-value aspect in their model is for them not enough to guarantee compliance: "(politicians) must be able to use policies that tie the continuation utility of a voter to their political success, or alternatively, if behavior is observable, allow voters to be punished if they renege on the exchange" (261). For Robinson and Verdier, reversibility (as a threat for punishment) is key to solving the commitment problem: "a job has the additional advantage that it can be withdrawn as punishment" (262), so "if the client deviates and the patron is elected, the client will be punished by being denied a public-sector job" (279). This also explains, in their view, why only true supporters – those with "intrinsic preferences" for the patron – are the beneficiaries of jobs. To reduce

---

[37] See Nichter (2009) for an interesting example of how clients in northeast Brazil strategically decide to reveal or hide their preferences for candidates according to their expectations of being rewarded or punished after the election.

[38] Recall that what Nichter (2009) calls prospective clientelism refers to clientelistic exchanges in which the benefit (in this case, a public sector job) is provided after the support (voting, in the case of Robinson and Verdier 2013) is received. The theory of self-enforcing patronage, in contrast, focuses on exchanges in which the benefit (the job) is provided before the support (political services) is received.

the moral-hazard problem and solve the commitment issue, jobs need to be distributed to members of the patron's group so the "patron can observe their effort with relatively high probability" (265). In the theory outlined here, by contrast, reversibility only matters because employees believe that a new incumbent could fire or demote them, which creates incentives for them to try to help keep the current incumbent in office, without any need for monitoring and punishment. Being perceived as a supporter is important not because it makes monitoring easy, but because perceived supporters are more afraid of a change in the administration, which makes their original commitment to provide political services credible.

2.5 ALTERNATIVE EXPLANATIONS

The literature has long recognized the commitment problem associated with clientelistic agreements that are sequenced and cannot be legally enforced (e.g., Piattoni 2001; Robinson and Verdier 2013; Stokes 2007). Two main theories have been advanced to explain what makes clientelism (in the case of this book, patronage) work: norms of reciprocity and fear of retaliation. According to the first set of theories, norms of reciprocity enforce the clientelistic exchange: clients fulfill their side of the agreement because they want to help those who have helped them. Receiving a benefit engenders feelings of personal obligation, trust, and gratitude; clients help the patron because of these feelings (Graziano 1976; Scott 1972). In fact, it is precisely the presence of these feelings that distinguishes patron–client relationships from relationships of pure coercion: "A patron may have some coercive power and he may hold an official position of authority. But if the force or authority at his command are alone sufficient to ensure the compliance of another, he has no need of patron–client ties which require some reciprocity" (Scott 1972, 93).

More recently, other scholars have also argued that reciprocity plays a central role in clientelistic relationships, particularly in vote-buying exchanges. According to Schaffer (2007, 193), for instance, "embedding vote-buying within ritual gift exchange helps engender feelings of obligation among recipients and can thus lower the rate of defection." Similarly, Lawson and Greene (2014, 61) argue that the receipt of benefits "creates feelings of indebtedness and gratitude among voters, who ... spontaneously support their political patrons." Finan and Schechter (2012) argue in turn that vote-buying agreements can be sustained by norms of reciprocity; they use survey and experimental data from Paraguay to show that brokers target reciprocal individuals. From the reciprocity perspective, public employees fulfill their side of the agreement and provide political services simply because they want to help the person who helped them. Moreover, in the case of patronage, in which the benefit received is a public sector job, feelings of reciprocity should be particularly effective. As Lawson and Greene (2014, 65) note, "variation in the value of benefits should also affect the degree of obligation."

The logic of the second set of theories, the one most accepted among scholars of clientelism, is very different. Clients comply because they are afraid that the patron will cut off their benefits if they fail to do so.[39] Much of the contemporary literature on clientelism has focused on the monitoring and commitment problems associated with this perspective (e.g., Brusco, Nazareno, and Stokes 2004; Nichter 2008; Robinson and Verdier 2013; Stokes 2005, 2007). For the authors who support this understanding of clientelism, the ability of the patron to identify and punish noncompliers is what makes an exchange truly clientelistic.[40] Kitschelt and Wilkinson (2007b, 9), for instance, consider a clientelistic exchange to comprise three components: "contingent direct exchange, predictability, and monitoring." Stokes et al. (2013, 13) also emphasize this point: "The voter suffers a punishment (or reasonable fears that he or she will suffer one) should he or she defect from the implicit bargain of a benefit for a vote; not (just) good will, but fear of punishment, turns distributive largess into votes." For these scholars, the defining feature of clientelistic exchanges is that they are contingent upon the client's behavior.[41] The conditional part of the bargain is so important in their understanding of clientelism that Stokes et al. (2013, 12) propose to use the term "non-conditional individual benefits" to describe individually targeted benefits with partisan bias in cases in which "recipients who defect and vote for a different party suffer no individual punishment."[42]

If clients do not behave according to their patron's wishes, the patron has the power to punish individual clients by withdrawing or withholding benefits. This means that the patron must be able to monitor clients' behavior, or at least that clients must believe that monitoring is possible. When the support provided by the client is electoral, monitoring requires some mechanism that violates the secrecy of the ballot or, alternatively, one that makes clients believe that such surveillance is a real possibility.[43] In these situations, party machines need to have an army of brokers "deeply embedded in social networks" to select appropriate clients and monitor their behavior (Stokes 2009, 14).[44] Patrons

---

[39] Lawson and Greene (2014) referred to this approach as the "instrumentalist approach"; Baldwin (2013, 2015) calls it "contingent exchange."

[40] See Chapter 1 for a discussion of definitions of clientelism based on the fear of punishment.

[41] For a similar perspective, see, among others, Grzymala-Busse (2007, 2008), Hicken (2011), Kitschelt and Altamirano (2015), Magaloni, Díaz-Cayeros, and Estévez (2007), Medina and Stokes (2007), Nichter (2008, 2014), Stokes (2007, 2009), and Weitz-Shapiro (2012, 2014).

[42] Others have argued that the monitoring and sanctioning of clients does not necessarily need to happen at the individual level, but by the collective monitoring of small groups (e.g., Cooperman 2019; Cruz 2019; Gingerich and Medina 2013; Rueda 2015, 2017).

[43] See Chandra (2007, 89–90), Cruz (2015, 2019, 399–401), Kitschelt and Wilkinson (2007b, 15–18), and Schaffer and Schedler (2007, 22–24) for examples of different techniques to monitor electoral preferences (or to make voters believe that they can be monitored), even with the secret ballot. For an analysis of perceptions of ballot integrity in the Argentinean case, see Oliveros (2019).

[44] See also Schaffer (2007) and Lehoucq (2007).

and brokers may also use other, more visible, ways to test their clients' loyalty, such as turnout (Nichter 2008), attendance at rallies (Szwarcberg 2012, 2015), or participation in local institutions (González-Ocantos et al. 2012). Regardless of the type (and visibility) of political support, the logic is the same; for a patron to be able to ensure that the political support associated with the benefit is in fact provided, the patron should be able to identify and credibly commit to punish noncompliers (and/or reward compliers). Clientelism is thus a "perverse" form of accountability in which parties hold voters accountable, not the other way around (Stokes 2005). From this perspective, the commitment problem is solved on the basis of a threat – patronage employees provide political services because they are afraid that the patron will cut off the benefit and fire them if they fail to do so.

My theory of self-enforcing patronage presents a different solution to the commitment problem that arises in clientelistic agreements. It is neither reciprocity nor the threat of punishment that ensures patronage employees uphold their part of the deal, but, rather, that their fates are tied to the political fate of their patron. Indeed, clients comply with clientelistic agreements because their incentives are aligned with those of their patrons – both the patron and client will benefit from the patron's success. Of course, this is not to say that fear of punishment or feelings of reciprocity are never present in clientelistic exchanges or that they are not possible, but rather that neither of these two factors is a *necessary* characteristic of these types of arrangements.[45] Patronage employees provide services because their incentives are aligned with the incentives of their patron. To the extent that patrons and clients share the same interests, monitoring is not necessary.

2.6 A NOTE ON THE COLLECTIVE ACTION PROBLEM

In the theory of self-enforcing patronage, public employees comply with patronage contracts because they believe that it is in their best interest to provide political services to help to keep their patron in power. More precisely, public employees believe that it is in their best interest that political services are provided *by someone,* so the incumbent politician gets reelected.

---

[45] The literature on clientelism that focuses on commitment issues has devoted considerable attention to whether it is possible to monitor voting behavior under the secret ballot (e.g., Brusco, Nazareno, and Stokes 2004; Nichter 2008; Stokes 2005, 2007). In the type of political support that I study here, political services, the possibility of monitoring is generally not an issue. Many of the political activities I look at are visible and thus potentially easy to monitor. However, just because these activities *can* be monitored does not mean that they *are*, in fact, being monitored. I do not claim that the political services provided by patronage employees are impossible or even difficult to monitor, but rather that monitoring behavior is not necessary under well-designed patronage contracts in which these jobs are distributed to supporters whose fates are tied to the fate of the incumbent.

What then are their individual incentives to contribute?[46] As with other public goods (such as the reelection of the incumbent) that depend on collective contributions (such as political services), there may be a temptation for each individual actor to let others exert the effort. In the words of Olson (1965, 21): "Though all the members of the group therefore have a common interest in obtaining this collective benefit, they have no common interest in paying the cost of providing that collective good. Each would prefer that the others pay the entire cost, and ordinarily would get any benefit provided whether he had borne part of the cost or not." In the absence of punishment, the benefit of the patron staying in power is non-excludable, so both those who comply with the patronage contract and provide political services and those who do not will equally enjoy the benefit of keeping the patron in power.

There are, however, at least four factors that reduce the likelihood of widespread free riding in the case of patronage, making cooperation more likely among patronage employees.[47] First and foremost, the important benefit at stake, a job, might be enough to provide a significant incentive for cooperation. Public sector jobs are indeed highly valued, both for the benefits associated with a formal position in the public administration, particularly in places like Latin America with high rates of informal employment, and for the remuneration, especially for low-skilled workers. For instance, in 2012, the average public employee in Latin America earned 38 percent more than a formal private employee and twice as much as an informal worker (Arcidiácono et al. 2014). In addition, the salary of the average public employee in Latin America increased 40 percent between 1992 and 2012, compared to a 19 percent increase for formal private workers (Arcidiácono et al. 2014). Moreover, public sector employees may enjoy job security, which has no equivalent in the private sector, and often receive better benefits than in the private sector.[48] Data from my own survey also reflect that local public administration positions are highly valued; the large majority of respondents reported being satisfied (59 percent) or very satisfied (31 percent) with their jobs.

With a benefit this large, patronage employees might be willing to pay the cost (provide political services) to make sure that the desirable outcome (the incumbent is reelected) actually happens. While some may be more comfortable with risk, the bigger the benefit, the fewer people there are who would risk missing the benefit. When there is a great deal at stake, more people will

---

[46] Others have raised similar concerns in relation to political brokers (e.g., Camp 2017; Stokes et al. 2013; Szwarcberg 2015). To create incentives for brokers to deliver, scholars have argued that political parties monitor their performance and offer them private rewards (e.g., Larreguy, Marshall, and Querubín 2016; Szwarcberg 2015).

[47] Both laboratory experiments and field studies have shown that collective action succeeds far more often than expected by Olson's theory. See Ostrom (2000) for a discussion of this point.

[48] For instance, while 83 percent of public sector employees have health insurance associated with their jobs, the proportion decreases to 67 percent for formal private employees (Arcidiácono et al. 2014). See also Chapter 7.

participate to avoid regretting their actions later, should the undesirable outcome (the incumbent losing the election, in this case) come to pass (Ferejohn and Fiorina 1974). At the same time, as Aytaç and Stokes (2019, 78) show for protest participation and voting, when individuals care greatly about the outcome, it "may just not feel right" to free ride on others – what the authors called "the cost of abstention." In this framework, individuals are not motivated by the idea that their actions might be pivotal for the outcome but by the desire to avoid the psychological disutility associated with not taking part. This disutility is higher when individuals care a great deal about the outcome. Whether individual employees' contributions to the reelection effort are to ensure that the incumbent is in fact reelected or to avoid the dissonance associated with not taking part in the electoral effort from which they would benefit, the fact that public sector jobs are such an important benefit increases the chances that employees will actually engage in the provision of political services.

Second, individual contributions to providing political services, in contrast to such contributions to voting, are not necessarily irrelevant to the outcome. While one particular individual's attendance at a rally may have little impact, the efforts of the person in charge of mobilizing many others to attend the rally may be important to its success. The argument, of course, is not that an individual employee's campaigning is pivotal to the electoral outcome (or that any employee would believe that it is), but that such efforts can be consequential. Monitoring elections, for instance, as described in Chapter 4, is a good example of a key activity with a potentially important effect on the election. The ability to deploy partisan electoral monitors to every single election booth is considered to be fundamental to winning elections in Argentina (e.g., Casas, Díaz, and Trindade 2017; De Luca, Jones, and Tula 2002, 2006; Zarazaga 2014). The contribution each patronage employee makes in her role as a partisan poll monitor is far from irrelevant to the electoral outcome.

Third, the cost of cooperation is not necessarily high. Political services are often provided during regular working hours, so public employees don't have to choose between, for example, attending a rally and staying at home, but, rather, between attending a rally and performing their regular "on-the-job" duties. Among the services analyzed in this book, the provision of favors is a good example of the type of services that are often provided during regular working hours (see Chapter 5). Many campaign events and rallies also take place during regular working hours (see Chapter 3). Political services, of course, are not as "low-cost" as voting (Aldrich 1993) but the benefit at stake (a highly-valued public sector job) makes the cost of providing political services seem comparatively low.[49]

---

[49] For Aldrich (1993, 261), turnout is a "low-cost, low-benefit action (...) a decision almost always made 'at the margin.'" For him, even small changes in costs and benefits, like the ones campaigns

Finally, in the theory of self-enforcing patronage developed in this book, patronage jobs are distributed to perceived supporters. As explained above, perceived support is not necessarily about ideological affinity but rather about proximity to the partisan network, which may or may not be due to ideological preferences. Among the group of perceived supporters, however, there may very well be a subgroup of truly committed supporters. In this case, in which there is a "true" ideological alignment with the politician, patronage employees are even less likely to renege on the agreement and are more likely to provide the promised political services. For those who truly support the party or the politician, the provision of political services is less costly.[50] Indeed, whenever there is ideological alignment, moral hazard is less of a problem and patronage employees are less likely to shirk on their commitments.[51]

The argument, of course, is not that collective action problems cannot or do not arise among patronage employees, but that the likelihood of free riding being widespread enough to be detrimental to outcomes is small.[52] In the end, in the absence of monitoring and punishment or some other form of pressure, the level of effort patronage employees expend providing political services might be suboptimal from the point of view of the politician but still significant.[53] The

make, can change the cost–benefit equation for voters. In the case of patronage jobs, the benefit is high, which makes the cost (even when higher than voting) seems low in comparison.

[50] Note that this is different from the argument in Robinson and Verdier (2013). In their model, members of the patron's group, true supporters, are less likely to shirk because they are easier to monitor, while the argument here is that true supporters are more likely to cooperate because of their ideological alignment. For the subgroup among perceived supporters that are truly committed to the party or the politician, cooperation is less costly.

[51] For instance, Mexican teachers affiliated with the Mexican National Education Workers Union (SNTE), a well-known political machine, are effective at mobilizing voters only when the effort favors their preferred party, the Institutional Revolutionary Party, or PRI (Larreguy, Montiel Olea, and Querubín 2017).

[52] Other scholars have argued that free riding might be harder in small groups. Free riding on others' efforts may be harder to sustain when those whom one is shirking are co-workers one must face daily. Using laboratory experiments, Ostrom and Walker (1997) show that face-to-face communication in a public-goods game produces substantial increases in cooperation (see also Ostrom and Walker 2003). When an individual is part of a community – in this case, a group of employees – social or reputational concerns may outweigh any benefit that would result from free riding on others (Chong 1991; Olson 1965).

[53] Although beyond the scope of this book, it is possible to think of situations in which free riding could be more extensive. First, any situation in which the cost of participation is increased might make it more tempting for clients to free ride. For instance, if participation in politics involves physical risks, clients might be more willing to free ride on others, although Aytaç and Stokes (2019) show that situations that increase the cost of participation sometimes also increase participation. Alternatively, if the benefit of the job is reduced, it might not be considered important enough to overcome the temptation of letting others do the work. For instance, when finding a job in the private sector is considered an attractive and easily achieved option, the incentives to free ride may be larger since less is at stake. It is also possible to imagine situations in which the contribution of each employee's participation becomes less relevant. With very low levels of electoral competition, for example, employees might feel that their cooperation

possibility of free riding is always present (and some amount of it is probably inevitable), but the specific (high) benefit and (low) cost involved in patronage contracts, the non-trivial contribution of the political services to the desired electoral outcome (the reelection of the incumbent and, thus, the preservation of status quo working conditions) as well as the fact that at least some patronage employees are committed ideological supporters make cooperation more likely.

2.7   EMPIRICAL IMPLICATIONS, ASSUMPTIONS, AND SCOPE CONDITIONS

In the theory of self-sustaining patronage developed in this book, patronage jobs are disproportionately distributed to perceived supporters, who appear more willing than non-supporters to provide political services in the future and, more importantly, can credibly commit to do so. Public employees believe that patronage jobs held by supporters and the working conditions associated with those jobs will be continued if the incumbent is reelected, but not if the challenger wins. Supporters thus have strong incentives to provide political services to help the incumbent remain in power. Because the incentives of the employees and the politician are aligned – they both want the incumbent reelected – patronage contracts are incentive compatible and therefore sustainable without the threat of punishment.

This theory of self-enforcing patronage has three main empirical implications, which are tested in the following chapters. First, patronage jobs are disproportionately distributed to supporters, those more closely connected to the partisan network. Not all jobs, of course, are patronage jobs, so this implication does not mean that all jobs – or even the majority of them – go to supporters. Empirically, the theory simply predicts that politicians hire a disproportionate number of their own supporters. Second, because most patronage jobs are distributed to supporters, more supporters than non-supporters are involved in the provision of political services. Third, supporters are more involved in the provision of political services because they believe that their jobs and working conditions are tied to the political success of the incumbent politician. I expect supporters to be more worried than non-supporters about a new politician replacing the incumbent.

A key assumption of the theory developed in this book is that patronage employees care about their jobs. It is not necessary to assume that patronage employees care *only* about their jobs. In fact, it may be that they care both about keeping their jobs and about helping the politician or the party they support (if

is not necessary for winning the election, which might encourage free riding. Finally, even though it is generally accepted that cooperation in small groups is easier because of the potential social or reputational costs of non-cooperation, it is possible to imagine employees who do not care about other people's opinions and will still chose to free ride on others. In the end, "the world contains multiple types of individuals" (Ostrom 2000, 138).

any), but it is an important assumption of this theory that job-related concerns predominate. If employees do not care enough about maintaining their jobs (or about maintaining the working conditions associated with those jobs), the theory has very little explanatory power. This yields another testable empirical implication. I expect employees who are less afraid of losing their jobs to be less involved in the provision of services. Two characteristics of employees are particularly correlated with anxiety about losing their jobs: education and type of contract. Those with more education, who thus have more outside options, and those with job security, who can be subjected to changes in their working conditions but cannot be fired, have less to lose from a change in the administration. I expect individuals who are less afraid of losing their jobs – namely tenured employees and those with a higher level of education – to be less willing to provide political services in order to help the incumbent stay in power.

More-educated employees have better prospects in the private sector labor market, so public jobs are less valuable to them than to less-educated employees, who have fewer outside options.[54] They are therefore generally less afraid of losing their jobs and will accept or comply with patronage contracts less often than will individuals who have more to lose from a change in the administration. Empirically, I expect to see more-educated employees to be less involved in the provision of political services and to be less afraid of suffering negative changes with a new administration.[55]

In addition to education, a second characteristic that affects patronage employees' job security and, as a consequence, their willingness to comply with the patronage agreement is the type of employment contract under which they are hired. In Argentina, as in many other countries with civil service rules, some employees enjoy job security, while others work under temporary contracts that need to be periodically renewed. Employees with job security cannot be legally fired, so they should have no fear of losing their jobs with a new administration. Public sector employees with these types of patronage jobs still fear negative changes in their working conditions under a new administration – such as being transferred, sidelined, or demoted – but they have no fear of losing their jobs (see Chapter 6). I expect that tenured employees will be less afraid of losing their jobs and that they be less involved in the provision of political

---

[54] On this point, see Calvo and Murillo (2004, 2019), Medina and Stokes (2002, 2007), and Robinson and Verdier (2013), among others. Moreover, as Calvo and Murillo (2004, 2019) show in Argentina and Arcidiácono et al. (2014) in Latin America, the wage premium derived from a public job is higher for less educated employees. Alesina, Danninger, and Rostagno (2001) find similar distributive effects of patronage in Italy.

[55] Recall that the types of political services that are the focus of this book are those usually provided by political workers on the ground. It is possible that more educated employees are involved in other types of services not analyzed here.

services than untenured employees, who have more to lose from a new administration.

From the point of view of the politician, hiring more-educated employees may involve a trade-off between "on-the-job" and "off-the-job" productivity. More-educated employees are less sensitive to patronage exchanges and therefore are less willing to provide political services. But education and skills are necessary for certain types of jobs, so politicians may need to "sacrifice" potential political productivity to gain on-the-job productivity in certain positions. Politicians might choose to concentrate their patronage appointments on certain positions and hire for others based on meritocratic criteria. Without a functioning bureaucracy, the potential electoral gains from the distribution of patronage jobs become counterproductive. Consequently, more-educated employees have less to fear from a change in the administration since they have outside options if they are fired, but they are also less likely to be fired because new incumbents might need their on-the-job productivity.

This trade-off, however, does not exist for employees with job security. Since untenured employees are more sensitive to patronage agreements, incumbents – all things being equal – should always prefer to hire patronage employees under temporary contracts rather than under civil service rules. Untenured employees have more to lose than tenured employees from a change in administration and will therefore more eagerly participate in efforts to keep the politician in power. The choice of contracts, however, is not at the complete discretion of the incumbent. There are legal limits to the amount of time that an employee can be kept on a temporary contract. Moreover, when taking office, every new incumbent inherits a set of tenured employees already in the administration. For the argument developed here, it is sufficient to consider that, although politicians may prefer temporary contracts to tenured ones, they face both legal and political limits on their ability to choose the type of contract.

While the theory of self-enforcing patronage developed in this book is a general one applicable beyond the Argentinean case where I test it, the theory does have some scope conditions. First, it examines the commitment issues associated with patronage agreements, but patronage agreements are only possible in contexts of weak or nonexistent civil service systems. These are the norm in most Latin American countries as well as in many other young democracies (see Chapter 7). The argument presented here should have less explanatory power about appointments in countries with more strict regulations about hiring and firing public sector employees.

Second, the theory focuses on patronage jobs distributed by an incumbent who aims to be reelected. The theory does not provide much insight into situations in which the incumbent is not seeking reelection, either because the law does not allow it or because the politician decides not to seek it. However, the theory is generalizable to situations in which the incumbent patron is not a politician but a political party. Depending on the context and the type of party system, the patron could be a political party instead of an individual politician, and the opposition might refer to a different party or a faction within the same party. At the same time, the theory presumes a minimal level of competition between parties or factions within those parties. In situations of very low competition, in which the likelihood of the incumbent losing an election is exceedingly low, employees might not be afraid of a change in administration and therefore would have no incentive to provide political services to help the incumbent win.

Finally, the theory assumes that partisan or political preferences are somewhat informative. Although supporters do not need to be "true" believers for the predictions of the theory to hold, their perceived support needs to be meaningful. If citizens can identify themselves with one party or politician, and then switch at no cost – as might be the case in countries with extremely weak party systems – then being perceived or branded as a supporter does not provide any valuable information to the incumbent or challenger. Under those circumstances, supporters could not credibly commit to provide political services in the future, and the predictions of the theory do not hold.

2.8 SUMMARY

Departing from existing explanations, the theory of self-enforcing patronage developed in this book posits that patronage employees (clients) engage in political activities that support the incumbent (their patron) because their interests are aligned with the political success of that incumbent. Patrons do not need to monitor patronage employees and threaten to punish noncompliers, nor need they rely on feelings of reciprocity. To make patronage contracts work, politicians just need to be able to screen supporters from non-supporters and distribute patronage contracts only to the former. When patronage jobs are distributed to supporters (or to those perceived as such), patronage contracts are incentive compatible. Only perceived supporters, those whose fates are tied to the political fate of the politician who hires them, can credibly commit to provide political support in the future. Patronage employees believe that their jobs and working conditions will be maintained by the incumbent but not by the opposition, because perceived supporters of the incumbent cannot credibly commit to provide political services for the opposition. Supporters thus have large incentives to provide political services to help their patron remain in power, and this alignment of interests between patrons and clients makes patronage contracts self-sustaining.

The theory does not claim that monitoring political behavior is impossible. Unlike voting behavior under the secret ballot, the various political services studied here are visible – with the possible exception of the provision of favors – and, thus, potentially easy to monitor. However, just because they can be monitored does not mean that they are in fact being monitored. When patronage jobs are distributed to perceived supporters, patronage contracts are incentive compatible and monitoring, with its threat of punishment, is not necessary to sustain the exchange. Patronage employees provide services because their incentives are aligned with those of their patron, not because they are afraid of being punished if they fail to do so. As long as patrons and clients share the same interests, monitoring and the threat of punishment are not necessary

3

Getting the Job

Patronage contracts are distributed to perceived supporters in exchange for political services. Politicians hire supporters for patronage positions because their commitment to provide these political services in the future is credible (see Chapter 2). Indeed, public sector employees under patronage contracts often help during elections by attending rallies, assisting the campaign with a variety of tasks, and acting as partisan poll watchers. Between elections, they also fulfill their side of the agreement by dispensing favors to voters. Chapters 3 to 6 test the theory of self-enforcing patronage using individual-level data I collected from a survey of public employees fielded in three Argentinean municipalities. I also rely on months of ethnographic work, during which I interviewed public sector employees, political brokers, high-level public officials, and politicians.

Even though patronage is a widespread phenomenon, the difficulty in collecting systematic data about it means that we know very little about how patronage employees are hired, what they do, and why they do it. Scholars have used different proxies, such as the number of public employees and spending on personnel, to overcome the difficulties of measuring patronage. However, neither a high number of employees nor a disproportionate amount of spending on public sector jobs necessarily means that these are patronage jobs. Moreover, the challenge is not limited to assessing whether or not public sector jobs are distributed in exchange for political services. It is also important to be able to establish the type and extent of the political support that public employees provide to their bosses, together with the reasons behind this support. Directly asking either patrons or clients is unlikely to yield useful insights because both have incentives to lie.[1]

---

[1] On the difficulties of studying patronage and the different solutions scholars have found, see Chapter 1.

Instead of using proxy measures or direct survey questions to test the empirical implications of the theory of self-enforcing patronage, I take a different approach, one that allows me to elicit accurate information from the actors involved by minimizing social response bias. I use an original face-to-face survey of 1,200 local public sector employees that incorporates two strategies to elicit honest responses. The first, following Scacco (2010), consists of employing a number of techniques to earn the respondents' trust by guaranteeing the confidentiality of the most sensitive questions. The second is the use of list experiments, a survey technique that protects the privacy of responses by using indirect questioning. I also conducted multiple interviews to illustrate and provide a thicker description of the main findings.

Using this data, I examine how public sector jobs are distributed and to whom, the electoral behavior of public employees, and, in the following two chapters, the type and extent of the political services the employees provide to politicians. The findings are consistent with the theoretical expectations of the theory of self-enforcing patronage outlined in Chapter 2. First, I show that most jobs are distributed through informal channels. Then I provide evidence that public sector jobs are disproportionally distributed to perceived supporters, who not only provide electoral support but also engage in a number of different political services, as laid out in Chapters 4 and 5. Consistent with the theory of self-enforcing patronage, these chapters also show that supporters are disproportionally more involved in the provision of political services than non-supporters. Chapter 6, in turn, shows that supporters engage in the provision of political services because their incentives are aligned with those of the incumbent who hired them.

This chapter is organized in three sections. In the first section, I detail the survey design and implementation protocol, interviews conducted, the logic for the selection of municipalities, and the main characteristics of the municipalities selected. In the second section, I focus on the ways that public sector employees obtain their jobs, showing the predominance of informal mechanisms of recruitment. In the third section, I use an instrumental variable design to show that public sector jobs are disproportionally distributed to supporters.

3.1   RESEARCH DESIGN

3.1.1   The Survey

Survey data were gathered during face-to-face interviews with 1,184 low- and mid-level local public sector employees in the Argentinean municipalities of Salta (Salta Province), Santa Fe (Santa Fe Province) and Tigre (Buenos Aires Province) in 2010–11.[2] Within each municipality, I generated a random sample

---

[2] For more information about the survey and the interviews conducted, see also Appendices A1 and A2.

from the complete list of public employees, excluding elected officials and high-level positions.[3] Information on public employment is not publicly available, and Argentinean politicians are reluctant to share it. The first challenge of the survey, therefore, was to get access to the data. This was only possible after I used personal connections to be introduced to various authorities and met with several high-level public officials over a period of weeks to explain the purpose of the study, obtain the lists of public employees, and, finally, receive authorization to conduct the survey.[4] That obtaining these lists was daunting and time consuming illustrates the opacity of Argentinean administration, and both the permission and the collaboration of the local authorities were critical.[5] To maximize the chances of getting official approval for the survey, I took two precautions. First, I excluded particularly direct, sensitive questions – especially questions related to mayors. Second, I designed the survey instrument to be as short as possible to ensure employees would not be kept away from their jobs for long periods of time while completing it. Local authorities in each municipality read the survey instrument but did not censor any of the proposed questions.

Interviewers received a random sample of names of public employees and their work addresses and directly approached the employees at their workplaces during work hours. Places of work ranged from city hall offices and decentralized offices (*delegaciones*) to parks, construction sites, cemeteries, hospitals, health centers, and the street itself. The jobs held by the respondents were also diverse. For instance, among workers with the highest-level positions who were interviewed were heads and directors of various departments (13 percent of the sample), doctors (3 percent), and advisers (2 percent). Among mid-level jobs, there were administrative employees (20 percent), different types of inspectors (7 percent), physical education teachers (2 percent), and nurses (2 percent). Examples of low-level jobs among the respondents were cleaning workers (5 percent), machine and

---

[3] Top positions at all levels of government (national, provincial, and local) are discretionally appointed, even where civil service regulations exist. Civil service systems usually limit political positions to higher ranks, where hiring based on political affiliation is legal (as opposed to career positions, for which hiring should be based on merit and qualifications). In most countries, top positions such as the heads of executive agencies, are "patronage appointments" (partisan appointed positions) (Fisman and Golden 2017, 39). Top positions were, therefore, excluded from the sample frame in this study.

[4] The survey was described to local authorities and public employees in broad terms as concerning the relationship of public sector employees with local public life (*la relación de los empleados públicos con la vida pública local*).

[5] Local authorities in Salta requested that I wait until after the local election to conduct the survey (a six-month delay). See more details in Appendix A2. In Tigre, the director of personnel waited until he had written authorization signed by the mayor in hand; he refused to share the data just with a phone call from a high-level official close to the mayor. In Santa Fe, after several failed attempts to get an appointment to discuss the survey, a phone call from a former National Deputy from the mayor's party facilitated access.

maintenance operators (5 percent), drivers (3 percent), street sweepers (2 percent), and night watchmen (1 percent). The interviewed sample also included, among many other jobs, seven musicians, three lifeguards, two gravediggers, two rangers, one photographer, one stretcher bearer, and one chaplain.[6] Figures 3.1–3.4 show some of the places where interviews took place.

When employees who had been randomly selected for an interview were not at the place of work at the time of the visit or if they preferred to answer the survey at a different time, interviewers made appointments to return later.[7] If the selected employee declined to respond to the survey, or the interview could not be conducted after a second attempt, the respondent was replaced with the next name on the interviewer's randomized list.[8] Interviewers were instructed to make detailed records of failed contacts and refusals.

The contact rate for the survey was 59 percent, the response rate 56 percent, and the refusal rate 3 percent. The margin of error was 2.7 percent. Across municipalities, the contact rate was slightly higher in Tigre (62 percent) and Santa Fe (61 percent) than in Salta (55 percent), while the response rate was 58 percent in Tigre and Santa Fe, compared to 53 percent in Salta.[9] As is clear from the low refusal rate, the principal challenge in conducting the survey lay more in finding the selected public sector employees than in getting them to agree to participate. In fact, once located, almost everyone agreed to complete the survey.

There were various reasons why some employees could not be located. To obtain the 1,184 surveys, a sample of 2,173 public employees was randomly selected from the lists provided by the local authorities (a sample frame of 11,197 employees, after excluding elected officials and high-level positions). Of this original sample of 2,173, 3 percent of the employees were no longer employed by the municipality by the time the survey took place; 13 percent happened not to be at their workplaces (twice) when the interviewer tried to contact them; 8 percent were people whom no one knew at their alleged places of work; 5 percent were known employees but were working somewhere else

---

[6] Jobs were self-reported in the survey; unfortunately, official data on this was not available from the local authorities.

[7] A few interviews were also scheduled by phone when the respondent worked in a place or at a time different from what the record indicated. Some employees – particularly ambulance drivers, nurses, doctors, and security guards – worked weekend and night shifts. Extra effort was made to interview them, but unfortunately some of the places were not safe to visit at night. As a result, employees who work night shifts may be slightly underrepresented.

[8] Of the 1,184 survey interviews conducted, 75 percent were conducted on the first attempt; the remaining 25 percent on a second or subsequent attempt. There was little variation across municipalities in this regard. In Tigre, 80 percent of the interviews were conducted on the first attempt, compared to 73 percent in Salta, and 71 percent in Santa Fe.

[9] Rates calculated according to the American Association of Public Opinion Research. For comparison, the response rate for the last LAPOP (Latin American Public Opinion Project) survey conducted in Argentina in 2018/9 was between 12 and 15 percent. Source: www.vanderbilt.edu/lapop/Argentina_AmericasBarometer_2018-19_Technical_Report_W_101019.pdf

FIGURE 3.1 Public employees working in green-area maintenance (Santa Fe)
Note: Photograph by the author

(and we couldn't reach them); 4 percent were on holidays or leave; and 9 percent were never sought out because the targeted number of surveys was achieved before we tried to contact all the sampled employees.[10]

To administer the list and survey experiments embedded in the survey instrument (described in Chapters 4 and 6), two versions of the questionnaire were used. With the exception of these survey experiment questions, respondents were interviewed using identical questionnaires. Interviewers used the two different questionnaires in sequential order, thus alternating the assignment of respondents to either the treatment or the control group.[11] On average, survey interviews lasted twenty-four minutes.

Because the survey was conducted face-to-face at public offices, getting truthful answers presented a challenge. While high-ranking public officials usually have their own offices, most public employees in Argentina share their workspaces, and public employees might be unwilling to reveal sensitive

---

[10] See Table A1 in Appendix A2 for more details.
[11] Ideally, respondents should have been randomly and independently assigned into each experimental condition for each survey experiment in order to minimize potential spillover effects (Gaines, Kuklinski, and Quirk 2007), but this was logistically too complicated to implement with a pencil-and-paper questionnaire.

FIGURE 3.2 Area where construction materials are kept (Santa Fe)
Note: Photograph by the author

FIGURE 3.3 Secretariat of Health Policy and Human Development (Tigre)
Note: Photograph by the author

FIGURE 3.4 *Delegación* (decentralized office), Rincón de Milberg (Tigre)
Note: Photograph by the author

information in front of others. Following standard survey procedures, all
interviews started with the interviewers explaining the purpose of the survey
and the confidentiality of all the data collected. Interviewers were instructed to
emphasize the strictly academic purpose of the survey and to assure respondents
that individualized information would not be shared with anyone. In addition
to this standard protocol, I implemented two distinct but complementary
strategies to elicit honest responses and minimize social response bias –
whether in the form of refusals or inaccurate answers.

First, I designed a series of list experiments – a technique that protects the
privacy of responses by using indirect questioning (see Chapter 4). Second,
I followed Scacco's (2010) strategy (originally developed to survey rioters in
Africa) and split the questionnaire into two parts. Part A included background
and general information about the respondent, as well as the less sensitive
questions and the list experiments. Part B included the more sensitive questions
about voting behavior, ideology, and political preferences. Each part of the
questionnaire was marked with a different survey identification number; these
could only be matched with a document not ever available to the interviewers.
Other than this number, Part B of the questionnaire contained no information –
such as age, gender, education, or occupation – that could be used to identify the
respondent.

Interviewers administered Part A of the questionnaire, while the sensitive Part B was read and filled out by the respondents themselves.[12] Other employees in the office therefore heard neither the questions nor the answers to Part B. This part of the questionnaire was purposely designed to be short and easy to understand and answer, with only closed-ended questions. At the end of the survey interview, respondents were asked to insert Part B of the questionnaire in a sealed cardboard box similar to a ballot box, which is familiar to respondents because paper ballots and cardboard ballot boxes are used in Argentinean elections. Interviewers were instructed to provide a detailed explanation of these procedures before handing Part B of the questionnaire to the respondents and to make sure respondents understood that the survey fully protected the confidentiality of their responses. Their understanding was fundamental to guaranteeing the success of the strategy.

3.1.2 Testing the Strategy

Was the strategy successful? To test the effect of the split questionnaire, I included an additional question in the Salta survey conducted between June and August 2011. This new question asked about voting intentions in the next presidential election, which was scheduled for October 2011.[13] Responses were coded 1 if respondents mentioned the mayor's party (Peronist) or any candidate from that party, and 0 otherwise.[14] Half of the respondents were asked this question directly by the enumerator at the end of Part A of the questionnaire, while the other half answered this question by themselves at the end of Part B. Table 3.1 presents the differences in means between the responses to the question when asked directly in Part A and when completed by respondents in private in Part B.

When asked directly about presidential voting intentions in Part A, 48 percent of the respondents answered that they would vote for the mayor's party (Peronist party). When the question was asked during the confidential section (Part B), the percentage reporting that they would vote for the Peronist party decreased to forty-two. The difference between these two means is not statistically significant.

This result is not surprising if, as predicted by the theory of self-enforcing patronage, patronage jobs are disproportionally distributed to supporters.[15] Having many Peronist employees in a municipality governed by the Peronist party since 1999 is to be expected, and Peronist supporters in a Peronist

---

[12] Literacy rates are high in Argentina, so there was no concern that the respondents would not be able to complete Part B of the questionnaires by themselves. According to the 2010 census, only 1.96 percent of the total population older than ten years old is illiterate.

[13] "Could you tell me for whom are you planning to vote in the next presidential elections?"

[14] All references to Peronist labels (Peronism, Kirchnerism, "*Frente para la Victoria*") as well as the name of the incumbent president running for reelection, Cristina Fernández de Kirchner, were coded as 1. The exception was Duhalde (seven respondents reported intending to vote for him), a Peronist who was running in clear opposition to the incumbent president.

[15] I provide empirical evidence of this in Section 3.3.

TABLE 3.1   *Respondents intending to vote for mayor's party in the 2011 presidential election, by way of asking*

Asked directly by enumerator (Part A)	0.48
	(0.04)
	N=193
Filled in by respondents themselves (Part B)	0.42
	(0.04)
	N=196
Difference	0.06
	(0.05)
	N=389

Note: Two-sample *t*-test with unequal variance. Standard errors in parentheses; *** $p < 0.01$, ** $p < 0.05$, * $p < 0.1$.

TABLE 3.2   *Respondents intending to vote for mayor's party in the 2011 presidential election, by way of asking and support for the mayor*

	Mayor voters	Non-mayor voters
Asked directly by enumerator (Part A)	0.54	0.21
	(0.04)	(0.07)
	N=147	N=33
Filled in by respondents themselves (Part B)	0.53	0.05
	(0.04)	(0.03)
	N=155	N=42
Difference	0.01	0.16**
	(0.06)	(0.08)
	N=302	N=75

Note: Two-sample *t*-test with unequal variance. Standard errors in parentheses; *** $p < 0.01$, ** $p < 0.05$, * $p < 0.1$.

municipality might be more willing to make their political preferences known in public. Only non-supporters would have an incentive to give untruthful responses about their political preferences when asked directly in front of others. To measure support for the mayor, I asked employees for whom they had voted in the last mayoral election (*Mayor Voters*), including the question in the confidential part of the questionnaire (Part B). Responses were coded 1 if the respondent voted for the incumbent mayor, and 0 otherwise. Table 3.2 presents the differences in means between the responses to the question about presidential voting intentions when asked directly (in Part A) and when completed by respondents (in Part B), by support for the mayor.

Among those who reported voting for the incumbent mayor in the last election (column 1), the different protocols do not make any difference. However, among those who did not vote for the incumbent (column 2), asking directly or indirectly yields different results. When asked directly, 21 percent of the non-mayor voters answered that they would vote for the mayor's party (Peronist) in the next presidential election. When asked in the private questionnaire (Part B), only 5 percent of non-mayor voters answered that they would vote for the Peronist presidential candidate. A two-tailed t-test confirms that this difference (16 percentage points) is statistically significant at the 95 percent level.

In sum, the change in procedure revealed no difference among those who voted for the mayor, but it revealed a significant difference among those who did not. This indicates that splitting the questionnaire worked as expected, making a difference for employees who might have had an incentive to lie.

3.1.3   The Interviews

Interviews with political brokers, politicians, high-level public officials, and public sector employees were conducted during multiple research trips to Buenos Aires, Salta, and Santa Fe between 2009 and 2011. Some interviews were conducted before the survey was implemented in order to help with the design of the survey instrument. Others were conducted in order to better understand the local dynamics in each municipality. The majority of the interviews, however, were conducted simultaneously with the survey implementation, with the goal of getting a thicker description of the dynamics of patronage in general and in each municipality in particular. Interviewees are not representative and were not selected at random; they were in many cases found through personal contacts and referrals and sometimes just by chance (see below). The descriptions and examples drawn from these interviews should therefore be considered illustrative, but not representative. All interviews were conducted by the author. Names are either changed or not provided to ensure anonymity.[16]

Most interviews with political brokers, who were found through personal contacts and referrals, were conducted before the implementation of the survey. The goal of these semi-structured interviews was to obtain a general sense of their political work and, in doing so, gain insights into campaign activities and political services – and the role of public employees in these activities and services – in order to design the survey instrument. A general framework rather than a fixed set of questions was used during the interviews, which generally lasted sixty to ninety minutes.

In each of the municipalities, semi-structured interviews with high-level public officials were conducted before starting the survey to gain a better understanding of the specific characteristics of the local public sector and to adjust the questionnaire as necessary. Other interviews with key informants, including brokers and

---

[16] See book Appendix A1 for a list of all the anonymized interviews conducted.

politicians as well as high-level officials, were also conducted with the goal of better understanding the specificities of local politics in each district, the politicization of the public sector, and the role of public employees in local politics. The duration of these interviews was generally around an hour.

Finally, several interviews were conducted with public sector employees. To select public employees for interviews, enumerators were instructed to obtain the contact information for employees who seemed willing to talk openly about the questions in the survey; they were later contacted to set up an appointment. These interviews generally lasted around sixty to ninety minutes. Many other semi-structured and conversational interviews arose spontaneously. I conducted 160 survey interviews myself, and while waiting to start a survey, or completing one, or while waiting for an interview, many employees were willing to talk. This informal setting often ended up being more conducive to interesting exchanges than was the more formal one. The duration of these unstructured interviews varied widely from only ten minutes to about an hour.

3.1.4   Selecting Municipalities within Argentina

Argentina has 1,195 municipalities spread over twenty-three provinces, so conducting the survey across a representative sample of municipalities was not feasible.[17] In order to make the research tractable and still obtain a sample with variation across municipalities, I selected three very distinct municipalities from three different provinces: Salta (province of Salta), Santa Fe (province of Santa Fe), and Tigre (Greater Buenos Aires, province of Buenos Aires). The three urban municipalities, while similar in population size, vary greatly in their political and economic characteristics. They therefore provide a good opportunity to test how the theory of self-enforcing patronage travels across different political and economic environments.

Salta (536,000 inhabitants) is located in the north of the country. It is the capital of its eponymous province and is the poorest of the three municipalities included in the survey. Over 21 percent of its residents live in poverty, and more than half of the population lacks health insurance.[18] Around 12 percent of

---

[17] The City of Buenos Aires, seat of the federal government, was excluded because of its unique status, which allows local authorities more prerogatives than a municipal government but fewer than a province. Including the smaller counterparts of municipalities, *comunas*, Argentina has more than 2,000 local governments.

[18] Poverty is measured using the most widely used measure of poverty in Argentina: "unsatisfied basic needs" or NBI (*necesidades básicas insatisfechas*). A household is considered to have unsatisfied basic needs if it meets at least one of the following criteria: density of more than three persons per room (crowding), living in a precarious house (housing), not having an indoor flush toilet (sanitation), having a child between six and twelve years old who is not attending school (school attendance), or having more than four members per employed member and the head of the household having two or fewer years of elementary school (subsistence capacity).

residents have not finished elementary school, 48 percent have not finished high school, and only 9 percent hold a college degree. The Peronist party has dominated Salta since the return of democracy in 1983, except when a provincial party (Partido Renovador de Salta or PRS) won the municipal executive post (1991–95 and 1997–99). Between 2003 and 2015, the Peronist Miguel Isa was the mayor, with the PRS as a minor partner. After his election in 2003, Isa was reelected in 2007 with 46 percent of the vote in a race against another Peronist candidate. He was reelected again in 2011 with 49 percent of the vote and a 20 percentage-point margin of victory.[19]

Santa Fe (485,000 inhabitants) is located in the central part of the country, in one of the richest provinces. It is the capital of and second-largest city in its eponymous province. With 59 percent of its residents having health insurance and 11 percent holding a college degree, it is the richest municipality included in the survey, yet 14 percent of its residents are poor. After being governed by the Peronist party for most of the period since 1983, both the city and the province of Santa Fe were at the time of the survey among the country's most competitive electoral arenas. In 2007, a coalition formed by the Radical party and the Socialist Party won both the gubernatorial and the Santa Fe mayoral elections, and the Radical Mario Barletta became the mayor with 33 percent of the vote and a margin of victory of less than two percentage points (around 3,000 votes) over the Peronist candidate.[20] Barletta was succeeded in July 2011, after the survey was completed, by another Radical, José Manuel Corral, who won with 45 percent of the vote and a margin of victory of seven points; he was reelected in 2015.[21]

Tigre (376,000 inhabitants) is located in Greater Buenos Aires, in a region known as Conurbano Bonaerense.[22] This region contains around 25 percent of the country's population, and it has attracted the attention of politicians, journalists, and academics alike. Much of the vast literature on Argentinean clientelism has focused on this area (e.g., Auyero 2001; Levitsky 2003; Zarazaga 2014). Because it composes such a large part of the Argentinean electorate, understanding how political competition works in this area is central to Argentinean politics. Although not among the poorest

[19] After finishing his term in the local administration, Isa became Salta's vice governor (2015–19) and subsequently ran for governor in 2019, but lost the primary. In 2015, Gustavo Sáenz, a Peronist from a different party faction than Isa, became the mayor of Salta; in 2019, Sáenz became governor of the province, and Bettina Romero, from the same faction as Sáenz, became the first woman mayor in the history of the city of Salta.

[20] In the 2009 elections for the city council, the coalition of the Radical party and the Socialist Party obtained 38 percent of the votes and a margin of victory of 13 percentage points.

[21] Barletta decided to run for governor rather than for reelection, but he lost the primary, and the electoral law in Santa Fe did not allow him to run for mayor after losing the gubernatorial primary.

[22] The Conurbano Bonaerense consists of twenty-four municipalities surrounding the City of Buenos Aires. It has a population of around 10,000,000 inhabitants (one quarter of Argentina's population). For an overview of this area, see Zarazaga and Ronconi (2018).

municipalities in the region, 20 percent of Tigre's residents live in poverty, and more than half of the population has no health insurance.[23] Around 17 percent of its residents have not finished elementary school, 55 percent have not finished high school, and only 7 percent have a college degree. The municipality of Tigre was governed by the Radical party between 1983 and 1987 and by a personalistic local party (Acción Comunal) from 1987 until the death of Ricardo Ubieto, its party leader, in 2006. The next year, Peronist Sergio Massa won the mayoral election with 46 percent of the vote and a margin of victory of four percentage points over Acción Comunal.[24] In 2011, after the survey was finished, Massa was reelected with the largest margin of victory of all districts in the Conurbano Bonaerense, receiving 73 percent of the vote to Acción Comunal's 6 percent.[25]

By including a municipality from the poorer north dominated by the Peronist party (Salta), a municipality from the relatively richer and more competitive center (Santa Fe), and one from Greater Buenos Aires (Tigre), the area most associated with clientelistic politics, I attempt to capture the regional diversity of Argentinean politics. Given the important differences in political and economic characteristics across the selected municipalities, a theory that works in all of them makes generalization from only three cases more plausible (Table 3.3).

The public sectors of the three municipalities shared a similar structure, a mix of tenured and untenured employees, resembling the way public sectors at the national and provincial levels are organized in Argentina. All tenured employees across districts and levels have similar contracts that include job security and the benefits associated with formal employment, such as health insurance, paid holidays, sick and maternity leaves, and a pension. All districts also have a category of formal temporary employees (usually on yearly contracts) who enjoy all the benefits of tenured employees except for job security. Often employees are hired in this category and then, after some time, move to the tenured category. In addition, municipalities have a variety of other, more flexible, short-term contracts. In Tigre, for instance, the most common of these is *monotributo*, a contract that pays by the hour and has no benefits, intended to be used for hiring freelancers.[26] In Salta, the

---

[23] Tigre is around average in terms of both population and poverty among the twenty-four municipalities that comprise the Conurbano. According to the 2001 census, the average population of the municipalities was 360,000 (compared to 300,400 in Tigre), while the percent of the population living in poverty in the region was 17.6 (compared to 20.3 percent in Tigre).

[24] In the 2009 council elections, the Peronist party increased its vote share to 53 percent, while Acción Comunal, in second place, received only 26 percent of the vote.

[25] In 2013, Massa stepped down as mayor to become a national deputy. In 2015, he ran for the presidency and finished in third place, with 21 percent of the vote. Julio Zamora, a long-term member of Massa's inner circle, became the interim mayor of Tigre (2013–15), and was later elected as mayor (2015) and then reelected (2019).

[26] According to high-level officials at Tigre's personnel office, there are around 200 employees who regularly work for the municipality every month under this type of contract. Almost all of them are doctors, and the reason to hire them under this contract is that it allows the municipality to

TABLE 3.3 *Socio-demographic and political characteristics of the municipalities*

	Salta	Santa Fe	Tigre
Province	Salta (North)	Santa Fe (Center)	Buenos Aires (CB)
Mayoral reelection rate (province)	0.40	0.47	0.46
Mayor	Miguel Angel Isa	Mario Barletta	Sergio Massa
Period	2003–15	2007–11	2007–13
Mayor's party	Peronist	Radical	Peronist
Electoral competition	Low	High	Middle/low
Population 2001	472,971	369,589	301,223
Population 2010	536,113	485,345	376,381
Less than elementary	12%	12%	17%
Less than high school	48%	45%	55%
With college degree	9%	11%	7%
With health insurance	48%	59%	45%
Under poverty level	21%	14%	20%

Note: Data from the 2001 Census, except for population, which is from the 2010 Census. (Other data from the 2010 Census were not available during municipality selection.) Mayors are those in power at the time of the survey (2010–11). Note that, in contrast to the low reelection rates for legislative representatives (Jones et al. 2002), the reelection rates for mayors in Argentina is relatively high (39 percent). Mayoral reelection rates by province correspond to the 1983–2007 period (Micozzi 2009).

most common short-term contract – around 11 percent of the payroll at the time of the survey – is called "political grouping" (*agrupamiento político*), which allows more flexibility in hiring, firing, and remuneration than regular temporary contracts. It has most of the benefits of other more permanent contracts (health insurance, pension, paid vacations, and leaves), but it ends with the mayor's term. Despite the "political grouping" name, these are not typical high-level political hires.[27] Indeed, among the thirty-six employees hired with this type of contract whom we interviewed (9 percent of the total interviews), there were fourteen administrative employees, a night watchman, a fiscal inspector, two telephone operators, and

pay them more than they could have under the formal salary structure (author interview, Tigre, July 15, 2010). All twenty-two of the employees with this type of contract who were interviewed in Tigre were indeed doctors.

[27] High-level officials or *funcionarios* are hired on a contract called "political structure" (*estructura política*).

a draftsman.[28] In Santa Fe, the most common of these short-term contracts, held by around 800 workers, is *practicancia*. It is formally a workfare municipal program, with no benefits and very low pay, but it is used to cover a significant portion of municipal low-skill jobs, such as cleaning and maintenance workers, as well as some administrative jobs.[29]

Besides this variation in short-term contracts, the most important way contracts across municipalities differ is in the proportion of employees with job security. The municipality of Santa Fe paid salaries to 5,070 people (1.04 percent of the local population). Excluding elected officials (the mayor and the thirteen council members), teachers, and top positions such as advisors, secretaries, deputy secretaries, directors, and deputy directors, the payroll consisted of 4,528 workers.[30] Of those, 2,611 (55 percent) enjoyed job security. Most employees (63 percent) were over forty years old, 36 percent were women, and 45 percent had been hired during the current administration.

Tigre paid salaries to 2,569 people (0.68 percent of the population). Excluding elected officials (the mayor and twenty-four council members) and top positions, the payroll consisted of 2,406 workers. Of those, only 475 (19.7 percent) had job security. Although comparative data is not available, anecdotal evidence suggests that the number of employees with job security is relatively smaller than in neighboring municipalities.[31] This is important because mayors can appoint new employees either by enlarging the public sector or by not renewing contracts and then hiring new employees. Because only 20 percent

---

[28] Just as with high-level officials hired on "political structure" contracts, 10 percent of the salaries of employees in the "political grouping" category is taken out of their paychecks to go to the party (author interviews, Salta, June 14 and 15, 2010; one of the employees who mentioned this showed me his pay slip).

[29] The program is financed in full by the municipality. At the time of the survey (July 2010), the remuneration was 600 pesos (around 150 dollars) for five hours of work a day. These contracts last six months, renewable for up to two years, but they are sometimes extended beyond that (author interview with the Santa Fe Deputy Secretary at the Civil Service Office, Santa Fe, June 10, 2010). A couple of survey respondents reported that they had two of these contracts and worked full time.

[30] Teachers were excluded for two reasons. First, not all Argentinean municipalities are in charge of education (Tigre and Salta, in particular, have no schools under their supervision), so I excluded teachers to keep the samples comparable. Second, the process of hiring and firing teachers in Argentina is different than for other types of public employees; their appointments and promotions are regulated by agencies that are relatively independent of the mayor. This does not mean, of course, that teachers are completely isolated from political pressures (see, for instance, Murillo and Ronconi 2004) but, in the Argentinean context, the scope for patronage is undeniably smaller than for other public employees. See also Chambers-Ju (2021).

[31] According to high-level officials at Tigre's personnel office, Tigre is an exception. According to them, municipalities in the area usually have an equal number of permanent and temporary employees (author interview, Tigre, July 15, 2010). According to Valeria, a high-ranking employee who had been at the personnel office since 2001, this policy of not granting job security is a legacy of the previous administration that the new one has continued. From the time that the new administration took office in 2007 through August 2010, only seven employees were granted job security (author interview, Tigre, August 23, 2010).

TABLE 3.4 *Characteristics of public sectors across municipalities*[32]

	Salta	Santa Fe	Tigre
Total N in payroll	4,619	5,070	2,569
As a % of the population	0.86%	1.04%	0.68%
Sample frame	4,263	4,528	2,406
Tenured employees	77%	55%	20%
Hired in current administration	47%	45%	45%
Women	37%	36%	45%
Older than 40	70%	63%	53%

Note: Data provided by each municipal government. Data from Santa Fe is from June 2010, data from Tigre is from July 2010, and data from Salta is from May 2011. See Tables A.2–A.4 in the book Appendix for more details on the three public administrations and survey sample representativeness. Sample frames exclude elected officials, high-level positions, and teachers.

of employees had job security, the opportunities for patronage were substantial. Women constituted 45 percent of the sample, and 53 percent of employees were older than forty. Among the 2,406 public sector employees in the sample, 45 percent (1,034) had been hired during the current administration.

Finally, the municipality of Salta paid salaries to 4,619 people (0.86 percent of the population). Excluding elected officials and top positions, the payroll consisted of 4,263 employees. Of those, 77 percent had job security and 47 percent were hired by the current administration. Almost half of the employees with job security (47 percent) had obtained it under the current administration (the Salta mayor had been in office since 2003). Women constituted 37 percent of the sample, and 70 percent of the employees in the sample were older than forty (see Table 3.4).

3.2 GETTING THE JOB

Consistent with conventional wisdom, most public employees reported having found their jobs through informal channels. Indeed, 64 percent of respondents found their job through some personal or political connection (see Table 3.5). Among them, 58 percent reported having learned of the position through someone – an acquaintance, friend, or relative – who worked at the municipality, and 6 percent reported that it was through political channels. A small group of respondents, 13 percent, reported that they submitted their

[32] Although official data on the educational background of public sector employees was not provided by the local authorities, the survey data suggest that Tigre's public employees are significantly more educated than employees in Salta and Santa Fe. Among survey respondents, 39 percent of Tigre's employees reported having a college degree, compared to 15 percent in Salta, and 14 percent in Santa Fe.

TABLE 3.5 *How did you find out about this job?*

	N	%	Through connections
Through someone/an acquaintance who worked at the municipality	352	30%	
Through a friend/relative who worked at the municipality	328	28%	64%
Through politics	69	6%	
Submitted a resume to the municipality	156	13%	
Previous beneficiary of a welfare program	55	5%	
Through an employment agency/the media/ newspapers/ ads	40	3%	
Previous internship at the municipality	25	2%	
Entrance examinations	18	2%	
Some other way and no reply	141	12%	
	1,184	100%	

information or resume to the municipality and were later contacted by the authorities. Another 5 percent had been beneficiaries of public workfare programs who were then hired as regular employees; 2 percent had been interns at the municipality and subsequently hired; and only 5 percent of the respondents learned of the job through public advertisement (3 percent) or publicly advertised entrance exams (2 percent).

Interestingly, some respondents who had found their jobs through political channels were open about it: "Through a politician," "Through politics," "Because I am an activist," "Through a local broker," "I used to work for a Peronist councilman," "I used to work in politics with someone at the municipality," "Because my (husband/wife/relative) works in politics." This, of course, does not mean that there were no political connections involved in other cases. Those who reported finding out about the job through an acquaintance, relative, or friend, may have had a political connection as well. Sabrina, a Santa Fe employee since 1985, explained that admitting the political connection might not be everyone's first choice: "It's always more dignified, I think, to earn one's job. I think we would all prefer that. No one wants to get the job because of one's best friend ... or later being singled out, 'look, he is the friend ... '"[33]

In Tigre, Valeria, a relatively high-level personnel office employee, estimated that there were around 200 new hires during the first four months of the new administration. According to her, "They came into office with a lot of people ...

---

[33] Author interview, Santa Fe, August 16, 2011.

of course, with all the political promises."[34] Another employee from Tigre, Francisco, a Peronist activist since the 1970s, reported that "the party" demanded that the mayor open up more "space in the government."[35] Daniela, an administrative employee in Salta's office of human resources, illustrated the importance of connections, explaining how department heads send in the resumes of people they intend to hire. Sometimes, she said, they are specific requests for a person with certain skills needed in their department, such as a lawyer or an architect. But her office also receives resumes for *designaciones políticas* (political appointments).[36] In those cases, the human resources department needs to figure out where to send the new hires, based on their characteristics, education, and skills, and based also on municipal budget considerations. According to her, the unions also send "lists" and resumes of potential hires, often the daughters and sons of current employees.[37] Fernando, a head of maintenance who supervises thirty to forty people and has been working for the municipality of Salta since 1982, described it this way: "They send people and one has to figure out what are they good for *(para qué sirven)*." To illustrate, he added, "If they send someone with only an elementary education you put him to clean, but if they send someone with a college degree, I won't put him as night watchman *(sereno)*."[38] Mauricio, a director in the public works department who has worked for the city since 1971 and is in charge of 250 municipal employees, tells a similar story: "They send us people" *(nos los mandan)*, and his department has no say in hiring decisions.[39]

Moreover, the majority of respondents perceived personal connections to be important for getting a job. Survey respondents were asked to evaluate the importance of different criteria for hiring decisions in their area within the administration. The majority of respondents (59 percent) considered personal connections to be important or very important in hiring decisions, following only education (74 percent) and work experience (66 percent) (see Figure 3.5).[40] The fact that work experience and education are still the main criteria is, of course, not surprising. Even in an administration with widespread patronage, not all public employees – not even a majority – are patronage employees.

Recall, however, that proximity to political networks (i.e., connections) does not necessarily mean ideological affinity or partisan affiliation. In the words of a Salta

---

[34] Some of them were later fired: "because some of those political hires thought they didn't have to work, but in this municipality one works *(se labura)*" (author interview, Tigre, August 23, 2010).

[35] Author interview, Tigre, September 22, 2010.

[36] Note that she defines political appointments as those that do not seem to be justified by a specific need of the administration.

[37] Author interview, Salta, August 5, 2011.

[38] Author interview, Salta, August 5, 2011.

[39] Author interview, Salta, June 13, 2011.

[40] Absolute numbers and percentages can be found in Table 3.9. Table 3.10 shows the importance of personal connections by municipality and that connections are perceived to be relatively more important in Salta. Both tables can be found in the Chapter Appendix.

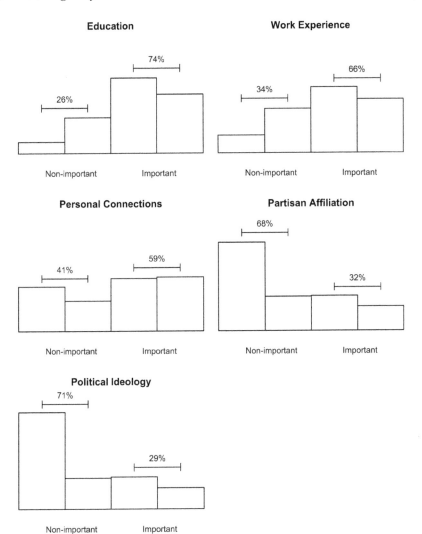

FIGURE 3.5 Perceived importance of different criteria for municipal hiring
Note: For ease of interpretation, percentages reported above the horizontal lines grouped "important" and "very important" into the "Important" category; while "not very important" and "not at all important" were grouped in the "Non-important" category. Absolute numbers and percentages can be found in Table 3.9 in the Chapter Appendix.

councilman from the opposition Radical party, "relatives, friends, brokers, sub-brokers … the machine is big (*el aparato es grande*)."[41] In line with the theory of self-enforcing patronage, public employees in fact reported that personal connections were more important than partisan affiliation and political ideology as hiring criteria for the administration. While 59 percent reported that personal connections were important and very important, only 32 percent gave the same ratings for partisan affiliation and 29 percent for ideology. What matters in a patronage exchange is not ideological or political commitment but being hired through informal channels – and thus owing the job to someone – with the expectation of providing political support in return. As explained by the Radical councilman, the administration is "full of people who have a close connection (*conexión estrechísima*). And what is the one thing they have to do in exchange? Work on the election."[42] What matters is not being a "true" supporter, just being perceived (or branded) as one. Patronage employees hired through personal connections are often perceived as supporters, even if they are not party affiliates or ideologically close to the politician or the party.

Laura, an employee from Tigre hired in 1988 when her brother was a councilman, explained it in simple terms: "Political affiliation, ideology, and personal contacts matter everywhere in the administration."[43] Ana, a 31-year-old administrative employee who had been on the Salta payroll since 2005, shared the same blunt assessment: "Everyone got their jobs through a connection." She added that the unions also manage to get jobs for "their" people, "particularly for employees' children."[44]

Other Salta employees also mentioned the importance of unions and how common it was to find the children of employees working for the municipality.[45] In fact, a few employees in Salta seemed upset because their children did not have a job in the administration. María, for instance, recounted that the unions "did not give her anything," but one of her coworkers, who "got her job though politics" (*entró por política*) two years earlier, "was already able to get her son a job." In contrast, María, who had been working for the city since 1997 and was the widow of another public employee, said she had submitted the resumes of four of her six children, and none of them got jobs.[46] Another Salta employee, Viviana, who got her job in 1979 by taking an entrance examination, never joined any union and "suffered the consequences," she said. "Those who are affiliated with the unions get jobs for their children . . . I couldn't get a job for my son even though I have been on

---

[42] Author interview (Radical City councilman), Salta, August 1, 2011.
[43] Author interview, Tigre, January 6, 2011.
[44] Author interview, Salta, June 15, 2011.
[45] The unions are important political actors in Salta, but less so in the other two municipalities. According to the survey responses, Salta had the highest rate of affiliation: 73 percent of respondents in Salta reported being union affiliates, compared to 62 percent in Santa Fe, and 36 percent in Tigre. The only union in Tigre seems to be particularly weak. According to Valeria, a relatively high-level employee from the local personnel office, who deals with union leaders regularly: "Here, the union is just another friend . . . and without a voice" (author interview, Tigre, August 23, 2010).
[46] Author interview, Salta, August 8, 2011.

the job for thirty-two years. They have ruined the civil service career."[47] Survey responses show that many employees' children do get jobs in the administration: 19 percent (74/389) of respondents in Salta reported getting their jobs through a parent.[48]

Political brokers are, of course, also important connections for hiring. Mariano, a relatively minor political broker who reported getting his job in the Salta administration "through politics," described the mechanism: "There are people who wait to get hired … they work – politically, on campaigns and attending rallies – for years and years, and the only thing they want is a job … . If they performed, showed up on time, if they attended the rallies, if they showed up at the place one wants them to show up at … yes, it is possible." He then explained that, of course, the availability of public sector jobs is limited, and that there are quotas for the different political groups (*agrupaciones*) as well as for the unions. Sometimes, he said, it is easier to get temporary workfare jobs for his followers. Even though Mariano himself is a broker working for the Peronist party, he still considers personal connections more important than partisanship and ideology when seeking a municipal job.[49]

3.3   WHO GETS HIRED?

The general understanding in the literature is that, in the absence of effective civil service rules, public sector jobs are disproportionally allocated to supporters (see Chapter 2). In spite of this general agreement, most of the evidence we have about public employees' voting behavior and partisan identification in the developing world is based on aggregate and often unreliable data.[50] Governments that extensively use patronage are reluctant to share information, and obtaining truthful answers about political behavior and partisan identification from public employees is difficult. Are public sector jobs being distributed to supporters, to those who are more closely connected to the party network? If so, we should see public sector jobs being distributed mainly through informal channels (as seen in Table 3.5), as well as finding a disproportionate number of the incumbent's supporters among public employees hired by the current administration. To identify support for the

---

[47] Author interview, Salta, August 3, 2011.
[48] For reasons described below, similar information about parental influence in hiring was not collected in the other two municipalities. The interviews, however, suggest that this was not at all common practice in Tigre and Santa Fe.
[49] Author interview, Salta, August 1, 2011.
[50] Some important exceptions include Brollo, Forquesato, and Gozzi (2017) and Colonnelli, Prem, and Teso (2018), who study patronage politics in Brazil. Others have used ethnicity to proxy for partisanship (e.g., Brierley 2021; Hassan 2017).

TABLE 3.6 *Public employees' self-reported mayoral vote*

	All respondents	Without "not-registered" voters	Without non-voters	Without missing, DK/NA, blank or null
Not registered	71 (6%)			
Did not vote	39 (3%)	4%		
Missing/ DK/NA	224 (19%)	20%	21%	
Blank or null	18 (2%)	2%	2%	
Others	151 (13%)	14%	14%	18%
Incumbent mayor	681 (58%)	61%	63%	82%
N	1,184	1,113	1,074	832

Note: "Not-registered" are voters who were registered to vote in another municipality (their legal residency) and a few non-citizens. Voting in Argentina is mandatory (with turnout around 70-80 percent), and registration is automatic.

mayor and the mayor's party, respondents were asked two questions.[51] The first asked for whom they had voted in the last mayoral election. Responses were coded 1 if the respondent reported voting for the current mayor (*Mayor Voter*) in the last mayoral election, and zero otherwise.[52] The second asked whether they identified themselves with a political party; those who replied affirmatively to this question were asked with which party they identified. This variable (*Mayor Party*) takes on the value 1 if the respondent reported identifying with the mayor's party, and zero otherwise.[53] Table 3.6 presents employees' self-reported mayoral vote in the last election before the survey.

A majority of employees reported having voted for the incumbent mayor. Of all respondents, 58 percent reported having voted for the current mayor in the last election. Excluding all the respondents who did not answer the question, voted blank or null, did not vote, or were not registered to vote in that municipality, the percentage rises to 82; only 18 percent reported having voted for another candidate.[54] As explained in Chapter 2, some supporters may be "true" supporters, committed to the party or the politician who hires

[51] Recall that the political questions were asked in a separate questionnaire (Part B) to improve the response rate and the accuracy of the responses. Question wording can be found in the book Appendix.

[52] Respondents who were not registered to vote in that municipality were coded as missing. Note that voting is mandatory in Argentina and, although the sanctions for not voting are hardly ever enforced, turnout is usually high (around 70–80 percent).

[53] Missing values were coded as zero, but an alternative codification of this variable with missing values coded as missing was also tried in all the analyses presented in Chapters 3 and 4. Those results were substantively identical.

[54] For context, recall that Massa (Tigre) won with 47 percent of the votes, Barletta (Santa Fe) with 33 percent, and Isa (Salta) with 49 percent.

TABLE 3.7   *Relationship between hiring administration and support for the mayor*

	Mayor voters	Mayor's party supporters
Current administration	0.72	0.42
	(0.02)	(0.02)
	N=492	N=499
Previous administrations	0.53	0.31
	(0.02)	(0.02)
	N=619	N=577
Difference	0.19**	0.11**
	(0.03)	(0.03)
	N=1,111	N=1,076

Note: Two-sample t-test with unequal variance. Standard errors in parentheses; *** $p < 0.01$, ** $p < 0.05$, * $p < 0.1$.

them; others may have been supporting the politician in order to obtain a job (or with the expectation of obtaining one). Indeed, using an innovative survey technique to measure the size of party networks and estimate their effect on voters' expectations, Calvo and Murillo (2019) show that the expectation of receiving a public sector job has a significant effect on the voting intentions of respondents, especially for voters who are more closely connected to the party network. Whether due to ideological commitment or expectations of employment, most public employees reported having voted for the incumbent.

At the same time, if public sector jobs are disproportionately distributed to supporters, we should also find a higher proportion of supporters of the incumbent mayor among employees hired during the current administration.[55] Table 3.7 compares the proportion of voters for the incumbent mayor and self-reported sympathizers with the mayor's party among employees hired during the current administration and those hired previously.

Table 3.7 shows more voters for the incumbent mayor and more supporters of the mayor's party among the employees who obtained their jobs during the current administration. Public employees hired during the current administration were far more likely (72 percent) to report having voted for the current mayor than those who were hired by previous administrations (53 percent). Employees hired by the current administration were also more likely (42 percent) to report being supporters of the mayor's party than workers

[55] Throughout this book, "current administration" refers to the administration of the incumbent mayor (not the incumbent party). Recall that in 2007 in both Santa Fe and Tigre there was a change in partisanship when Barletta (Radical) and Massa (Peronist) took office, following a Peronist and an independent mayor, respectively. In the case of Salta, Isa (Peronist) took office in 2003 following another Peronist mayor.

hired by previous administrations (31 percent). A two-tailed t-test confirms that both differences (19 and 11 percentage points, respectively) are statistically significant at the 95 percent level. Table 3.7 appears to show that public jobs are, in fact, disproportionally distributed to supporters.

Two important caveats, however, are worth mentioning. It is possible that employees, in general, are overreporting their support for the incumbent mayors and their parties. While both questions were included in the private part of the questionnaire (Part B, filled out by employees themselves), it is still possible that at least some employees were overreporting support for the mayor. The estimates presented here are thus conservative.

The second caveat is related to the direction of the relationship between being a supporter and getting the job. According to the theory of self-enforcing patronage, public sector jobs are disproportionally distributed to perceived supporters, those closer to the mayor's network. The evidence shown here, however, is also consistent with a story of independents, or even opposition voters, who became supporters of the incumbent after getting the job. In other words, those hired during the current administration could be more likely to identify themselves with the mayor's party precisely because they did get the job. Thus, it is possible that instead of having obtained the job because they were perceived to be supporters of the mayor's party or in close proximity to the party network, public employees could be supporters of the mayor's party because they obtained a job.

I test for this possibility of reverse causation using an instrumental variable (IV) approach. In simple terms, an instrument is a variable that is related to the independent variable and only related to the outcome variable through its impact on the independent variable (exclusion restriction). Following Stokes et al. (2013), I use a question about the party identification of the respondents' parents when they were young to instrument for the partisan identification of respondents. The correlation between the respondent identifying with the mayor's party and both parents identifying with the same party is 0.30.[56] In this case, the partisan identification of the parents when the employee was young is related to the partisan identification of the respondent because party identity is partially a product of family socialization. It is also generally unlikely that parents' identification with the mayor's party when the employee was young caused the mayor to hire the respondent years later, except through the effect of the parents' partisan identity on their child's partisan identity. If these assumptions are valid, a relationship between the partisanship of the parents

---

[56] The correlation between a father and the respondent identifying with the mayor's party is 0.29, whereas the correlation with the mother's partisan identity is 0.36. Although mother and father's party identification were highly correlated (0.54), I opted to use the partisan identification of both parents together. Stokes et al. (2013, 58) find similar correlations in their survey of Argentinean voters. Using the partisanship of either parent as the instrument yielded similar results (not shown). Question wording can be found in the book Appendix.

and the respondent obtaining a public job indicates the effect of the partisan identification of the respondent on the likelihood of receiving a job.

Strangely enough, the municipality of Salta gives priority to the children of public employees when hiring. As seen earlier, almost 20 percent of Salta respondents reported getting the job through a parent due to this practice. In this case, the exclusion restriction is violated because when the parents are public employees, the instrument – the parents' partisanship – has a direct effect on the hiring of the son or daughter that is not a result of the family socialization of partisanship. For this reason, those seventy-four respondents were excluded from the analysis below.[57]

Table 3.8 reports the results of the IV analysis. In all three columns, the dependent variable is a dummy variable for whether the employee was hired during the current administration (*Current Mayor*). The main independent variable is the self-reported partisan identification, coded 1 for employees who identified themselves with the mayor's party and 0 otherwise (*Mayor Party*). The instrument is a dummy variable for whether both of the respondent's parents had the same partisanship as the current mayor when the respondent was young, coded 1 for those whose parents shared the partisanship of the mayor and 0 otherwise (*Mayor Party Parents*). Controls for the age of the respondent (*Age*), education (*Education*), gender (*Female*), and municipal dummies were also included.

Column 1 reports the result of a simple regression in which *Current Mayor* is regressed on the respondent's self-reported partisan identification; Column 2 reports the IV regression instrumenting the respondent's partisan identification with the partisan identification of the parents; and Column 3 reports the reduced-form regression in which *Current Mayor* is regressed directly on the instrument *Mayor Party Parents*. In line with the *t*-test (cf. Table 3.7), the naive estimation of Column 1 shows a strong and positive relationship between the employee's partisan identification with the mayor's party and being hired

---

[57] Even after excluding this group, the exclusion restriction is a problematic assumption for this analysis. If some other employees got their jobs because of their parents, the exclusion restriction would be violated. To deal with this, it would have been ideal to have information about the specific employees who obtained their jobs through their parents. Unfortunately, although we asked an open-ended question about how employees got their jobs, the responses were coded in a way that makes it impossible to separate employees who were hired through their parents from those who were hired through another relative or a friend. Only in Salta, due to the aforementioned regulation, was data collected in a way that made it possible to separate out those who got their jobs through their parents. Outside Salta, however, almost no employee mentioned parents as the source for their job when answering the survey or during interviews. Nevertheless, as a robustness check, I ran the IV regression excluding all employees who reported having obtained their jobs though a friend or a relative in Tigre and Santa Fe (125 employees), while still excluding the aforementioned Salta employees (74). The results from this IV regression are substantively equivalent to the ones reported here. The coefficients are slightly smaller, but still significant at the 95 percent level. See Table 3.11 in the Chapter Appendix.

TABLE 3.8 *The effect of being a supporter on hiring (IV regression)*

	Current mayor	IV current mayor	Reduced-form current mayor
Mayor Party	0.15***	0.29***	
	(0.03)	(0.11)	
Mayor Party Parents			0.09***
			(0.03)
Age	−0.22***	−0.22***	−0.22***
	(0.01)	(0.01)	(0.01)
Female	0.06**	0.06**	0.05*
	(0.03)	(0.03)	(0.03)
Education	0.01	0.01	0.01
	(0.02)	(0.02)	(0.02)
Salta	0.13***	0.09**	0.17***
	(0.04)	(0.04)	(0.03)
Santa Fe	0.03	0.06	0.03
	(0.03)	(0.04)	(0.03)
Constant	1.01***	0.97***	1.04***
	(0.06)	(0.07)	(0.06)
Observations	1,004	1,004	1,104
R–squared	0.32	0.30	0.31

Note: The age variable takes on values from 1 to 5, corresponding to respondents who are 18–25, 26–35, 36–45, 46–55, and older. The education variable takes on values from 1 to 3, corresponding to completed primary school, secondary school, and university or tertiary education. The female variable takes the value 1 when the respondent is female, and 0 otherwise. Tigre (the base category) was excluded. Robust standard errors in parentheses, *** $p < 0.01$, ** $p < 0.05$, * $p < 0.1$.

during the current administration. The IV estimator in Column 2 yields the expected positive estimated coefficient, significant at the 99 percent level. The last column reports the reduced-form regression, in which the coefficient is also positive and significant at the 99 percent level. In sum, the results from the IV regression also show – conditional on age, education, gender, and municipality – a positive relationship between the respondent sharing partisan identification with the current mayor and receiving a job during the current administration. Therefore, the results do not support the alternative hypothesis of employees becoming supporters of the mayor's party because they obtained a job. The correlation between being a supporter of the mayor's party and obtaining a job during the current administration (cf. Table 3.7) cannot be attributed to the reverse causation story of employees becoming supporters after getting their jobs.[58]

Note that this does not imply anything about supporters' ideological commitment. Again, being a supporter can be interpreted as being more closely connected to the party network, as described in Chapter 2. The reason why some voters are closer to the partisan network than others could be ideological or instrumental (they may have drawn closer to the party in order to get a job), or some combination of the two. The results above simply show that the correlation between declared support for the party and being hired cannot be attributed to the reverse causation story of declaring support *because* they were hired.

3.4   CHAPTER APPENDIX: ADDITIONAL TABLES

TABLE 3.9 *Importance of different criteria for hiring*

	Not important at all	A little important	Important	Very important	N
Education	6% (N=72)	20% (N=228)	42% (N=481)	32% (N=376)	1157
	26%		74%		
Work experience	10% (N=114)	24% (N=282)	36% (N=419)	30% (N=342)	1157
	34%		66%		
Personal connections	24% (N=281)	17% (N=191)	29% (N=334)	30% (N=342)	1148
	41%		59%		
Partisan affiliation	49% (N=552)	19% (N=213)	19% (N=217)	13% (N=151)	1133
	68%		32%		
Political ideology	53% (N=594)	17% (N=190)	18% (N=197)	12% (N=130)	1111
	71%		29%		

Note: Question wording can be found in the book Appendix.

---

[58] Stokes et al. (2013, 58–59) find similar (but weaker) results in their study of vote buying. They instrument partisan ideology with the ideology of the voter's father and find that loyal supporters (core voters) in Argentina attract more campaign gifts and subsidies than non-supporters (swing voters).

TABLE 3.10 *Importance of personal connections for hiring, by municipality*

	Not important at all	A little important	Important	Very important	N
Salta	10% (N=38)	13% (N=49)	30% (N=111)	47% (N=175)	373
	23%		77%		
Santa Fe	44% (N=170)	17% (N=66)	22% (N=84)	17% (N=66)	386
	61%		39%		
Tigre	19% (N=73)	20% (N=76)	36% (N=139)	26% (N=101)	389
	38%		62%		

Note: Question wording can be found in the book Appendix.

TABLE 3.11 *IV regression, excluding employees who obtained their jobs through friends or relatives*

	Current mayor	IV current mayor	Reduced-form current mayor
Mayor Party	0.16***	0.24**	
	(0.03)	(0.12)	
Mayor Party Parents			0.08**
			(0.04)
Age	−0.21***	−0.22***	−0.22***
	(0.01)	(0.01)	(0.01)
Female	0.06*	0.06*	0.05*
	(0.03)	(0.03)	(0.03)
Education	0.00	0.00	0.01
	(0.02)	(0.02)	(0.02)
Salta	0.08**	0.06	0.14***
	(0.04)	(0.05)	(0.03)
Santa Fe	−0.02	−0.01	−0.01
	(0.04)	(0.04)	(0.04)
Constant	1.05***	1.02***	1.07***
	(0.07)	(0.08)	(0.07)
Observations	824	824	910
R-squared	0.30	0.30	0.29

Note: The effect of partisanship on being hired by the current mayor (IV regression), excluding employees who got their job through parents (in Salta) and friends or relatives (in Santa Fe and Tigre). The age variable takes on values from 1 to 5, corresponding to respondents who are 18–25, 26–35, 36–45, 46–55, and older than 55. The education variable takes on values from 1 to 3, corresponding to completed primary school, secondary school, and university or tertiary education. The female variable takes the value 1 when the respondent is female, and 0 otherwise. Tigre (the base category) was excluded. Robust standard errors in parentheses; *** $p < 0.01$, ** $p < 0.05$, * $p < 0.1$.

4

Patronage Contracts and Political Services: Evidence from List Experiments

In office, politicians distribute many low- and mid-level public sector jobs in order to maintain a network of activists on the ground who perform various political activities. These activities, if enough of them and successful, can improve a politician's electoral returns. Incumbents use the perceived support of potential employees at the time of hiring as a proxy for their willingness to provide political services: only perceived supporters can credibly commit to provide political services in the future (see Chapter 2). This chapter provides a detailed description of three different political activities performed by public employees during elections. Using the list experiment technique described below, I estimate the proportion of employees – particularly supporters – who help with campaigns, attend rallies, and monitor elections. These are not the only types of political services that patronage employees provide, but they are among the most important ones provided by mid- and low-level local employees in the Argentinean context.[1]

4.1 EMPIRICAL STRATEGY: LIST EXPERIMENTS

Along with questions on voting behavior and political preferences, questions about political services were the hardest to ask. Employees could be unwilling to reveal that kind of information in front of others (recall that the interviews were conducted at public offices), but it was also possible that they would be unwilling to reveal that information in private or, even worse, provide inaccurate responses.[2] To get around this problem,

---

[1] Chapter 2 provides a description of other political services; Chapter 5 focuses on another common political service – the provision of favors.

[2] List experiments (and indirect questioning in general) are typically used to improve measurement of behavior or beliefs the respondents would prefer to hide. In the case of the political services studied

survey questions about political services included both relatively direct questions in the sensitive part of the survey (Part B, filled out by employees on their own) and list experiments.[3]

The logic of the list experiment technique is straightforward. First, the survey sample is split into random halves: a treatment and a control group. Each group is read the same question and shown a card with a number of response options.[4] Cards for the control and treatment group differ only in the number of response categories. List experiments work by integrating the item one cares about (the "treatment" or "sensitive" item) into a list of other items. Respondents are asked to report the number of items on the list that apply to them, but not which ones. The question does not ask respondents to mention specific activities, only *how many* of those activities they did. Thus, as long as respondents understand that the anonymity of their responses is protected, list experiments generate more accurate responses and more valid estimates than direct questioning (Coutts and Jann 2011; Kiewiet de Jonge and Nickerson 2014).[5] Because

here, however, it is possible that some employees would actually want to broadcast their contributions and loyalty to the incumbent. The issue is that whether an employee would prefer to broadcast or hide his or her political contributions is not random. For instance, most interviews with low-skilled workers took place in front of others, including sometimes their own bosses. If bosses or coworkers were supporters of the incumbent, one would expect that the employee may have had an incentive to over-report his/her political contribution. But bosses or coworkers could also be employees appointed by the previous administration or merit/examination hires, in which case employees might prefer to hide their political activities. The advantage of list experiments is that they prevent both under-reporting and overreporting.

[3] To see the effects of social desirability bias on responses to a similar topic, see González-Ocantos et al. (2012). By comparing responses to direct questions with responses to list experiments, they show the existence of important social desirability bias on questions about clientelism. For advice on how to design list experiments, see Glynn (2013).

[4] The list of responses was not read aloud to increase privacy.

[5] To protect anonymity, it is crucial to avoid lists that would result in respondents choosing none or all of the items, generating "floor" or "ceiling" effects, respectively (see Kuklinski et al. 1997). Ceiling effects occur when respondents select the entire list of possible responses. In that case, the respondent would be claiming performance of all activities (including the sensitive one) so the anonymity that the list experiment is supposed to achieve would be ruined. To avoid selecting all items and admitting to the sensitive one, respondents would probably lie or refuse to answer. Floor effects, in turn, may arise if the control questions are expected to be negative for many respondents. To minimize ceiling effects, all the lists included unusual activities or activities that were not possible to perform concurrently. The strategy was successful since only around 1 percent of respondents in the control groups reported all four of the control items. The inclusion of high-prevalence activities to minimize the risk of floor effects was less successful (see Table 4.3 in the Chapter Appendix). Note, however, that the presence of either ceiling or floor effects would lead to the underestimation of the sensitive activity (Blair and Imai 2012); the estimates presented here are thus conservative. Using the method developed by Blair and Imai to test the validity of the experiments, I failed to reject the null hypothesis for design effects in all the list experiments. See Appendix A3 for the wording of the experiments and Table 4.3 for the distribution of responses across groups.

respondents are randomly assigned to either the treatment or the control group, the two groups are, on average, indistinguishable on both observable and unobservable characteristics.[6] Therefore, an estimate of the proportion of respondents delivering political services can be obtained by subtracting the average number of items reported by the control group from the average number reported by the treatment group.[7] Differences in the means between the two groups provide a point estimate of the number of respondents who performed political services.[8]

List experiments are not the only method of obtaining valid estimates of attitudes and activities thought to be subject to social desirability bias. Two interesting alternatives are the randomized response technique and the crosswise model.[9] I chose to use list experiments over alternatives, such as the randomized response technique, mainly for their simplicity. Instructions are easy to understand, and respondents tend to trust that the anonymity of their responses will be protected (Coutts and Jann 2011). Since the survey respondents were low- and mid-level employees, some with low levels of education, this simplicity was an important advantage over the alternatives.

Although the list experiment technique is fairly easy to implement and understand, it is still more demanding than direct questioning. Careful survey implementation was crucial for obtaining accurate responses.[10] Had the interviewers not provided clear instructions, respondents might not have

---

[6] See Tables A.5 and A.6 in Appendix A2 for covariate balance.

[7] List experiments' internal validity relies on the assumption that the list length has no effect on the responses, independent of the list content. Kiewiet de Jonge and Nickerson (2014) find that list experiments do not overestimate the incidence of behaviors or attitudes and that, for high-incidence behaviors, they actually tend to underestimate it.

[8] Although there have been developments on the use of list experiments with multivariate regression analysis (see, for instance, Blair and Imai 2012; Corstange 2009; Glynn 2013; Imai 2011), difference-in-means estimators are still considered standard for analyzing list experiments (González-Ocantos et al. 2012). An advantage of using a difference-in-means estimator is that no functional form assumption is needed.

[9] The randomized response technique works by introducing noise to responses (respondents use a coin or a spinner to determine whether to answer the sensitive question or the non-sensitive one), which protects individual answers but enables the researcher (who knows the probability distribution of the realizations of the device used) to estimate the frequency of the behavior under study. See Gingerich (2010, 2013b) for an application of this technique to the study of political corruption. The crosswise model is a version of the randomized response technique, but it is administered without a randomizing device (Gingerich et al. 2016). See Corbacho, Gingerich, Oliveros, and Ruiz-Vega (2016) for an application to the study of corruption. Corstange (2009) discusses different techniques to neutralize response bias.

[10] Careful implementation is always important when conducting surveys, but this is particularly crucial with list experiments because there is an unavoidable efficiency cost associated with the use of the technique. List experiments reduce bias by minimizing the incentives for respondents to lie, but they do so at the cost of efficiency; the standard errors for the list experiment estimates are larger than they would have been for a direct question with no response bias (Blair and Imai 2012; Corstange 2009).

understood that the anonymity of their responses was protected and, as a consequence, they might have provided inaccurate responses or refused to answer. Besides the extensive training that the interviewers received, three precautions were taken to ensure that respondents understood the instructions.

First, interviewers were directed to give the instructions for the list experiment questions clearly and slowly and to provide a scripted example. Second, the cards listed the items by letter (A, B, C) instead of by number to facilitate the detection of respondents confused by the directions. During the pilot, we had uncovered two types of error responses by respondents who did not follow the instructions. One type occurred when respondents gave a count of the frequency of doing each of the items instead of counting the items that applied to them on the list. The second type of error was identifying the item or items by using their numbers on the list, causing confusion about whether they were referring to the number of activities that applied to them or to a specific activity on the list (which was not what we wanted). In this latter case, the use of letters instead of numbers to order the list made the confusion with the instructions more evident to the interviewers, who were told to repeat the instructions if respondents showed any lack of understanding. Because the survey included four list experiments, interviewers had a chance to explain the procedure again if the response on the first experiment alerted them to a misunderstanding. Finally, I put the list experiment with the least sensitive item first (providing favors, see Chapter 5). If respondents did not understand the instructions but did not feel any social desirability bias in answering the question, they would be more likely to just identify the items on the list one by one (instead of refusing to answer or providing untruthful responses). This gave the interviewers a chance to detect the lack of understanding and repeat the instructions before going on to the more sensitive items.[11] Using this technique, the survey instrument included questions about four different political services: helping with electoral campaigns, attending rallies, monitoring elections, and providing favors (see Chapter 5).

4.2 POLITICAL SERVICES DURING ELECTIONS

Helping with Electoral Campaigns Since the return of democracy in 1983, there has been an undeniable modernization of Argentine electioneering

---

[11] While interviewers gave the instructions as many times as necessary, they never explained how the list experiment worked and which one was the item on the list we cared about. This is important to prevent respondents to overreport the sensitive item just to please the interviewers, as Ahart and Sackett (2004) suggested could have been driving the list experiment results in Dalton et al. (1994).

(Waisbord 1996). Electoral campaigns in Latin America in general and in Argentina in particular, however, still often combine modern modes of campaigning with more traditional ones (De la Torre and Conaghan 2009; Muñoz 2018; Waisbord 1996). This is particularly true at the local level, where politicians have limited resources for financing professional campaigns that include extensive use of the media (Kemahlioğlu 2012; Zarazaga 2014). At the local level in Argentina, labor-intensive activities such as painting graffiti, putting up posters, meeting with voters, organizing and attending rallies, and canvassing door-to-door are still essential parts of campaigning. Over the years, fewer and fewer activists have volunteered to perform these activities (Levitsky 2003; Scherlis 2010; Waisbord 1996), making the role of public employees crucial.[12] In addition to organizing and participating in rallies, which are discussed below, there is a diverse array of other activities conducted during campaigns.

One common activity that political parties undertake, especially in poorer neighborhoods, is organizing door-to-door campaigns (*rastrillajes*). Gerónimo, a recently elected councilman and Peronist broker in Malvinas Argentinas (Greater Buenos Aires), describes how, as soon as the candidates are announced and the campaign defined, they "start walking, ringing bells, talking with the neighbors."[13] Sergio, a Peronist public employee and political broker from La Matanza (Greater Buenos Aires), explains that this is an activity that the Peronist party does "everywhere" in the province. They usually start three or four months before the election, and each broker takes care of his or her own area. The people in charge are always from that area; Sergio said that it is more "efficient" that way because "you know the neighbors."[14]

Door-to-door campaigning is always accompanied by the distribution of paper ballots, the same ones that voters would find at the polls on Election Day. In Argentina, voters can vote with ballots they receive directly from party activists or with the ones available inside the voting booth. Argentina does not use an official ballot with all the candidates on it (i.e., the Australian ballot).[15] In contrast, and although the government is in charge of ballot distribution to the voting cites (schools in the case of Argentina) on Election Day, each political

---

[12] Jorge Fernández, a Peronist politician from Santa Fe, described this change: "Up to 1986 or 1987 there was a high level of political mobilization. There were robust political organizations with a strong presence of volunteer activists. There were neighborhood organizations and unions linked to the parties. With very scarce resources you ran a campaign. You hardly had to pay for anything, because everything was done by volunteers; people even contribute with their own money. But now, nothing of that is left" (cited by Scherlis 2010, 209).

[13] Author interview, Malvinas Argentinas, August 20, 2009.

[14] Author interview, La Matanza, August 10, 2009.

[15] Although sometimes confused with the secret ballot, the Australian ballot refers to ballots that the government or the electoral authorities produce, listing all political parties or candidates for office in the same ballot.

party is responsible for producing its own ballots, ones that include only their list of candidates. The dissemination of these ballots, either door-to-door or on a busy city corner, in the weeks before the election is considered crucial by all political parties. It helps voters get to know the candidates and familiarize themselves with the ballot they will choose on Election Day. This could be key for finding the preferred ballot at the voting booth, which often – especially when federal and local elections are held concurrently – contains an overwhelming number of ballots. On Election Day, many voters bring their own ballots to the polls.[16] At the same time, the distribution of ballots before the election has been associated with vote buying. A common practice among brokers is to distribute paper ballots together with handouts, making it clear where the handout is coming from and, as Brusco, Nazareno, and Stokes (2004) point out, perhaps reinforcing the message that a vote is expected in return.[17]

Other important campaign activities that require the people power of supporters include painting graffiti, hanging banners, and plastering walls with posters highlighting the name of the candidate or the party. Activities like these are an essential part of campaigning, especially for local politicians who cannot afford more expensive types of advertising, such as billboards. Those helping with the campaign take these activities very seriously, to the point of fighting over available wall space. In his study of Argentinean brokers, Zarazaga (2014) reports that eighteen of 120 brokers interviewed affirmed having been involved in shootouts with other brokers while they were painting graffiti.

Campaigning in Argentina also involves organizing political meetings with voters – sometimes referred to as *mateadas* because attendees often share the green tea known as *mate* – and other activities such as seminars, social gatherings, and cultural events. Among the 120 brokers interviewed by Zarazaga (2014), seventy-two (64 percent) said they had organized meetings for voters to meet the candidate. In Tigre, the decentralized offices (*delegaciones*) help organize meetings and dinners. According to Laura, a longtime administrative employee in one of these offices, they all help with these events: "People need to be invited and neighbors need to be brought in." A key part of organizing is inviting people: "You know already which groups of neighbors you can count on ... institutions, schools, clubs, senior centers." During the 2009 election, "there was something every weekend and smaller

---

[16] In a survey conducted in three Argentinean provinces in 2001–02, Brusco, Nazareno, and Stokes (2004) find that 15 percent of respondents reported having voted in the last election with ballots that they brought with them. In the 2015 Argentinean presidential election runoff, in which there were only two ballots to choose from, 6 percent of respondents from a representative national survey still reported bringing their preferred ballot to the voting booth (Lupu et al. 2015).

[17] Brusco, Nazareno, and Stokes (2004) find that voters who vote with a ballot provided by a broker are more likely to have received handouts, and those who receive both a ballot and a handout are more likely to report that the handout influenced their vote.

things during the week." During campaigns, employees often work on weekends: "It was the same before [with the previous administration], employees already know." But some things have changed; according to Laura, the previous administration had less money, so public employees used to act as waiters at some events. That is no longer the case.[18]

Valeria, another employee from Tigre, who was hired in 2001, corroborated that decentralized offices are important resources for campaigning, a legacy of the previous administration. In fact, employees who have been on the job longer are "used to helping with campaigns ... Every two years they knew they had to collaborate ... They are better trained (*están más entrenados*)." According to her, employees at decentralized offices work long hours during elections, and when the campaign organizes dinners, they help to set up the tables and accommodate the guests. Valeria, who works in the personnel office, verified that employees get overtime pay when they work at these campaign events after hours.[19]

Table 4.1 presents the result of the list experiment where the treatment category is "Work/help in the electoral campaign" in the last election.[20] The average number of activities reported by respondents in the control group (with only four list items) was 1.19, while the average among respondents whose list included the treatment item (political campaigns) was 1.41. Thus, the estimated percentage of public employees who helped in the last election is 22 percent (significant at the 99 percent level).[21]

Attending Political Rallies Another important activity for parties, especially in the months before an election, is conducting political rallies. Although rallies are no longer as important as they used to be in Argentinean politics, political parties still invest a lot of time and effort into organizing them. A crucial part of their organization is making sure that enough people will show up. Qualitative work has pointed out that public employees and beneficiaries of social welfare and workfare programs are expected to turn out to rallies (e.g., Auyero 2001; Quirós 2006; Szwarcberg 2015; Vommaro and Quirós 2011; Zarazaga 2014). Sometimes, those in charge of the mobilization get "paid." According to an

---

[18] Author interview, Tigre, January 6, 2011.

[19] Author interview, Tigre, August 23, 2010.

[20] Exact wording and baseline response categories for all the list experiments can be found in Appendix A3.

[21] For comparison, in the 2012 Latin American Public Opinion Project (LAPOP) survey (the closest to the 2009–10 survey of public employees), 8 percent of respondents in Argentina reported to have worked for a candidate or party during the last presidential campaign, in 2011. Among those who reported working for the state (at any level of the administration) or for a state company, 12 percent reported to have worked on the campaign (compared to 7 percent of salaried employees in the private sector). Source: The AmericasBarometer by LAPOP, www .LapopSurveys.org.

important activist (*operador político*) for the Peronist party in the province of Buenos Aires, some are "paid" with public sector jobs, some get paid "under the table," and some receive "favors for their neighborhoods."[22] To facilitate and increase attendance, transportation is often provided. A telephone operator from Salta, Josefina, recalled that the last time she attended a rally was when a councilman from the mayor's party took office: "They brought us from here," she said, emphasizing how the municipality had provided transportation.[23] In Malvinas Argentinas, a municipality located on a suburban railway line in Greater Buenos Aires, when they have to mobilize for national rallies, they "rent one or two trains." The train "makes its stops and the activists or the ones attending the rally keep on boarding the train. Then we get off in Retiro [downtown Buenos Aires] and walk to the Plaza de Mayo [the square in front of the Presidential House, a common place for rallies]."[24]

Political rallies play diverse and important roles in Argentinean politics. They serve the straightforward purpose of advertising and allowing candidates to display their power to voters and other politicians. Indeed, as in Peru (Muñoz 2014, 2018), Bolivia (Lazar 2004), Ecuador (De la Torre and Conaghan 2009), and Mexico (Holzner 2010; Szwarcberg 2015), rallies in Argentina are still an important mechanism to establish and signal candidates' electoral viability, especially at the local level. Attendance at rallies is also considered a way for potential clients to show loyalty (e.g., Auyero 2001; Quirós 2006; Szwarcberg 2012, 2015; Vommaro and Quirós 2011). In Auyero's words (2001, 163), attending rallies is "a way of showing a broker that one is loyal, responsible, and ready to help out when needed – and therefore deserving of a job if and when one becomes available." Rallies (as well as the other campaign activities discussed above) give citizens the opportunity to be visible to brokers and politicians, publicly signaling their support and their willingness to provide political services, with the expectation of getting a job (or some other benefit) in the future. As in Bolivia, "a record of involvement in party activity, can lead to a chance of employment" (Lazar 2004, 232). In the words of Sofía, an administrative employee from Salta: "I've told you that I got this job through politics, but the thing is that I was politically active *in order to* get a job."[25]

Politicians and brokers, in turn, take these signaling efforts seriously. Mauricio, a director in the Salta public works department who has worked

---

[22] Author interview (Lucas), La Plata, August 5, 2009.
[23] Author interview, Salta, June 15, 2011.
[24] Author interview (Gerónimo), Malvinas Argentinas, August 20, 2009.
[25] Author interview, Salta, June 8, 2011. In line with the expectations of the theory outlined in this book, when asked about the criteria for hiring in her sector, she considered personal connections to be more important than political ideology and partisan affiliation.

for the municipality since 1971, explained this point bluntly, "*Acá el que toca el bombo, tiene trabajo* (Here, whoever plays the drums gets a job)," referring to the usual presence of drums at political rallies in Argentina.[26] Another employee from Salta who had helped during the campaign and, at the time of the interview, was working in close proximity to the mayor, provides a similar account: "If a person has contributed to the mayor's victory, she has a right (*tiene cierto derecho*) [to get a job]."[27] Mariano, a relatively minor Peronist broker in Salta, talks about people "waiting": they "wait to get a job ... there are people who work for you (politically) for years and years, and all they want is a job."[28] The key is *acompañar*; voters who *acompañan políticamente* (politically accompany), who show up when needed, increase their chances of getting a job.

At the same time, the number of followers each broker can mobilize to rallies provides party leaders with important information about the power of each broker. Rallies give brokers the opportunity to show the size of their network of supporters. In a survey of 800 brokers conducted in Argentina, Stokes et al. (2013, 122–23) asked them to name the most important activity for brokers interested in a political career. About 10 percent replied that mobilizing voters for a political rally was more important than mobilizing voters for a primary or a general election. Some scholars have argued that party leaders use this information to monitor brokers and reward or punish them according to their ability to mobilize people to those rallies (Stokes et al. 2013; Szwarcberg 2015; Zarazaga 2014).

Brokers are well aware of the importance of mobilizing for rallies. José, the local broker and provincial public employee from Buenos Aires mentioned at the beginning of this book, does not have a lot of *his* people to mobilize for rallies. When asked about mobilization, he replied: "I have people ... I have agreements ... They [the people] are not mine ... I have an agreement with territorial brokers (*referentes territoriales*) with whom we exchange things." He further explained what he meant by "things": "because of my political connections I can maybe get resources ... Maybe they don't have access to the social welfare ministry ... or to obtain material resources (*mercadería*) to be able to help people." He has an agreement to help other brokers with "things" and those other brokers help him with "people" when he needs to mobilize for rallies.[29] Mariano, another Peronist broker (albeit less politically relevant than José) and public employee from Salta, considered mobilization for rallies to be a relatively easy task: "I think it's a little easier [than turning out the vote] when there are rallies." He described the types of voters he often mobilizes and how: "Young people (*chicos*) from the neighborhood ... How does one make them go there? By giving them t-shirts, making a barbecue, things like that ... They

---

[26] Author interview, Salta, June 13, 2011.
[27] Author interview (Micaela), Salta, August 10, 2011.
[28] Author interview, Salta, August 1, 2011.
[29] Author interview, La Plata, August 5, 2009.

are often young people who do nothing, who spend a lot of time on the streets ... And we have buses and trucks."[30]

Table 4.1 presents the results of the list experiment in which the treatment category is "Attend Political Rallies" during the last election. The average number of activities reported by respondents in the control group (with only four list items) was 1.39, while the average among respondents whose list included the treatment item (political rallies) was 1.60. Thus, the estimated percentage of public employees who attended rallies during the last election is 21 percent (significant at the 99 percent level).[31]

Monitoring Elections In Argentina, voting takes place in schools, and voters are preassigned to a voting booth (called *mesa*) that is typically a classroom. Outside each one, tables are set up for the polling officials and the ballot box. Windows in the classroom, if any, are covered, and any other doors blocked to guarantee the secrecy of the vote; the sealed classroom is then called the "dark room" (*cuarto oscuro*). After showing identification, voters receive a signed, official envelope and, alone, enter the assigned classroom, where the paper ballots for each party are kept. Once inside, voters pick their preferred ballot, put it inside the envelope, and exit the classroom to deposit the envelope in the ballot box.

The electoral law requires two or three official poll workers (*autoridades de mesa*) – a president and one or two surrogates – at each voting booth to monitor the election and count the votes. These poll workers, selected by the government from among local residents, are responsible for arranging the paper ballots inside the classroom at the beginning of the day, keeping on top of restocking ballots when they run out, checking voters' IDs, and signing identification cards after votes are cast.[32] At the end of the day, they count the votes and fill in the official forms reporting the electoral results. The ballot boxes and forms are then sent off to the proper ministries. On Election Day, if none of the appointed poll workers are present, voters in line to vote at that particular polling station take on their duties, but turnout of the official poll workers is usually high.[33] Each party that competes in the election has the right to assign one partisan

---

[30] Author interview, Salta, August 1, 2011.

[31] For comparison, in the 2012 LAPOP survey mentioned above, 8 percent of the respondents in Argentina reported participating in a rally or protest (*manifestación o protesta pública*) in the last twelve months. Among public sector employees (at all levels of the administration) and employees of state companies, the percentage rises to 14 percent compared to 10 percent among salaried private sector employees. Source: The AmericasBarometer by the Latin American Public Opinion Project (LAPOP), www.LapopSurveys.org.

[32] This signature has not been required since 2013. Now, in 2020, the official poll workers give voters a signed piece of paper as proof of voting. (Recall that voting is mandatory in Argentina.)

[33] According to a study conducted by the Argentinean NGO CIPPEC, 95 percent of all polling stations in the Greater Buenos Aires area in 2013 and 96 percent in 2015 were covered by the designated official poll workers (Leiras et al. 2016). See Ascencio and Rueda (2019) for an

monitor or poll watcher (*fiscal de mesa*) to each voting booth, plus a partisan monitor head (*fiscal general*) to each school.[34] The citizens selected by the government – the official poll workers – are the ones in charge and the only ones with legal authority to decide on electoral issues, yet Argentinean political parties consider the presence of party representatives at polling stations on Election Day essential to guaranteeing fair elections.

Probably the most important role that partisan monitors play in the country's elections is ensuring that each booth is stocked with enough of their party ballots throughout the day. Accusations of missing ballots are frequent in Argentinean elections, and the conventional wisdom posits that parties steal other parties' ballots from the voting booths, preventing citizens from voting for their preferred candidate. Among the 120 political brokers interviewed by Zarazaga (2014) in 2009–10 in Greater Buenos Aires, twenty-two (18%) admitted to having sent followers to steal opposition ballots. Among the 200 official poll workers interviewed by the NGO CIPPEC during the 2015 election in Greater Buenos Aires, 8 percent reported that stolen ballots were an issue in the voting booth that they were assigned to (Leiras et al. 2016). During the 2015 election, even the eventual winner of the presidential election, Mauricio Macri (PRO, 2015–19), expressed concerns: "the national sport of stealing ballots has started (*empezó el deporte nacional del robo de boletas*)."[35] The media reports anecdotally on several incidents of this kind during every election in Argentina, but they are rarely legally denounced, let alone prosecuted.[36]

Another illegal trick that has been reported is the introduction of fake ballots. Brokers send supporters to replace the official ballots with fake ones that look similar to the original ones when citizens enter the classroom to vote; subsequently, distracted voters cannot tell the difference, and vote using these

---

analysis of the effects of a similar rule in Mexico, where parties place supporters first in line to be ready to replace official poll workers if the opportunity arises.

[34] Partisan monitors need a party permit to be able to perform their role. The poll workers are the ones in charge of checking these permits.

[35] "Mauricio Macri: 'Empezó el robo de boletas; algunos entran flacos y salen gordos del cuarto oscuro'" (*La Nación*, 08/09/15).

[36] See, for example: "Partidos opositores denuncian robo de boletas" (*El Litoral*, 10/28/07), "Principales fuerzas de la oposición denunciaron robo de boletas" (*La Capital*, 10/28/07), and "Una elección donde ganó la denuncia" (*La Nación*, 10/29/07), for the 2007 election; "La oposición denunció robos y faltantes de boletas" (*Clarín*, 08/14/11) and "Para la oposición fue 'sistematizado y organizado' el robo de boletas" (*La Nación*, 08/15/11), for the 2011 election; and "El PRO denunció robo de boletas y el oficialismo negó irregularidades" (*Clarín*, 08/10/15), "Macri denunció el 'robo de boletas'" (*Ámbito*, 08/09/15), and "Macri y Michetti denunciaron que hubo robo de boletas" (*Infobae*, 08/09/15), for the 2015 election. On the lack of legal denunciations, see: "Lo que faltó fueron las denuncias" (*Página12*, 08/12/15); "Ningún candidato formalizó denuncias por robo de boletas" (*Infobae*, 08/09/15).

fake ballots. They are then nullified when the votes are counted.[37] While the official poll workers are in charge of making sure ballots from all parties are available and preventing these tricks from happening, parties consider it essential to have their own monitors in place to stop their ballots from being stolen or switched out.

Monitors are also crucial in the event of a vote that could be counted as null.[38] If the party that the vote is intended to go to has no partisan monitor present, the likelihood of counting that vote as null is higher. An experienced monitor would argue with the poll workers to make it count for her or his party. The final decision on all these issues is always in the hands of the official poll workers, but it is not unusual to find inexperienced citizens serving as poll workers. They sometimes do not know the rules well enough or are simply not willing to argue with partisan monitors.[39] Among the 200 official poll workers interviewed by CIPPEC in the survey mentioned above, only 63 percent of them have participated in some sort of training (up from 40 percent in 2013) and around 40 percent were acting as poll workers for the first time (Leiras et al. 2016).

Finally, partisan monitors are also considered essential for monitoring turnout and vote-buying (Brusco, Nazareno, and Stokes 2004; Szwarcberg 2012, 2015). As in Mexico (Ascencio and Rueda 2019), this is facilitated by poll workers being instructed to read the names of voters aloud as voters are handed the envelopes to cast their ballots, and partisan monitors are given the list of registered voters in each voting booth. The purpose of this practice is to prevent multiple voting but, as Ascencio and Rueda (2019) point out for the Mexican case, it is a practice that exemplifies how partisan monitors are in a position to become either protectors or manipulators of the electoral process.

There is some evidence that partisan monitors do have an effect on electoral outcomes. Using a natural experiment generated by the alphabetical assignment of voters to voting booths within schools, a study of the 2011 legislative election in Argentina finds that the presence of a partisan monitor increased the vote count for the monitor's party by 1.5 percent on average, with the effect reaching up to 6 percent

---

[37] Zarazaga (2014) reports having witnessed this trick firsthand during the 2009 election in Greater Buenos Aires.

[38] Null votes are those where the preferred choice is not clear. This could be because the ballot put in the envelope is not the official one, the ballot is damaged, two ballots for the same position were submitted, or something other than the official ballot was put in the envelope. For an analysis of the causes of invalid voting in Latin America, see Cohen (2018).

[39] To get a better sense of the work of monitors, I volunteered as a partisan monitor for the Socialist Party in the city of Rosario (Santa Fe), where I had some contacts, for the 2011 local elections. When the first vote that could be considered a null vote came up, the highest official authority (*presidente de mesa*), who was a teacher in her early twenties, told me and the monitors from the other two parties to decide among ourselves what *we* wanted to do with that vote.

for some parties. The authors argue that this is caused by paper ballots disappearing from the voting booth (Casas, Díaz, and Trindade 2017).[40] In Mexico, Ascencio and Rueda (2019) also find a positive correlation between the presence of partisan monitors and the vote share of those monitors' party. In addition, they find that the presence of partisan monitors increases turnout (presumably as a consequence of vote and turnout buying) and reduces the share of null votes, especially when the other parties have no partisan monitors present. Despite the relatively limited evidence of the effect of partisan monitors on electoral outcomes, Argentinean parties consider them essential to guaranteeing fair elections and devote significant resources to making sure that their own monitors are present in every voting booth.

When asked about the types of activities employees are asked to do during elections, Valeria, the employee from Tigre mentioned above, named just one activity: "monitoring elections." When asked about other things, she added other events, but her first response was only electoral monitoring; this gives a sense of how common requests for monitoring are among public employees. In a survey of 420 partisan monitors conducted by the NGO CIPPEC in Greater Buenos Aires during the 2015 election, 34 percent reported being public sector employees (Leiras et al. 2016). Valeria monitored the 2007 election for *Acción Comunal*, the party in power at the time, and for the incumbent Peronist party in 2009. She is always asked to monitor, probably because she has been working at the municipality since 2001 ("maybe they call the well-known ones," she says), and she has a master's degree. According to her, parties try to get more educated employees to act as partisan poll monitors.[41]

Having partisan monitors in every voting booth is considered so important that parties that cannot recruit enough "volunteers" frequently pay for the service; this is often necessary when the party is not in power. Pablo and José, the two Peronist brokers from Greater Buenos Aires mentioned in Chapter 1, explained the differences between their districts: "[They] are different because Peronism is not in power in A, but it is in power in B. In A, partisan monitors are paid, in B monitors are not paid .... Why are monitors not paid? Because they get a salary." José referred to the fact that in municipalities in which their party is in power, public employees, who "get a salary" from the state, are the ones

---

[40] There are good reasons to expect these effects to be larger for primaries. In contrast to general elections, very few people used to participate in primaries in Argentina. Fewer voters means that the opportunities for electoral manipulation are higher (De Luca, Jones, and Tula 2002, 2006). Since 2011 (after the survey was concluded), primary elections have been mandatory (for both parties and voters) for presidential and national legislative positions. In August 2011, the first primary elections were held under this law, and the turnout was above 70 percent.

[41] Author interview, Tigre, August 23, 2010.

who monitor the election.[42] Lucas, the President of the local branch of the Peronist party in a traditionally opposing municipality in another district in Greater Buenos Aires, estimated that around 200 out of the 750 monitors who participated in the 2009 election in his district were paid (50 pesos).[43] In Salta, even though Peronism was in power, a few employees mentioned that Peronist monitors were paid in the last election. One of them reported that those who were general monitors (*fiscales generales*), such as herself, received 100 pesos and a handout of food (*un bolsón*).[44] Mariano, the Peronist broker mentioned above, reported that he had gotten his aunt some money and two bunk beds that she needed in exchange for her services as a partisan monitor.[45] A Salta city councilman from the opposition Radical party explained that the majority of monitors from all parties get paid, except those who already get a salary from the state (*los que ya están contenidos*). To illustrate, he gave an example: "If I hire you in the public administration and you earn 3000 pesos (*mangos*), imagine if on top of that I would have to pay you! No way, you go and take care of the school. That's how the system works."[46] In the CIPPEC survey of partisan monitors in Greater Buenos Aires mentioned above, 25 percent of respondents reported having been paid (Leiras et al. 2016).

On Election Day in Salta, in addition to partisan monitors, there are what they called "lawyers by school" (*abogados por escuela*). These are lawyers recruited by the administration to be present on Election Day (two per school) to resolve disputes. They have no legal authority; there is no legislation that regulates their role; and this practice, to the best of my knowledge, exists only in Salta Province.[47] The role of these "legal" monitors was confirmed in several interviews with employees who themselves had acted as "lawyers by school" in previous elections. Interviewees agreed that all lawyers in the administration get asked to do this, and almost all of them agree. As Marisa, a lawyer from Salta, said: "We already know – it's a mandate."[48] According to Jaime, another lawyer who had taken on the role in several elections, the official poll workers call the lawyers when they have a question or there is an issue; the poll

---

[42] Author interview, La Plata, August 5, 2009. The names of the municipalities are not provided to protect anonymity.

[43] Author interview, La Plata, August 5, 2009. In June 2009, fifty Argentinean pesos were around thirteen US dollars.

[44] Author interview, Salta, June 6, 2011. In June 2011, 100 pesos were around twenty-four US dollars. For the same job, the Radical party was paying between fifty and seventy pesos. Author interview (Radical city councilman), August 1, 2011.

[45] Author interview, Salta, August 1, 2011.

[46] Author interview (Radical city councilman), Salta, August 1, 2011.

[47] According to a city councilman from the Radical party (the opposition at the time), this is done in other Salta municipalities as well. Author interview, Salta, August 1, 2011.

[48] Author interview, Salta, June 8, 2011.

TABLE 4.1   *Political services – List experiment estimates*

	Electoral campaigns	Rallies	Monitoring
Treatment	1.41	1.60	1.05
	(0.04)	(0.04)	(0.03)
	N=587	N=586	N=585
Control	1.19	1.39	0.93
	(0.03)	(0.04)	(0.02)
	N=582	N=584	N=587
Estimated proportion	0.22***	0.21***	0.12***
	(0.05)	(0.06)	(0.04)
	N=1,169	N=1,170	N=1,172

Note: List-experiment control and treatment values are the mean number of items identified by respondents (Rows 1 & 2). Row 3 displays the estimated proportion of respondents participating in each activity. Two-sample *t*-test with unequal variance. Standard errors in parentheses; ***$p < 0.01$, **$p < 0.05$, *$p < 0.1$.

workers, who are often not familiar with the law, "assume that the lawyers have more authority."[49] Marisa confirmed his account. This assumption, of course, gives these lawyers, who have in fact no legal authority to make any decisions, a significant amount of power.[50]

Table 4.1 presents the result of the list experiment where the sensitive category is "Being an election monitor" in the last election. The average number of activities reported by the respondents in the control group (with only four list items) was 0.93, while the average among respondents whose list included the treatment item (election monitor) was 1.05. Thus, 12 percent of public employees reported having acted as election monitors in the last election (significant at the 99 percent level).[51]

[49] Author interview, Salta, June 15, 2011. To illustrate this point, he described an incident from a previous election. Another lawyer was bothering the official poll workers, and he had to explain to them that they had the authority to have this lawyer removed from the school; indeed, the poll workers can get anyone removed from the school by the police if they find it necessary, but the poll workers did not know this.

[50] According to a city councilman from the Radical party, in the unequal Salta society, where social status and last names matter, there is an exaggerated respect for lawyers (*un respeto exagerado por el doctor*) that gives them even more power. Author interview, Salta, August 1, 2011.

[51] To assess the magnitude of these numbers, I collected information about the number of monitors needed in the Tigre election. In Tigre, 225,493 voters were registered to vote in the 2009 election, and there were 652 voting booths or *mesas* (official data from the provincial electoral authorities, *Junta Electoral, provincia de Buenos Aires*). Parties assigned one monitor to each booth plus a head monitor, who is usually a relatively important broker, to each school. Excluding head monitors, 652 monitors were needed to cover every voting booth in the district. Recall that the total number of employees in

The use of list experiments allowed me to provide an accurate estimate of the proportion of employees involved in each political service during the last election: 22 percent reported helping with the electoral campaign, 21 percent reported attending a political rally, and 12 percent reported monitoring the last election.[52]

4.3 POLITICAL SERVICES AND SUPPORT FOR THE MAYOR

According to the theory of self-enforcing patronage, patronage jobs are distributed to perceived supporters. Employees more closely connected to the mayor's network, those perceived as supporters, are the ones who have more to fear from a change in administration, which makes their original commitment to provide political services credible and works as a strong incentive for them to provide these services (see Chapter 6). We should then find more supporters than non-supporters involved in the provision of political services. This section provides evidence that supporters are, in fact, more involved in the provision of the services described in the previous section.

To determine whether the provision of political services varies across different types of public sector employees, I estimate the difference-in-means across subgroups. I also corroborate the main results with regression analyses in which the list experiment counts are the dependent variables and the treatment (the list experiment including the sensitive activity) is interacted with each independent variable. Support for the mayor is measured with a question that asked respondents whether they identified themselves with the party of the mayor (*Mayor Party*).[53] Figure 4.1 displays the list experiment estimates of the three political services according to this measure of support for the mayor.[54] Results are presented graphically. For example, the left plot in the figure shows the proportion of respondents who participated in the electoral campaign, contrasting employees who identified themselves with the party of the mayor (Supporter) and those who do not (Non-Supporter). Black circles indicate the proportion of employees in each subgroup. The dashed line represents the quantity of greatest interest, because a steeper slope indicates a larger difference between supporters and non-supporters. The number over the dashed line provides the numeric value of the difference, and vertical lines represent 95 percent confidence intervals.

Tigre was 2,406 (excluding elected officials and high-ranking positions). If 337 (14 percent, which is the estimated number of monitors for the case of Tigre) of those 2,406 employees served as election monitors in the 2009 election, more than half (52 percent, 337 of 652) of the people needed to monitor the 2009 election were local low- and mid-level public employees, even though fewer than 1 percent of Tigre's voters are local public employees.

[52] The estimated percentages by municipality are: 29%*** in Salta, 24%*** in Santa Fe, and 13%* in Tigre for helping with the campaign; 23%** in Salta, 21%** in Santa Fe, and 21%** in Tigre for attending rallies; and 10% in Salta, 14%* in Santa Fe, and 14%* in Tigre for monitoring elections (***$p < 0.01$, **$p < 0.05$, *$p < 0.1$).

[53] See Appendix A3 for question wording. This question was included in the protected part of the questionnaire (Part B) that employees filled out by themselves.

[54] Table 4.4 in the Chapter Appendix presents the numeric values displayed in the figure.

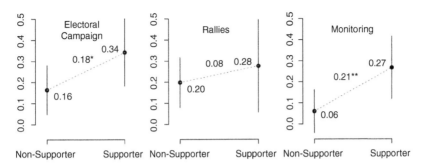

FIGURE 4.1   List experiment estimates of political services, by support for the mayor
Note: Estimated proportion of respondents participating in each activity calculated as the difference between the treatment and the control group (t-test with unequal variance). Black circles indicate the proportion of employees in each subgroup who performed each service. Vertical lines represent 95 percent confidence intervals. *** $p < 0.01$, ** $p < 0.05$, * $p < 0.1$.

In line with expectations, Figure 4.1 shows that supporters engage in more political services than non-supporters. Among the subgroup who self-identified with the mayor's party, the proportion of those helping with the campaign is 34 percent, while the proportion for those who did not self-identify with the mayor's party is 16 percent. The 18-percentage-point difference between these groups is significant at the 90 percent level. The other political services show a similar pattern. Among supporters, 28 percent report attending rallies, while among non-supporters the proportion drops to 20 (although the 8 percentage-point difference is non-significant). Among supporters, 27 percent acted as partisan election monitors in the last election, while among non-supporters the proportion is not statistically distinguishable from zero. The 21-percentage-point difference between the proportion of supporters and non-supporters who reported being monitors in the previous election is significant at the 95 percent level.[55]

To evaluate these findings more rigorously and control for other characteristics that could affect the provision of services, I conducted multivariate analysis. There are two respondent characteristics that could also condition the provision of political services: type of contract and level of education. I expect employees without job security to be more involved in political services than those who enjoy tenure rights. In the theory of self-enforcing patronage, employees without job security have more to lose with a change in the administration because they can legally be fired, which is a strong incentive to provide political services in an effort to keep the mayor in power. The sensitivity of public employees to patronage contracts also

---

[55] The list experiments did not ask for which party the political services were provided, so it is possible that some respondents were providing services for the opposition. The estimates presented throughout the book are therefore conservative.

depends on the employees' skills and labor market expectations (Calvo and Murillo 2004; Medina and Stokes 2007; Robinson and Verdier 2013). Less-educated workers have more to fear from losing their jobs with a change in administration, so it is also expected that they would be more willing to comply with their part of the patronage contract and provide political services.

The multivariate analysis also allows me to control for the main alternative explanations for the provision of services: reciprocity and fear of punishment. Recall that according to reciprocity theories, clients fulfill their side of the agreement because they want to help those who have helped them. Receiving a benefit – a job in this case – engenders feelings of obligation and gratitude, and employees help the politician by providing political services because of these feelings (e.g., Finan and Schechter 2012; Lawson and Greene 2014; Scott 1972). According to punishment theories, in contrast, employees comply with patronage agreements providing political services because they are afraid that the politician will fire them if they fail to do so (e.g., Brusco, Nazareno, and Stokes 2004; Nichter 2008; Robinson and Verdier 2013; Stokes 2005).

If reciprocity theories of clientelism were correct, respondents with more favorable attitudes toward reciprocity should be more involved in the provision of services out of feelings of gratitude, particularly those appointed by the current administration. If punishment theories were correct, respondents without tenure rights should be more involved in the provision of services, out of fear of being fired. To measure attitudes toward reciprocity (*Reciprocal*), respondents were asked about their agreement with the following statement: "We always have to return the favors that others have done for us." Those who strongly agreed or agreed more than disagreed were coded as reciprocal (1); those who strongly disagreed or disagreed more than agreed were coded as non-reciprocal (0).[56] To account for the possibility that employees may feel gratitude toward the politician who hired them in particular, this variable is interacted with *Current Mayor*, which takes the value of one for those hired by the current mayor, and zero otherwise. *Tenure* takes the value of one for those with job security, and zero otherwise. Control variables include *Female* (0–1), *College* (0–1), *Age* (1–5), and dummies for municipalities.[57] In all the models, the main variable of interest (*Supporter*) is measured, as in the previous section, with a question that asks about partisan self-identification.

Table 4.2 presents the results of the multivariate analysis. All the models are ordinary least squares regressions with the list experiment counts as dependent variables. Following González-Ocantos et al. (2012) and González-Ocantos, Kiewiet de Jonge, and Nickerson (2015), the models include a dummy variable

---

[56] This way of measuring reciprocity is far from ideal. Measuring levels of reciprocity is, however, not an easy task. See Chapter 6 (Section 6.5.2) for a brief discussion of alternative measures of reciprocity and a closer look at this alternative explanation.

[57] See Table A7 in Appendix A3 for descriptive statistics.

TABLE 4.2 *Political services – OLS regressions*

	Political campaigns			Political rallies			Election monitors		
Supporter	0.22**	0.18*	0.18*	0.09	0.06	0.06	0.24**	0.25**	0.24**
	(0.10)	(0.10)	(0.10)	(0.13)	(0.13)	(0.13)	(0.10)	(0.10)	(0.10)
College	−0.03	−0.04	−0.04	−0.09	−0.08	−0.06	0.01	0.01	−0.00
	(0.11)	(0.11)	(0.11)	(0.13)	(0.13)	(0.13)	(0.11)	(0.11)	(0.11)
Tenure	0.08	0.08	−0.01	−0.06	−0.04	−0.05	−0.18	−0.17	−0.17
	(0.12)	(0.12)	(0.14)	(0.14)	(0.14)	(0.16)	(0.11)	(0.11)	(0.13)
Reciprocal		0.01	0.09		0.11	−0.12		0.03	0.09
		(0.14)	(0.18)		(0.14)	(0.17)		(0.13)	(0.17)
Current Mayor			0.02			−0.55**			0.20
			(0.27)			(0.28)			(0.25)
Current Mayor *Reciprocal			−0.20			0.59**			−0.19
			(0.28)			(0.28)			(0.25)
Constant	0.21	0.22	0.29	0.04	−0.05	0.17	0.21	0.18	0.10
	(0.16)	(0.20)	(0.24)	(0.18)	(0.22)	(0.26)	(0.15)	(0.19)	(0.24)
N	1,165	1,157	1,154	1,166	1,159	1,156	1,168	1,160	1,157
R-squared	0.12	0.13	0.13	0.16	0.16	0.17	0.09	0.09	0.10

Note: OLS regressions with the list experiment counts as dependent variables. All coefficients are interactions between each independent variable and the treatment (the list experiment condition including the sensitive activity). All regressions include controls for age, gender, and municipality (not shown). Table 4.5 in the Chapter Appendix reports the coefficients for all the variables in these models. Robust standard errors in parentheses. *** $p < 0.01$, ** $p < 0.05$, * $p < 0.1$.

indicating the treatment assignment (i.e., the list experiment condition), interactions between this variable and all the independent variables, and non-interacted versions of all the variables.[58] The estimates for the political services are derived from the interacted coefficients, while the non-interacted coefficients (not reported here) provide estimates for the activities on the control lists. All models include controls for age, gender, municipality (not shown), college, and tenure. Models 2, 5, and 7 add a dummy for reciprocity, while Models 3, 6, and 9 include an interaction between reciprocity and being hired by the current mayor.

The results from the different models show that being a supporter is positively associated with the provision of services, even when controlling for

---

[58] Although Blair and Imai (2012) propose more efficient estimators than the one implemented here, my attempts to use their estimators were unsuccessful. Similar issues were reported by others (e.g., González-Ocantos, Kiewiet de Jonge, and Nickerson 2015; González-Ocantos, Kiewiet de Jonge, and Meseguer 2018; Mares and Young 2018). Note, however, that the less efficient (and therefore conservative) OLS fixed-interaction approach used here still produces unbiased estimates (Blair and Imai 2012; Imai 2011).

other relevant covariates and the two main alternative explanations. As in the difference-in-means analysis, in all models the sign of the coefficients for the *Supporter* variable is positive and statistically significant for helping with the campaign and monitoring elections, while positive but not significant for attending rallies. Depending on the model, supporters are between 18 and 22 percentage points more likely to be involved in the campaign, between 24 and 25 percentage points more likely to act as partisan election monitors, and between 6 and 9 percentage points more likely to participate in rallies (albeit this latter difference is not significant) in comparison to non-supporters. Neither the *Reciprocal* variable nor the *Tenure* variable is statistically distinguishable from zero in any of the models. The only variables (beyond *Supporter*) that achieved statistical significance are *Current Mayor* and its interaction with *Reciprocal* for the case of rallies. All in all, controlling for the main alternative explanations and other relevant covariates, being a supporter seems to be the best predictor of the provision of services.

Indeed, the theory of self-enforcing patronage posits that the main explanatory variable for the provision of services is support for the mayor. Supporters are more involved in the provision of political services because they have more to lose from a change in administration. Non-supporters, with or without job security, more or less educated, and more or less reciprocal, have nothing to fear from a new government. The reason why public sector employees comply with their side of the agreement is not fear of being punished or feelings of reciprocity, but the belief that they could lose their jobs (or suffer negative changes in their working conditions) with a change in the administration. Chapter 6 tests this claim.

4.4 SUMMARY

This chapter presents the first systematic evidence of the type and extent of political services that public sector employees provide for the incumbent. The evidence strongly supports the theory of self-enforcing patronage. In Chapter 3, I showed that most jobs are distributed through informal channels and that public sector jobs are disproportionally distributed to supporters. In this chapter, I provide empirical evidence that, in exchange for their public sector jobs, patronage employees engage in a number of political services at election time that go far beyond their electoral loyalty: they help with electoral campaigns, attend political rallies, and monitor elections. Using different techniques to obtain truthful responses and improve response rates, I show that a considerable proportion of employees, ranging from 12 to 22 percent, participate in one or more of these activities during elections. Moreover, and consistent with the expectations of the theory of self-enforcing patronage, I show that an incumbent's supporters are more involved in the provision of these services than non-supporters. The next chapter focuses on an activity that public employees engage in *between* elections: providing favors.

4.5   CHAPTER APPENDIX: ADDITIONAL TABLES

TABLE 4.3 *Distribution of responses for the list experiments*

	Rallies			Electoral campaign			Monitoring		
	Control		Treatment		Control		Treatment		Control		Treatment
0	76	13%	61	10%	79	14%	79	13%	162	28%	130	22%
1	277	47%	259	44%	334	57%	271	46%	319	54%	319	55%
2	162	28%	158	27%	153	26%	175	30%	93	16%	112	19%
3	66	11%	70	12%	13	2%	47	8%	12	2%	24	4%
4	3	1%	36	6%	3	1%	12	2%	1	0%		0%
5			2	0%			3	1%				0%
Estimate		0.21***				0.22***				0.12***	
N	584		586		582		587		587		585

Note: To minimize ceiling effects, the lists included rare activities or activities that one cannot perform concurrently (see Appendix A3) and only around 1 percent of respondents in the control groups reported all four of the control items. The inclusion of high-prevalence activities to minimize the risk of floor effects was less successful. Although I am not aware of any systematic study of this issue, anecdotal evidence from the survey interviews that I conducted suggests that at least some of those zero responses are indeed "DN/NA." List experiments do not include this as a response option so when respondents were in a hurry or did not want to answer for any reason, a "zero" response seemed to be the choice. The presence of either ceiling or floor effects, however, would lead to the underestimation of the sensitive activity (Blair and Imai 2012); the estimates presented here are thus conservative. *** $p < 0.01$, ** $p < 0.05$, * $p < 0.1$.

TABLE 4.4 *List experiment estimates of political services, by support for the mayor*

		Political campaigns	Political rallies	Election monitors
Mayor Party supporter	Yes	0.34***	0.28**	0.27***
		(0.08)	(0.11)	(0.08)
		N=379	N=380	N=381
	No	0.16***	0.20***	0.06
		(0.06)	(0.06)	(0.05)
		N=790	N=790	N=791
	Difference in means	0.18*	0.08	0.21**
		(0.10)	(0.13)	(0.09)
		N=1,169	N=1,170	N=1,172

Note: Estimated proportion of respondents participating in each activity calculated as the difference between the treatment and the control groups. Standard errors in parentheses. *** $p < 0.01$, ** $p < 0.05$, * $p < 0.1$.

TABLE 4.5 *Political services – OLS regressions: Coefficients for the treatment lists*

	Political campaigns				Political rallies				Election monitors			
Supporter	0.194*	0.217**	0.177*	0.180*	0.078	0.089	0.055	0.061	0.212**	0.236**	0.254**	0.237**
	(0.102)	(0.103)	(0.103)	(0.104)	(0.129)	(0.133)	(0.133)	(0.132)	(0.093)	(0.099)	(0.100)	(0.100)
Tenure		0.076	0.081	-0.013		-0.055	-0.044	-0.052		-0.175	-0.167	-0.166
		(0.120)	(0.121)	(0.141)		(0.139)	(0.138)	(0.161)		(0.109)	(0.109)	(0.129)
Reciprocal			0.015	0.094			0.112	-0.118			0.031	0.094
			(0.135)	(0.183)			(0.143)	(0.172)			(0.128)	(0.167)
Current Mayor				0.015				-0.55**				0.196
				(0.267)				(0.276)				(0.253)
Current Mayor *Reciprocal				-0.198				0.592**				-0.191
				(0.276)				(0.281)				(0.255)
Female	-0.019	-0.043	-0.023	-0.015	0.09	0.044	0.062	0.055	-0.021	-0.02	-0.025	-0.028
	(0.102)	(0.098)	(0.097)	(0.098)	(0.116)	(0.111)	(0.111)	(0.111)	(0.091)	(0.090)	(0.090)	(0.090)
College	-0.087	-0.033	-0.038	-0.040	-0.084	-0.086	-0.076	-0.060	0.011	0.005	0.009	-0.00
	(0.110)	(0.111)	(0.111)	(0.111)	(0.130)	(0.128)	(0.129)	(0.130)	(0.108)	(0.112)	(0.113)	(0.114)
Age	-0.024	-0.045	-0.047	-0.064	0.041	0.060	0.052	0.046	-0.069*	-0.036	-0.04	-0.032
	(0.042)	(0.046)	(0.046)	(0.047)	(0.047)	(0.054)	(0.054)	(0.057)	(0.037)	(0.041)	(0.042)	(0.043)
Salta		0.096	0.099	0.154		-0.003	0.004	0.017		0.005	-0.001	-0.001
		(0.120)	(0.120)	(0.129)		(0.147)	(0.147)	(0.158)		(0.111)	(0.111)	(0.117)
Santa Fe		0.139	0.134	0.16		-0.006	-0.011	0.006		0.137	0.148	0.138
		(0.125)	(0.126)	(0.129)		(0.129)	(0.130)	(0.137)		(0.123)	(0.123)	(0.125)

(continued)

Treatment constant	0.26	0.214	0.217	0.292	0.036	0.035	-0.048	0.174	0.288**	0.214	0.184	0.105
	(0.167)	(0.162)	(0.198)	(0.240)	(0.180)	(0.181)	(0.218)	(0.265)	(0.144)	(0.146)	(0.191)	(0.242)
N	1,166	1,165	1,157	1,154	1,167	1,166	1,159	1,156	1,169	1,168	1,160	1,157
R-squared	0.037	0.124	0.129	0.132	0.082	0.165	0.165	0.173	0.043	0.09	0.094	0.098

Note: OLS regressions with the list experiment counts as dependent variables. All coefficients are interactions between each independent variable and the treatment (the list experiment condition with the sensitive activity). Coefficients for the non-interacted variables available upon request. The municipality of Tigre (the base category) was excluded. Robust standard errors in parentheses. *** $p < 0.01$, ** $p < 0.05$, * $p < 0.1$.

5

Patronage, Favors, and the Personalization of Public Administration

In countries around the world – from Bolivia (e.g., Lazar 2004) and Ghana (e.g., Brierley 2021; Driscoll 2018) to Mexico (e.g., Chambers-Ju 2021; Larreguy, Montiel Olea, and Querubín 2017) and Pakistan (e.g., Callen, Gulzar, and Rezaee 2020) – public sector employees are involved in electoral mobilization. In Argentina, the number of public employees involved in this mobilization by helping with electoral campaigns, attending rallies, and monitoring elections is in the range of 12–22 percent (see Chapter 4). One of the advantages that incumbents enjoy in utilizing public employees as political workers is that patronage agreements do not end on Election Day; patronage employees also provide political services between elections. In this chapter, I focus on one of the main activities that patronage employees perform between elections: the provision of favors.

The bulk of the literature on clientelism refers interchangeably to favors and gifts (or material goods or benefits) to denote the types of "things" exchanged in clientelistic relationships. Surveys on clientelism often ask respondents whether they have received a "gift or favor" from a broker or political activist during the last election (e.g., González-Ocantos et al. 2012; Stokes et al. 2013). Similarly, the Latin American Public Opinion Project (LAPOP), the largest ongoing survey on the Americas, includes a question asking whether the respondent has been offered "a favor, food, or some other thing or benefit."[1] But favors and material benefits are not functional equivalents. The actors distributing favors are usually public employees, particularly those who typically interact with citizens – called "street-level bureaucrats" by Lipsky (1980) – or other agents with access to public employees and state resources. From the point of view of the politician, these favors are then "free": public employees, on a salary paid by

---

[1] Others have opted to ask only about material benefits (or even just money), without referring to favors or services (e.g., Calvo and Murillo 2013, 2019; Cruz 2019; Finan and Schechter 2012; González-Ocantos, Kiewiet de Jonge, and Nickerson 2014; Kramon 2016b; Stokes 2005).

the state, can provide favors to voters while doing their regular jobs. Political parties thus do not have to invest in complex territorial machines or in procuring actual material goods to deliver to voters.

Patronage employees do not have to go out of their way to provide real favors: they just need to frame their interactions with citizens to make them look like personalized exchanges and claim credit for them. Like the "particularized benefits" described by Mayhew (1974, 54), these administrative favors have two main properties: (1) they are given to specific individuals or groups; and (2) each favor "is given out in apparently ad hoc fashion." Consequently, public employees can often turn a regular administrative task into a personal favor. When normal administration becomes a constant personalization of even the most routine tasks – transforming the provision of favors into the normal way of dealing with citizens – public administration can be easily used for political gain. These types of administrative favors are then different from the distribution of material goods that most of the literature has focused on because they are directly and necessarily channeled via the state apparatus by patronage employees, thus routinizing and disguising eminently political relations.

While others have extensively documented the distribution of material goods for political support, the literature has paid less attention to the distribution of administrative favors.[2] The provision of favors, however, deserves much more attention for a number of reasons. First, from a politician's perspective, the provision of favors by public sector employees can be an effective and extremely cheap way of obtaining and maintaining votes.[3] The recurrent use of discretion – or *perceived* discretion – in the everyday actions of public employees and the consequent personalization of problem-solving helps give voters the impression that personal relationships are essential for getting things done. Once established, these personal connections can work as a strong incentive for voters to try to preserve the political status quo. If a citizen has established a personal connection with someone in the public sector who provides help when needed – or with someone who has regular access to such a person – why would she vote for another party that might fire her contact? Voters have an incentive to want to keep the incumbent in office so the connection to the state will remain intact. Self-interested voters living in clientelistic environments understand the benefits of maintaining their personal connections to the public administration and may vote accordingly. At the same time, because the link between the favor and the administration is so immediate and clear, it significantly facilitates credit claiming (Mayhew 1974; Müller 2007). Finally – and probably most worrisome – because these

---

[2] With some important exceptions (e.g., Auyero 2001; Chubb 1981, 1982; Mares, Muntean, and Petrova 2017; Mares and Young 2019a).

[3] For the potential cost of clientelism, however, see Weitz-Shapiro (2012, 2014) and Mares and Young (2019a).

services are explicitly connected to the public administration, they can potentially affect equality of access to the state.

Given these characteristics, it is surprising that we do not have a more precise assessment of who is engaged in the provision of these administrative favors, how widespread the practice is, and its political logic. Part of the reason we know so little is that obtaining reliable and systematic data is extremely difficult. In this chapter, I draw on the survey of local public employees described in Chapter 3 as well as on months of ethnographic work, during which I conducted interviews with public sector employees, political brokers, and politicians.[4] The chapter proceeds as follows. In the following two sections, I describe the type of favors that public employees often provide as well as how they manage to claim personal credit for those favors. Next, I use a list experiment survey question to estimate the extent of the practice and provide evidence that incumbent supporters grant more favors than non-supporters. After that, I show that supporters get asked to grant favors more often than non-supporters and that those who ask for favors tend to be known by public employees, especially in the case of supporter employees. Finally, I show that supporters tend to be more helpful than non-supporters.

5.1   GRANTING FAVORS

The literature on distributive politics provides extensive evidence that rules about the distribution of material benefits are often manipulated for political gain by politicians and state officials around the world.[5] In Argentina, for instance, Giraudy (2007), Lodola (2005), Nazareno, Stokes, and Brusco (2006), and Weitz-Shapiro (2006) provide evidence of significant political bias in the distribution of funds across provinces for a workfare program for the unemployed (Plan Trabajar). In Mexico, Magaloni (2006) finds that the PRI (Partido Revolucionario Institucional) favored moderately competitive districts in the distribution of social programs and punished those controlled by the opposition, while Palmer-Rubin (2016) shows partisan bias in the distribution of benefits to small-business organizations. In Peru, Schady (2000) finds that elections have a significant effect on the timing and geographical distribution of expenditures for the anti-poverty program implemented by the Fujimori government (FONCODES). In Zambia, Baldwin (2013, 2015) finds evidence that more classrooms are constructed in chiefdoms where the chief has a good relationship with the member of parliament. In Turkey, Aytaç (2014) shows that for a conditional cash transfer program, the incumbent party channels disproportionately more resources to districts with an ideologically close challenger. In Pakistan, Callen et al. (2020) find that areas dominated by the

---

[4] See Chapter 3 and the Appendix for more details about the interviews, a full description of the survey, and the logic for the selection of the municipalities.

[5] For a review of this literature, see Golden and Min (2013).

governing party receive more doctors than areas governed by opposition parties.

This political manipulation in the administration of government-funded programs and resources – often anti-poverty or workfare programs – can also be found at the individual level. In places with weak institutions like Argentina, elected and unelected public officials enjoy considerable discretion on how and when to enforce rules.[6] In this situation, many people – especially the poor – find that it is crucial to have regular access to someone in the government or to someone with access to government officials, who can provide solutions to specific problems or make exceptions when needed.

Discretion and bias can then be found both at the aggregate level – in the distribution of resources across regions or groups – and at the individual level, as this chapter documents. For instance, in Venezuela, supporters of former president Hugo Chávez were more likely to receive land grants in states governed by pro-Chávez governors and less likely to receive grants in states governed by the opposition (Albertus 2015). Mayors in Hungary and Romania (Mares and Young 2019a, 76–84) and in Argentina (Weitz-Shapiro 2012, 2014) use significant discretion in the allocation of social assistance benefits for the poor. In cities across Latin America, mayors manipulate the enforcement of rules ("forbearance") regarding street vending and squatting (Holland 2017). In the city of Palermo, Italy, "the party intervenes in the processes of ordinary administration ... All relationships are highly personalized and politicized, even those regarding the most trivial administrative procedures" (Chubb 1981, 120). Szwarcberg (2009, 51) describes a similar situation in Argentina: "Anyone visiting local legislative offices on any business day will notice people waiting to talk with a councilor in the hopes that he or she can help solve a personal problem."[7] In addition, Auyero (2000, 2001) provides numerous examples of the kind of problems – from information about government-funded food distribution to access to medicine, food packages, and mattresses – that brokers connected to the local administration solve for poor people in an Argentinean slum.

Although the poor are both most vulnerable to the arbitrariness of the state and most in need of its protection, the need (or desire) for favors from government officials and street-level bureaucrats when dealing with the state

---

[6] For Kitschelt and Wilkinson (2007b, 12), this is a situation that politicians often find convenient: "Clientelistic politicians (...) prefer rules and regulations for the authoritative allocation of costs and benefits that leave the maximum political discretion to the implementation phase (...) Politicians then may cast their net narrowly and aim at identifying particular individuals and small groups whose support can be obtained by material inducements tailored to their personal needs and serviced by political appointees in public bureaucracies who do the governing parties' bidding." Golden (2003) makes a similar argument about the Italian public administration. Cruz and Keefer (2015), in turn, show that public sector reforms are less successful in the presence of non-programmatic parties, those more likely to rely on clientelistic appeals.

[7] A similar description of Argentinean local offices can be found in Ortiz de Rozas (2017).

is not restricted to them.[8] In the city of Palermo, the selective enforcement by the city police of rules regarding vending and commercial licenses for shops provides a classic example: "there are literally thousands of ways in which a vigilant police officer can either perform a favor or make life miserable for a shopkeeper or a street vendor" (Chubb 1981, 119). Moreover, the types of favors provided by political appointees in high-level positions rarely benefit the poor. Government activities such as business and market regulations, subsidies, loans, and procurement contracts for government infrastructure are all activities that allow discretion and case-by-case targeting (Kitschelt and Wilkinson 2007b).[9]

Regulation generates ample opportunities for political manipulation, particularly when those in charge of the enforcement are supporters of the politician or party who would benefit from the manipulation. In Turkey, construction regulations are consistently relaxed during election periods to keep voters who want to build or expand their houses happy, and this is particularly noticeable in places where politicians have more control over bureaucrats (Bozçağa and Holland 2018). In Brazil, mayors from the presidential coalition running for reelection strategically manipulate the enforcement of the school attendance requirement for cash transfer recipients so enforcement is weaker before elections, particularly in schools with "politically connected principals" (Brollo, Kaufmann, and La Ferrara 2020). In these cases, as well as in the ones described above, having supporters appointed to relevant positions makes it easier for parties and politicians to get public employees to do them favors, bend the rules, or make exceptions as needed.

This chapter focuses on the favors that low- and mid-level public sector employees grant to citizens and to the political brokers who often act on behalf of those citizens. Since most of the literature has focused on the exchange of votes for material benefits, the manipulation of public policies that distribute those benefits has received a great deal of attention. Such manipulation is certainly important. For example, with regards to adding beneficiaries to the rosters of public welfare programs, Sergio, a local broker and public employee from La Matanza (Greater Buenos Aires), explained that they find most people in need through their network of activists: "The majority are activists, the ones who come to me with the names of the people who need help . . . many of them [the beneficiaries] are politically active and I know them

---

[8] Among the poor, slum dwellers are the most vulnerable (Murillo, Oliveros, and Zarazaga 2021).

[9] More than forty years ago, Wolfinger (1972, 389) explained this clearly: "(T)here is no reason why the advantages of political influence appeal only to the poor. In places where the political culture supports expectations that official discretion will be exercised in accordance with political considerations, the constituency for machine politics extends across the socio-economic spectrum."

personally."[10] Mariano, a public employee and relatively minor Peronist broker from Salta, recounted that he became involved in politics in order to help people; he then managed to get "handouts, mattresses, bunk beds, medicine" from the municipality to distribute to "people with those needs."[11] But public employees – both brokers and less-important patronage employees – do a lot more than distribute or manipulate the distribution of material benefits.

The day of my interview with Sergio, for instance, he was about to meet with someone who wanted his help with the organization of an art exhibition. As he pointed out, not all favors are about "issues of extreme need and urgency, of food. ... To the extent that you can, you help with a bunch of [different] things."[12] José, another local broker and public employee, gave other examples:

From a person who does not want to wait in line to get his driver's license, and he calls us and says: "Is there any way that I can get the license without having to wait in line?" ... To someone who has a problem because his father fell and broke his leg and needs to go to the hospital, and instead of calling the hospital directly, he calls us for us to send his father to the hospital. ... To a group of young people that calls me because they want to meet with me to organize a party at the university.[13]

In most of these cases more than one person is involved. Less influential employees can only get certain types of favors done, usually the ones that are closely related to their sector in the administration. But brokers – often patronage employees themselves – can provide a wider range of favors because they have connections to other patronage employees who can help them help others. Another example illustrates this point:

Imagine a guy whose father died and who does not have a place to hold a wake ... But he knows that there is a broker (*referente*) who is a friend of the Secretary of Social Welfare at the municipality, also in charge of the cemetery ... So you pick up the phone and in five minutes you are saying: "Go see –, the director of the cemetery: *he* will give you a service, a coffin, a wreath, six hours in a place to hold a wake."[14] (emphasis added)

When a broker gets something done for someone else, other public employees are almost always involved – in this example, the director of the cemetery. So even in the cases in which brokers themselves do not hold public sector jobs,

---

[10] Author interview, La Matanza, August 10, 2009. Recall also the conversation related in the introduction to this book, in which two public employees, both important brokers, were discussing the distribution of welfare benefits to people they knew. Although there is evidence (both in the scholarly literature and in journalists' accounts) of bias in the distribution of material benefits in Argentina, it is extremely rare to find anti-poverty benefits distributed to the non-poor. In most cases, it is not about distributing benefits to those who do not qualify for the benefit, but about which among those who qualify receive it or receive it sooner.

[11] Author interview, Salta, August 1, 2011.

[12] Author interview, La Matanza, August 10, 2009.

[13] Author interview, La Plata, August 5, 2009.

[14] Name was omitted to ensure anonymity. The person he named was the director at the time of the municipal cemetery. Author interview (José), La Plata, August 5, 2009.

they use their "bureaucratic connectivity" (Auerbach and Thachil 2018) to get things done.[15] A broker cited by Zarazaga (2015, 373) emphasizes this point: "90 percent of my problem is to keep connections in the municipality. If you have friends there, then doors will open when you knock. It is not easy, you need to be here in the streets of the neighborhood listening to people's needs, but also at the municipality getting resources."[16] Repeatedly, the brokers interviewed referred to picking up the phone to solve problems; the person on the other end is almost always a public official. When the favor is very important, this public official may be an elected official or someone who works closely with one. When the favors are relatively minor, like the ones I look at in this chapter, often the person who facilitates the resolution of the problem is a low- or mid-level public employee.

5.2 MAKING IT PERSONAL

The existing literature as well as my own research thus suggests that politicians and bureaucrats enjoy significant discretion to manipulate public resources for political gain. Frequently, however, patronage employees do not manipulate the rules or provide any *real* favors. Normal administrative tasks can be perceived as personal favors if patronage employees manage to personally claim credit for them – if they can appear to be helping.[17] Without breaking any rules, maybe just by making an exception or providing some information that the citizen does not have, in other words, by simply doing their jobs or speeding things up, patronage employees can give the impression that *they* are the reason problems get solved and services provided. If they manage to successfully create the perception that they – rather than the municipality as an institution – are personally responsible for the task accomplished, they can claim credit for it.

Patronage employees – especially the most active ones, political brokers – understand this logic perfectly; they are fully aware of the importance of these personal connections that facilitate credit claiming. For instance, in discussing the difference between collecting food assistance with an ATM card (a new system) as opposed to receiving a bag of food directly from the person in charge of distribution, a local broker puts it clearly: "It is not the same thing because

---

[15] Sometimes, brokers are public employees at the national or provincial level but politically active at the local level. In fact, the broker cited (José) is a provincial public employee (and former municipal employee) in Buenos Aires province, who continues to be an important broker at the local level. In these cases, connections with local patronage employees are fundamental to being able to "deliver" at the local level.

[16] In his description of congressional offices, Mayhew (1974, 55) highlights the same point: "Each office has skilled professionals who can play the bureaucracy like an organ – pushing the right pedals to produce the desired effects."

[17] Weitz-Shapiro (2014) makes a similar argument about how mayors can create an image of having discretion over the distribution of benefits to be able to enforce clientelistic exchanges. For her, however, this is done in order to convince voters that the politician is responsible for program distribution and that he can actually *punish* defectors (those who do not vote as expected) by withdrawing the benefits.

the ATM card does not listen to you, does not speak to you, does not understand you (*no te contiene*), does not ask you how you are doing."[18] In contrast, another broker claimed to be happy with the ATM card system because it would actually reduce poor people's "broker dependence" (*dependencia punteril*). Somewhat ironically, he communicated this change by *personally* calling all the beneficiaries he knew and, when he did not know the beneficiary personally, he called the activist who referred the beneficiary so that the activist could let him/her know.[19] Gerónimo, a Peronist councilman and broker from Greater Buenos Aires, also describes the importance of personal connections: "People ask me for things . . . A lot of people ask me for jobs . . . I don't have jobs . . . But, at least, I stop to listen. I think people want social and political leaders or brokers (*dirigentes o referentes*) to love them (*que los quieras*). People can tell."[20]

Government programs' design sometimes facilitates this personalization of credit claiming. In Malvinas Argentinas, the municipality where Gerónimo is a councilman, for instance, the PROMUNIF program (Programa Municipal para la Infancia y la Familia) addresses the needs of the poor, such as "prosthetics, housing improvements, long (health) treatments, hearing aids." Brokers are key actors in connecting those in need with the administration: "the political brokers (*referentes*) *themselves* are the ones who bring the requests, the requests they receive on the street: 'I need a wheelchair'; 'I need a special hearing aid for my son'; 'I need an orthopedic bed for my mum.'"[21]

Another example can be found in Tigre, where the department of social assistance hires "territorial agents" (*agentes territoriales*). These public employees are in charge of "the construction, implementation, and development of the municipal social policy in the neighborhoods. With that purpose, they have to mediate (*mediatizar*) the needs of the community."[22] Their job is to identify the needs of the poor and connect them to the resources available in the municipality for solutions. These positions, however, are viewed as political and are occupied by supporters of the incumbent. Valeria, a Tigre employee who has worked at the personnel office for about ten years, explained that the only ones who lost their jobs with the change of administration in 2007 were those who were "very politically identified" (*muy identificados políticamente*) with the old administration. Among those, she explains, were these territorial agents "whom all politicians have and are representatives of each neighborhood." They were replaced with "connections that this administration had in each neighborhood."[23] On the dataset of public employees provided by the municipality for the survey,

---

[18]   Author interview (Pablo), La Plata, August 5, 2009.
[19]   Author interview (Sergio), La Matanza, August 10, 2009.
[20]   Author interview, Malvinas Argentinas, August 8, 2009.
[21]   Author interview (Gerónimo), Malvinas Argentinas, August 8, 2009, emphasis added.
[22]   Municipality of Tigre website, accessed on June 27, 2018. www.tigre.gov.ar/salud/asistencia-social/
[23]   Author interview, Tigre, August 23, 2010.

there were seventeen employees officially identified as territorial agents; sixteen of them hired by the new administration after 2007. According to Valeria, there are actually more than sixty.

Beatriz, the daughter of two Peronists, exemplifies the type of employee who often occupies this position. She was hired by the new administration as a territorial agent in 2008, finding out about the job through someone who was working at the municipality, and she was Peronist affiliated before joining the administration. She had been doing volunteer work in poor neighborhoods since 2002. When asked what were the most important factors for hiring new employees in her area of work, she named political ideology and personal connections. Beatriz also reported being very interested in politics. Not surprisingly, when asked about the provision of favors, she said she was asked for favors every day.[24]

Why do voters – especially the poor – reach out to these intermediaries instead of making demands directly to the administration? In poor neighborhoods, the only intermittent presence of the state and the politicization of access to scarce basic public services and resources turn brokers connected to political networks into essential actors (e.g., Auerbach and Thachil 2018; Auyero 2001; Szwarcberg 2015; Zarazaga 2014). Controlling access to scarce resources in a setting where resources are desperately needed makes brokers key to the daily lives of the poor. In the words of a Peronist broker: "The broker is like a model for them (*el referente es como un referente para ellos*). He is close. It's a person that, in a moment of desperation, they can reach out to to get the problem solved. And that's why they believe in him (*creen en él*)."[25] More broadly, even in the case of more well-off voters, reaching out to intermediaries is perfectly reasonable in a context in which, as shown below, personal connections are essential for getting things done.

My own fieldwork and prior qualitative studies provide substantial evidence of the widespread practice of favor provision by public sector employees. This qualitative approach, however, is limited in its ability to measure the extent of the phenomenon. To better understand the political logic behind the provision of favors by public employees, individual-level data and a reliable measure are needed. Therefore, I now turn to the survey and survey experimental evidence collected across local public administrations in Argentina.

5.3 HOW WIDESPREAD IS THE PROVISION OF FAVORS?

In this section, I use a list experiment to measure the extent to which public employees provide favors.[26] Table 5.1 presents the results of a list experiment in which the treatment category is having helped someone at the city hall during

---

[24] Author interview, Tigre, August 17, 2010.
[25] Author interview (José), La Plata, August 5, 2009.
[26] The list experiment technique is described in detail in Chapter 4.

the previous week.[27] Note that the question asks about helping "someone," which could mean either directly helping citizens or helping other patronage employees – often brokers – help citizens.

List experiments guarantee the anonymity of responses because respondents are not asked to answer about specific activities, only about the number of listed activities performed. The technique is thus particularly useful for studying sensitive behaviors. Considering the provision of favors a sensitive issue, however, might be counterintuitive. After all, a favor is about helping others. It is true that in some cases, employees show pride in being helpful. In other cases, especially during interviews when questions about favors were asked directly, the sensitivity of the issue became evident. Sergio, a broker and public employee from La Matanza, provides a good example of how someone could get slightly offended by the implication that employees provide favors. After a couple of questions about favors, he replied emphatically: "But politics is not a favor machine! (*una máquina de hacer favores*)."[28] Pablo, another Peronist broker and public employee, wanted to make sure not to give the impression that providing favors was a broker's main role: "Peronism is not just helping people (*no es solamente asistencia*) ... Peronism is an ideal (*un modelo de país*) ... Assisting people is just a small part ... "[29]

The average number of activities reported by respondents in the control group (with four list items) was 1.14, while the average among respondents whose list included the sensitive item (provide favors) was 1.58. Because respondents were alternatively assigned to the treatment and control groups, the difference in means can be attributed to employees who report providing favors. The estimated percentage of public employees helping others with errands or tasks at the city hall in the week prior to the interview is a significant 44 percent (at the 99 percent level).[30] This figure indicates that the provision of favors is a frequent phenomenon in these Argentinean municipalities, providing the first systematic test of the conventional wisdom on this topic.

To be sure, I am not claiming that 44 percent of public employees were involved in clientelistic arrangements in which help is provided with the expectation of receiving political support in return. Personalized interactions between public employees and voters, however, are a necessary – albeit not sufficient – condition for generating clientelistic

---

[27] See Appendix A3 for question wording and Table 5.3 in the Chapter Appendix for the distribution of responses across groups.

[28] Author interview, La Matanza, August 10, 2009.

[29] Author interview, La Plata, August 5, 2009.

[30] The estimated percentages by municipality are: 48 percent in Salta, 37 percent in Tigre, and 47 percent in Santa Fe (all significant at the 99 percent level).

TABLE 5.1 *Granting favors – List experiment estimates*

	Favors
Treatment	1.58 (0.05) N=591
Control	1.14 (0.05) N=590
Estimated proportion	0.44*** (0.07) N=1181

Note: List-experiment control and treatment values are the mean number of items identified by respondents in each group (Rows 1 & 2). Row 3 displays the estimated proportion of respondents providing favors. Two-sample *t*-test with unequal variance. Standard errors in parentheses. ***$p < 0.01$, **$p < 0.05$, *$p < 0.1$.

relations. Clientelistic exchanges are not feasible in an impersonal administration. It is critical to explore – as this chapter does – whether the provision of these favors is politically biased and potentially consequential for political gain.

5.4   FAVORS AND SUPPORT FOR THE MAYOR

According to the theory of self-enforcing patronage developed in this book, a higher proportion of public sector employees who support the incumbent should be involved in the provision of favors. If jobs are in fact disproportionally distributed to supporters in exchange for their political services, one should observe a disproportionate number of supporters involved in service provision. I also expect supporters to be more involved in the provision of political services because they believe that their jobs are tied to the political success of the incumbent politician (an expectation tested in Chapter 6). Providing favors to voters is one of the concrete ways in which public employees can help the incumbent stay in office. In the words of a Tigre employee: "Public employees identify themselves with the job and collaborate with (*acompañan*) the administration. By identifying yourself with the job and doing it right,

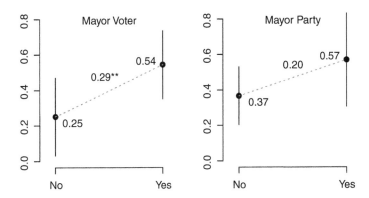

FIGURE 5.1 Granting favors – List experiment estimates, by support for the mayor
Note: Black circles indicate the estimated proportion of respondents granting favors
calculated as the difference between the treatment and the control groups. Vertical lines
represent 95 percent confidence intervals. Two-sample t-test with unequal variance.
$*** p < 0.01$, $** p < 0.05$, $* p < 0.1$.

one knows that it has a positive effect within the organization (*repercute
en forma buena dentro de la organización*)."[31]

To determine whether the provision of favors differs across supporters and
non-supporters, I calculate the difference in the list experiment estimate across
sub-groups (the same strategy used in Chapter 4). As in previous chapters,
support for the mayor (*Mayor Party*) is measured by asking respondents
whether they identify themselves with the mayor's party. As an alternative
measure, I use *Mayor Voter*, public sector employees who reported having
voted for the current mayor in the last election.[32] Figure 5.1 presents the list
experiment estimates for the provision of favors across supporters and non-
supporters and the difference in means estimates. Results are presented
graphically. For instance, the left plot shows the proportion of respondents
who provided favors across employees who voted for the mayor ("Yes") and
those who did not ("No"). Black circles indicate the proportion of respondents
in each subgroup. A steeper slope in the dashed line connecting these black
circles indicates a larger difference across subgroups. The number over the

[31] Author interview (Valeria), Tigre, August 23, 2010.
[32] Because some employees identify with the mayor's party but not with the mayor himself, and vice
versa, two different measures of support (*Mayor Party* and *Mayor Voter*) are used. Electoral
identification is a weaker commitment than partisan identification: it is perfectly possible to vote
for a candidate and not identify with his/her party (especially in Argentina, where voting is
mandatory). In addition, in both Salta and Santa Fe the mayor was elected by a coalition of
parties, so voters who voted for the mayor do not necessarily identify themselves with the
mayor's party. For all these reasons, while positively correlated, both measures are only correlated at 0.4.

dashed line provides the numeric value of the difference. Vertical lines represent 95 percent confidence intervals.

Figure 5.1 shows that there are large differences in means in the expected direction.[33] Supporters are indeed more likely to be involved in helping others. Among the subgroups of employees who reported having voted for the current mayor (*Mayor Voter*), the proportion of those who reported helping someone is 54 percent; among those who reported not voting for the current mayor, the proportion is 25 percent. The 29 percentage-point difference is significant at the 95 percent level. Among the subgroups of employees who self-identified with the mayor's party (*Mayor Party*), the proportion of those who reported providing favors is 57 percent; among those who did not identify with the mayor's party, the proportion diminishes to 37 percent (although this 20 percentage-point difference is not significant). Taken together, these results suggest that the mayor's supporters grant favors more often than non-supporters.

5.5   GETTING ASKED FOR FAVORS

Supporters' greater level of involvement in helping others is consistent both with situations in which supporters are more often asked for favors and with situations in which supporters and non-supporters are equally likely to be asked for favors, but in the latter case, supporters are more willing to grant those favors. This distinction has different implications. The first scenario may indicate a general public that understands the advantages of approaching public employees who have political connections or who are more willing (or able) to help. Voters may anticipate that such connections will facilitate getting things done or that supporters would simply be more willing to help, so they choose supporters over non-supporters. The second scenario may suggest a different attitude among supporters and non-supporters who get asked for favors equally frequently, with the former being more responsive to these requests and thus doing favors more often. This section presents evidence in favor of the first scenario. A higher proportion of supporters – both those who reported voting for the incumbent mayor (*Mayor Voter*) and those who identified themselves with the mayor's party (*Mayor Party*) – provide favors, at least partially because they are *asked* for favors more often.

To test this claim, employees were asked: "How frequently do people come to you to ask you for favors related to your work here at the municipality?"[34] Responses options were: (1) never, (2) a couple of times a year, (3) a couple of times a month, (4) 1–2 times a week, (5) 3 times a week or more, and (6) every day. *Mayor Voter* and *Mayor Party* were used again to measure support. I also include controls for the variables that, according to the theory of self-enforcing patronage, might affect employees' willingness or ability to provide political services: education and type of contract. Employees without job

---

[33] See Table 5.4 in the Chapter Appendix.
[34] See Chapter 3 for a description of the survey.

security – who can get fired – or less education – who have fewer outside employment options – have more to fear from a new administration and thus are likely to be more motivated to provide favors to help the electoral chances of the incumbent. At the same time, more educated employees occupy positions with more power, so they may have more opportunities to grant favors. The education variable (*College*) is coded 1 when respondents have a college degree, and zero otherwise. The contract variable (*Tenure*) is coded 1 when respondents enjoy tenure rights, and zero otherwise.

The models also include controls for age, gender, time of hiring, and municipality to control for regional effects. The age variable (*Age*) takes on values from 1 to 5, corresponding to respondents who are 18–25, 26–35, 36–45, 46–55, and older than 55. The gender variable (*Female*) is coded 1 for female respondents and zero otherwise. The time of hiring (*Current Mayor*) is coded 1 if the respondent was hired by the current administration and zero otherwise. The models also include a variable to control for personal propensity to help others (*Reciprocal*). This variable was measured with the following question: "How much do you agree or disagree with the following statement: 'We always have to return the favors that people do us.'" Response options were as follows: strongly agree, agree more than disagree, disagree more than agree, and strongly disagree.[35] This variable is coded 1 if respondents opted for "strongly agree" or "agree more than disagree," and zero otherwise.[36] An interaction between *Current Mayor* and *Reciprocal* was also included to account for the possibility that employees more thankful for their jobs may be more willing to help others. This may be because they are thankful for their jobs in general or, as the theory of reciprocity suggests, because they are thankful to their bosses for their jobs and providing political services (in this case, favors to voters) is their way to reciprocate.

Table 5.2 presents the results of a series of OLS regressions in which the outcome variable takes on values from 1 to 6, with higher numbers corresponding to higher frequencies of being asked for favors. The regression results reported in Models 1–3 measure support using the previous vote for the incumbent mayor (*Mayor Voter*), whereas results reported in Models 4–6 measure support using self-identification with the party of the incumbent mayor (*Mayor Party*). Models 1 and 4 include controls for age, gender, education, and municipality; Models 2 and 5 add controls for type of contract, time of hiring, and reciprocity; Models 3 and 6 add an interaction between reciprocity and time of hiring.

The main results from the different models are quite similar and consistent with the theoretical expectations. As expected, the coefficients on *Mayor Voter* and *Mayor Party* are both positive and significant across all models,

---

[35] The distribution of responses was: 66 percent strongly agree, 20 percent agree more than disagree, 8 percent disagree more than agree, and 6 percent strongly disagree.

[36] An alternative coding grouping the last three responses together was also tried (because the distribution of responses was skewed) and the results were similar.

TABLE 5.2 *Frequency of requests for favors – OLS regressions*

	Model 1	Model 2	Model 3	Model 4	Model 5	Model 6
Mayor Voter	0.50***	0.54***	0.54***			
	(0.12)	(0.12)	(0.12)			
Mayor Party				0.45***	0.49***	0.49***
				(0.12)	(0.12)	(0.12)
Age	0.04	−0.06	−0.06	0.02	−0.08	−0.08
	(0.05)	(0.06)	(0.06)	(0.05)	(0.06)	(0.06)
Female	0.42***	0.44***	0.45***	0.45***	0.47***	0.48***
	(0.11)	(0.12)	(0.12)	(0.11)	(0.11)	(0.11)
College	−0.45***	−0.44***	−0.45***	−0.50***	−0.49***	−0.50***
	(0.14)	(0.14)	(0.14)	(0.13)	(0.13)	(0.13)
Salta	0.04	0.03	0.03	0.08	0.09	0.08
	(0.14)	(0.16)	(0.16)	(0.13)	(0.15)	(0.15)
Santa Fe	−0.02	−0.04	−0.04	−0.01	−0.02	−0.02
	(0.14)	(0.15)	(0.15)	(0.14)	(0.14)	(0.14)
Tenure		0.22	0.22		0.17	0.16
		(0.17)	(0.17)		(0.16)	(0.16)
Current Mayor		−0.24	−0.06		−0.28*	−0.08
		(0.16)	(0.32)		(0.15)	(0.30)
Reciprocal		−0.10	−0.02		−0.11	−0.01
		(0.16)	(0.21)		(0.15)	(0.20)
Current Mayor *Reciprocal			−0.21			−0.23
			(0.33)			(0.20)
Constant	2.77***	3.15***	3.09***	2.97***	3.41***	3.33***
	(0.20)	(0.27)	(0.29)	(0.18)	(0.26)	(0.28)
Observations	1,106	1,095	1,095	1,177	1,165	1,165
R-squared	0.04	0.05	0.05	0.04	0.05	0.05

Note: An alternative specification using ordered probit yields similar results. The municipality of Tigre (the base category) was excluded. Robust standard errors in parentheses. *** $p < 0.01$, ** $p < 0.05$, * $p < 0.1$.

indicating that being a supporter is correlated with a higher frequency of requests for favors. Both measures of support are associated with about a 0.5-unit significant increase in the frequency of demand for favors (measured on a 1–6 scale).

Two other results are worth mentioning. The first is the significant and negative relationship between the outcome variable and education: those without college degrees are more frequently asked for favors. In spite of that, the list experiment estimate for the provision of favors across those with and without a degree shows no significant difference across groups.[37] Using a more nuanced measure of education shows that the negative relationship between education and the frequency of demands for favors is non-linear. Respondents who have a secondary education are more frequently asked for favors than are those with only a primary education or those with a college degree.[38] Estimates from the list experiment also show that respondents with secondary education provide more favors. Among the subgroup with secondary education, the proportion of those who reported helping someone is 56 percent, compared to 30 percent for those with primary education or less and 42 percent for those with a college degree (all estimates are significant at the 99 percent level).[39] Public sector employees with medium levels of education (a secondary degree) – that is, those probably more likely to be street-level bureaucrats who regularly and directly interact with citizens (Lipsky 1980) – are both more frequently asked for favors and more frequently deliver on those requests.

Another interesting result is the strong and positive relation between being a woman and the frequency of requests for favors. One possible explanation is that, in Argentina, women are more commonly in positions that involve face-to-face interactions with citizens, which allows for more direct requests for favors than jobs that are out of the view of ordinary citizens. Calculating the difference in the size of the list experiment estimate across gender shows that among female employees, the proportion of those who reported providing favors is 55 percent; among male employees, the proportion diminishes to 34 percent (though the 20 percentage-point difference is not significant).[40] Note, however, that female public employees are significantly more educated than their male counterparts, with the majority of women having finished high school.[41] Limiting the comparison to those with secondary education (the group more involved in the provision of favors), the gender gap is even larger. Among female employees with secondary education, 76 percent reported providing favors; among male employees with secondary education, the proportion drops to 36 percent. Taken together, these results suggest an important gender gap both in the requests for favors and in granting favors: women get asked more frequently for favors, and they provide favors more often than their male counterparts.

---

[37] Among the subgroups with a college degree, the proportion of those who reported helping someone is 42 percent; among those without a degree the proportion is 44 percent (the 2 percentage-point difference is not significant). See Table 5.5 in the Chapter Appendix.

[38] See Table 5.6 in the Chapter Appendix.

[39] See Table 5.7 in the Chapter Appendix.

[40] See Table 5.5 in the Chapter Appendix.

[41] Indeed, while 51 percent of women have secondary education and 34 percent hold college degrees, only 14 percent have a primary education or less. Among male employees, 45 percent have a primary education or less, 41 percent have secondary education, and only 14 percent have college degrees.

In sum, supporters are more frequently asked for favors than non-supporters. It is possible, as Calvo and Ujhelyi (2012) argue, that employees who are more willing to provide political services self-select into positions that allow them to grant more favors. Calvo and Ujhelyi (2012) need this mechanism of self-selection because they argue that, at the time of hiring, potential employees' political preferences is private information not available to the politician. By contrast, in the argument developed in this book, personal connections and referrals are used for political screening, and politicians use perceived political preferences at the time of hiring to screen supporters from non-supporters. Politicians may also use this information to assign patronage employees to positions that afford more opportunities to grant favors. The story of Gerónimo, the Peronist councilman from Malvinas Argentina mentioned above, illustrates how supporters might end up in these positions. Gerónimo has been a political activist since the age of 14 and was trained as a turner,[42] but he left that job to work in a public hospital. He explains: "That was not because I was making more money in the public administration than I had been making as a turner, but ... because I was working at a hospital I was able to provide solutions to people's issues or problems (*darle solución a algunos temitas o problemas que tenía la gente*), with a medical appointment, with some medicine, with ... And, well, I felt that was my place, and not the turner job."[43]

However, a situation in which citizens choose to ask favors from supporters, regardless of their positions in the administration, is also consistent with the data. Citizens may just prefer public sector employees with "incumbent partisan connectivity" (Auerbach and Thachil 2018). But how do citizens know how to distinguish supporters from non-supporters? And, if they prefer supporters, is there any evidence that supporters respond differently to these types of petitions? The next two sections provide answers to these questions.

5.6   THE PERSONAL CONNECTION

How can citizens screen supporters from non-supporters when asking for favors? Although the most influential patronage employees, political brokers, are well known to everyone, differentiating supporters from non-supporters may be harder with respect to less influential patronage employees. In this section, I provide evidence that people asking for favors are able to target supporters because they actually know them. Requests for favors go to friends and acquaintances, not strangers.

To test this claim, the following question was used: "How likely is it that the person who is asking you for a favor is: a) a friend or acquaintance, b) a relative, c) a stranger sent by someone you know, or d) a complete stranger." The

---

[42] A turner is a person who manufactures and assembles metal components for tools and machinery.
[43] Author interview, Malvinas Argentinas, August 20, 2009.

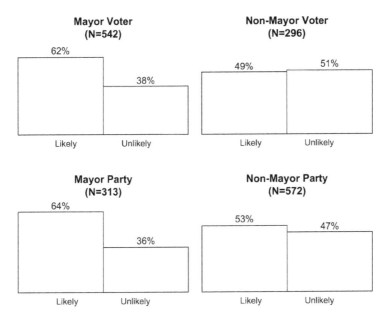

FIGURE 5.2 Likelihood that the person asking for a favor is a friend or acquaintance, by support for the mayor

response options were: very likely, likely, not very likely, and unlikely. To facilitate the analysis, the former two options were coded as "likely" and the latter two as "unlikely." Figure 5.2 displays the responses for option "a" (friend or acquaintance), across supporters (left panels) and non-supporters (right panels).

Figure 5.2 shows that supporters responded differently than non-supporters. About 60 percent of those who reported voting for the mayor in the previous election (top-left panel) replied that it was likely or very likely that the person who asked for a favor was a friend or acquaintance, while a little less than 40 percent responded that such a request was not very likely or unlikely. In contrast, among non-mayor voters, the responses were equally distributed among the two categories (49 and 51 percent, respectively). The 13 percentage-point difference between mayor voters (62 percent) and non-mayor voters (49 percent) who reported that they were likely to be asked for favors by friends and acquaintances is significant at the 99 percent level (two-sample t-test with unequal variance). Similarly, among those who self-identified with the mayor's party, 64 percent reported that it was likely or very likely that a person who asked for a favor was a friend or an acquaintance, while only 36 percent responded that such a request was not very likely or unlikely. In contrast, among those who did not identify with the mayor's party, while we still find slightly more responses in the likely or very likely category (53 percent), the difference with the other category (47 percent) is only six percentage points. The 11 percentage-point difference between party supporters (64 percent) and non-supporters (53 percent) who reported that it was likely that those asking for favors were friends and acquaintances is significant at the 99 percent level (two-sample *t*-test with unequal variance).

In sum, supporters get asked for favors disproportionately by friends and acquaintances, suggesting that most people understand the importance of political connections. When possible (i.e., when someone knows a supporter), supporters are chosen over non-supporters. The testimony of Ana, an administrative employee from Salta, illustrates the importance of knowing the right person. Besides working for the city, she was involved in voluntary work as the head of a neighborhood center. These types of centers organize social and cultural events, and, in poor neighborhoods like hers, they are also often used as soup kitchens and as distribution points for food assistance benefits. When asked about how much interest she had in politics, she replied emphatically: "Very interested! All the contacts [you need] to bring things to your neighborhood are political contacts."[44]

Moreover, the fact that citizens prefer supporters they know when in need of help reinforces the idea that such requests are considered favors and not regular administrative tasks that any employee would do. As discussed in previous sections, a regular administrative task can be framed and perceived as a favor. To the extent that employees can appear to be helping in a personal way, they can claim credit for it, and the evidence presented here strongly suggests that citizens consider personal connections to be important for getting things done. If citizens did not see these connections as relevant, they would not choose supporters over non-supporters, and employees they knew over strangers. When knowing a public employee who can provide this type of personalized help becomes important to citizens, the public administration can be easily used for political gain.

Note that those asking for favors could be the voters themselves or political brokers acting on their behalf. Many of the "friends and acquaintances" who ask for favors may actually be brokers asking for something for one of their clients. Brokers, of course, know perfectly well which employees can help and where they can be found. Recall the conversation quoted earlier in this chapter about a broker calling the director of the cemetery, *his friend*, to help organize a wake. Brokers themselves are also well known. A conversation with Sergio, a local broker from La Matanza, illustrates this point. When I told him, "For

---

[44] Author interview, Salta, June 15, 2011. In the terminology of Holland and Palmer-Rubin (2015), she is an "organizational broker," a broker embedded in an interest organization who attempts to extract benefits for the members of her association. At the time of the interview, her center managed a program that distributed flour to the poor (Plan Pan Casero), and she was trying to get another program that provides breakfast and afternoon snacks to poor children (Copa de Leche).

instance, if I had a problem, I wouldn't think about calling you," Sergio replied, "Because you don't know me!" He then described the kind of people who usually come to him for help: "All kinds of people ... It can be people who know you because you have a friendship relationship, a neighborhood relationship, people who know you are in politics ... I am 55 years old, and I've been politically active (*milito*) since age 16 ... People know me one way or the other (*Alguno que otro me conoce*)."[45]

Whether the favor comes directly from a public employee or from a broker – who may or may not be a public employee herself – knowing the right person seems to be essential to getting things done. Voters may know a broker who might act on their behalf or they may know a less influential employee. Brokers, in turn, are known by everyone, and they know better than anyone who can be asked to do what. This allows them to provide a very diverse portfolio of favors – more than regular employees, who might only be able to help people within their own area of work. Brokers are, in Auyero's words, at the center of the "problem solving network."

5.7 ARE INCUMBENTS' SUPPORTERS MORE HELPFUL?

Supporters more frequently grant favors, and they are also more frequently asked for favors, especially by friends and acquaintances. The reason supporters are more involved in providing political services – favors, in this case – is that patronage jobs are disproportionally distributed to supporters who believe that their fates are tied to the political fate of the mayor (see Chapter 2). Supporters of the incumbent believe that their patronage jobs and working conditions will be maintained by the incumbent but not by a competing politician. From the patronage employees' point of view, then, helping those who ask for favors is in their best interest. Voters who believe that personal connections matter may be more likely to vote for the incumbent, and employees help voters in order to help the incumbent politician remain in power. From the voters' point of view, to the extent that the incumbent's supporters are more eager (or able) to help than others, it is reasonable to ask them (rather than non-supporters) for help.

To study differences in responsiveness among employees, we used the following question: "Now I am going to ask about a hypothetical situation. Imagine that someone comes to you and asks you for a favor, but the thing she is asking for is actually handled by another office or person; you would: A) tell her that you are not the person in charge of that, B) tell her which office she should go to, or C) tell her which office she should go to and give her the name of someone you know at that office to make sure that the problem gets solved." About 3 percent responded "A," about 40 percent responded "B," and about 57 percent responded "C." To test whether these replies vary by support for the mayor, Figure 5.3 presents the set of responses split across those who reported

---

[45] Author interview, La Matanza, August 10, 2009.

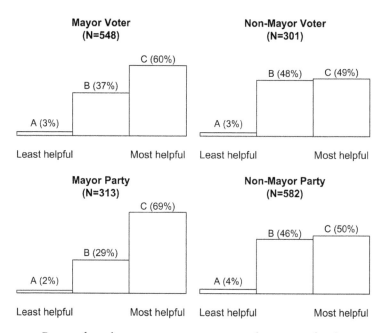

FIGURE 5.3 Range of employees responses to requests, by support for the mayor
Note: Numbers (and percentages) exclude respondents who answer "never" to the question about frequency of favor requests. "A," "B," and "C" correspond to possible employee responses to requests for favors, as described in the text.

voting for the incumbent mayor in the previous election and those who did not (top panels) and those who self-identified with the mayor's party and those who did not (bottom panels).

Figure 5.3 shows that supporters responded differently than non-supporters to the hypothetical question. The least helpful of the three options (option "A"), was chosen by very few respondents across all groups (2–4 percent), so I focus on discussing the other two, more popular, response options. About 60 percent of those who reported voting for the incumbent mayor (top-left panel) choose option "C," the most helpful one, while about 37 percent chose option "B," a less helpful option. Among non-mayor voters (top-right panel), responses are equally distributed; 49 percent chose "C" while 48 percent chose "B." The 11 percentage-point difference between mayor voters (60 percent) and non-mayor voters (49 percent) who opted for the most helpful option ("C") is significant at the 99 percent level (two-sample *t*-test with unequal variance). A similar pattern appears when comparing supporters of the mayor's party to non-supporters. About 69 percent of those who self-identified with the mayor's party (bottom-left panel) chose the most helpful option, "C," while 29 percent chose the less helpful one, "B." In contrast, about 50 percent of non-supporters of the mayor's party chose the most helpful option, while 46 percent chose the less helpful option. The almost 20 percentage-point difference between mayor party supporters and non-supporters who responded "C," the most helpful option, is significant at the 99 percent level (two-sample *t*-test with unequal variance).

Note that these different responses across supporters and non-supporters are not based on years in the administration and potentially knowing more people who could help because of that. Comparing the responses of those who got their jobs during the incumbent mayor's administration with those who got their jobs earlier yields no significant difference.[46] New jobs are disproportionally distributed to supporters, so they have, on average, fewer years on the job than non-supporters. Supporters, however, are more willing (or able) to help than non-supporters.

These results show that supporters are more likely to try to help voters, or brokers acting on behalf of voters, suggesting that it makes perfect sense for citizens to seek supporters when in need of a favor. Whether this is because supporters are more eager to provide political services to help their patron stay in power, or because supporters are better equipped to provide favors to citizens – they may know the right person to ask – citizens preferences for seeking help from supporters seem to be based on real differences in public employees responsiveness.

5.8   SUMMARY

In line with the theory of self-enforcing patronage and the findings on other political services, this chapter shows that supporters of the incumbent are disproportionally more involved in granting favors than non-supporters. Supporters are more involved in all the four types of political services studied in this book – monitoring elections, helping with electoral campaigns, attending rallies, and providing favors – because patronage jobs are disproportionally distributed to supporters who believe that their fates are tied to the electoral fate of the mayor.[47] Supporters believe that their patronage jobs and working conditions will be maintained by the incumbent politician but not by a competing politician. As a result, supporters have large incentives to provide political services to help the incumbent stay in power.

This chapter focuses on a particular type of political service, the provision of favors, that is not necessarily attached to the electoral cycle. As an employee from Tigre bluntly explained it, "people get needy" (*la gente se pone más densa*) around elections, but favors are requested and granted on an ongoing basis.[48] The fact that patronage employees provide favors is important not only because it is an activity that is done continually but, more significantly, because it is a cheap and potentially effective way for the incumbent to gain and maintain electoral support. As Mayhew (1974, 53) writes regarding members of congress: "The political logic

---

[46] See Table 5.8 in the Chapter Appendix.
[47] The next chapter provides empirical evidence for this statement.
[48] Author interview (Laura), Tigre, January 6, 2011.

of this, from the congressman's point of view, is that an actor who believes that a member can make pleasing things happen will no doubt wish to keep him in office so that he can make pleasing things happen in the future."

Far from the Weberian ideal of an impartial bureaucracy, in Argentina's public administration, the use or perceived use of discretion in the everyday tasks of public sector employees gives voters the impression that personal relations are important for getting things done. Once established, these personal connections can work as strong incentives favoring the maintenance of the status quo. Citizens who receive help from state officials or intermediaries understand that their personal connection has been critical. If a citizen has established a personal connection with someone in the public administration, or with easy access to such a person, one who provides help when needed, why would she vote for another party? Citizens seem to have good reasons to want to maintain things as they are, keeping their connection with the state intact by keeping the incumbent in office.

5.9   CHAPTER APPENDIX: ADDITIONAL TABLES

TABLE 5.3 *Distribution of responses from the list experiment on granting favors*

	Control		Treatment	
0	214	36%	136	23%
1	175	30%	189	32%
2	125	21%	137	23%
3	57	10%	71	12%
4	19	3%	35	6%
5			23	4%
Estimate		0.44***		
N	590		591	

Note: To minimize ceiling effects, the list of activities included one unusual activity ("Have a serious fight with someone due to political differences"). The strategy proved successful since only around three percent of respondents in the control group reported all four of the control items. The inclusion of a high-prevalence activity ("Talk about politics with someone") to minimize the risk of floor effects was less successful. The presence of either ceiling or floor effects, however, could lead to the underestimation of the sensitive activity (Blair and Imai 2012), so the estimates presented here are conservative. Using the method developed by Blair and Imai to test the validity of the experiments, I failed to reject the null hypothesis for design effects in the list experiment. See Appendix A3 for the complete wording of the experiment. *** $p < 0.01$, ** $p < 0.05$, * $p < 0.1$.

TABLE 5.4 *Granting favors – List experiment estimates, by support for the mayor*

Characteristic	No	Yes	Difference
Mayor Voter	0.25**	0.54***	0.29**
	(0.11)	(0.10)	(0.15)
	N=430	N=680	N=1,110
Mayor Party	0.37***	0.57***	0.20
	(0.08)	(0.13)	(0.15)
	N=797	N=384	N=1,181

Note: Estimated proportion of respondents granting favors calculated as the difference between the treatment and the control groups (Columns 1 and 2). Column 3 presents the differences in proportions. Two-sample *t*-test with unequal variance. Standard errors in parentheses; *** $p < 0.01$, ** $p < 0.05$, * $p < 0.1$.

TABLE 5.5 *Granting favors – List experiment estimates, by education and gender*

Characteristic	No	Yes	Difference
College Degree	0.44***	0.42***	0.02
	(0.08)	(0.15)	(0.17)
	N=911	N=267	N=1,178
Female	0.34***	0.55***	0.20
	(0.09)	(0.11)	(0.14)
	N=655	N=526	N=1,181

Note: Estimated proportion of respondents granting favors calculated as the difference between the treatment and the control groups (Columns 1 and 2). Column 3 presents the differences in proportions. Two-sample *t*-test with unequal variance. Standard errors in parentheses; *** $p < 0.01$, ** $p < 0.05$, * $p < 0.1$.

TABLE 5.6 *Frequency of requests for favors (with alternative measure for education) – OLS regressions*

	Model 1	Model 2	Model 3	Model 4	Model 5	Model 6
Mayor Voter	0.50***	0.54***	0.54***			
	(0.12)	(0.12)	(0.12)			
Mayor Party				0.44***	0.48***	0.48***
				(0.12)	(0.12)	(0.12)
Age	0.05	−0.05	−0.05	0.03	−0.07	−0.07
	(0.05)	(0.06)	(0.06)	(0.05)	(0.06)	(0.06)
Female	0.38***	0.41***	0.41***	0.42***	0.45***	0.46***
	(0.12)	(0.12)	(0.12)	(0.11)	(0.11)	(0.11)
Primary Ed.	0.32*	0.32*	0.33*	0.41**	0.42***	0.43***
	(0.17)	(0.17)	(0.17)	(0.16)	(0.16)	(0.16)
Secondary Ed.	0.51***	0.49***	0.50***	0.54***	0.52***	0.53***
	(0.15)	(0.15)	(0.15)	(0.14)	(0.14)	(0.14)
Salta	0.01	0.00	−0.00	0.06	0.07	0.07
	(0.14)	(0.16)	(0.16)	(0.14)	(0.15)	(0.15)
Santa Fe	−0.02	−0.04	−0.05	−0.01	−0.03	−0.03
	(0.14)	(0.15)	(0.15)	(0.14)	(0.14)	(0.14)
Tenure		0.23	0.23		0.17	0.17
		(0.17)	(0.17)		(0.16)	(0.16)
Current Mayor		−0.23	−0.04		−0.28*	−0.07
		(0.16)	(0.32)		(0.15)	(0.30)
Reciprocal		−0.10	−0.01		−0.11	−0.01
		(0.16)	(0.21)		(0.15)	(0.20)
Current Mayor *Reciprocal			−0.21			−0.24
			(0.33)			(0.31)
Constant	2.31***	2.70***	2.62***	2.47***	2.90***	2.81***
	(0.21)	(0.27)	(0.30)	(0.19)	(0.26)	(0.29)
Observations	1,106	1,095	1,095	1,177	1,165	1,165
R-squared	0.04	0.05	0.05	0.04	0.05	0.05

Note: Primary education corresponds to respondents with at least some primary education or who have completed it; secondary education corresponds to respondents who have completed secondary education; and college (the base category) corresponds to respondents who have completed university or tertiary education. The municipality of Tigre (the base category) was excluded. An alternative specification using ordered probit yields similar results. Robust standard errors in parentheses; *** $p < 0.01$, ** $p < 0.05$, * $p < 0.1$.

TABLE 5.7 *Granting favors – List experiment estimates, by levels of education*

	Primary Education	Secondary Education	College
Treatment	1.23	1.77	1.68
	(0.09)	(0.09)	(0.11)
	N=191	N=258	N=141
Control	0.93	1.21	1.26
	(0.08)	(0.07)	(0.10)
	N=178	N=284	N=126
Estimated proportion	0.30***	0.56***	0.42***
	(0.12)	(0.11)	(0.15)
	N=369	N=542	N=267

Note: List-experiment control and treatment values are the mean number of items identified by respondents (Rows 1 & 2). Row 3 displays the estimated proportion of respondents reporting granting favors. Two-sample t-test with unequal variance. Standard errors in parentheses; *** $p < 0.01$, ** $p < 0.05$, * $p < 0.1$.

TABLE 5.8 *Helpful responses, by time of hiring*

Responses	Hired during previous administrations	Hired during current administration	Total N
Not the person in charge	3% (N=15)	3% (N=13)	28
Provides information about which office to visit	41% (N=202)	40% (N=157)	359
			505
Provides information about which office to visit and the name of someone who you know at that office to make sure that the problem gets solved	56% (N=280)	57% (N=225)	
	497 (100%)	395 (100%)	892

Note: Two-sample t-tests with unequal variance show that the responses of employees hired by the current administration and those of the ones hired by previous administrations are statistically equivalent.

6

Self-Enforcing Patronage Contracts

Why do public sector employees provide political services? Since the exchange of political support for jobs is sequenced and the law cannot be used to enforce the exchange, patronage contracts leave ample opportunity for deception and betrayal (see Chapter 2). When the political support is expected *after* the benefit has been received, individuals who receive public sector jobs can always opt to renege on their side of the agreement by refusing to provide the promised support (e.g., Calvo and Ujhelyi 2012; James 2006; Robinson and Verdier 2013).[1] Most of the literature argues that clients comply with their side of the agreement – by providing electoral support or broader political support – because of either the threat of punishment or norms of reciprocity. The theory of self-enforcing patronage set forth in this book posits that public employees under patronage contracts provide political services because their incentives are aligned with those of the politician who hired them. Using two survey experiments embedded in the survey of public employees described in Chapter 3, as well as interviews with political brokers, politicians, and public sector employees, this chapter tests this claim – the main empirical implication of the theory.

One reason for the incentive alignment between patronage employees and politicians is that politicians are generally able to appoint perceived supporters – those more closely connected to the partisan network – who are more likely to provide political services in the first place (Chapter 3). Evidence from list experiments show that, as hypothesized, supporters are far more likely to provide political services (Chapters 4 and 5). Such supporters, however, are more involved in providing these services not only because patronage jobs are disproportionally distributed to them for that purpose, but also because they

---

[1] Although not the focus of this book, when political support is provided before the benefit is received, there is also the possibility of betrayal on the part of politicians, who can simply refuse to comply with their side of the agreement once in office. This risk, however, is lower when the benefit exchanged is a public sector job (see Chapter 2).

have more to lose from a change in the administration. Patronage employees believe that their jobs and working conditions are safe if the incumbent stays in power but could be in jeopardy if the opposition wins. Following the same logic that an incumbent uses to choose supporters for patronage jobs – they can credibly commit to provide political services – a new politician will want their own supporters in patronage positions. As a consequence, current patronage employees believe that they could be fired, demoted, or sidelined. Their desire to prevent this makes their original commitment to provide political services credible.

This chapter shows that patronage employees believe their jobs are tied to the electoral fate of the incumbent. To identify the potential effects of a change in the partisan alignment of the administration, I designed two survey experiments. Half of the respondents were asked to estimate the likelihood of losing their jobs and of suffering changes in working conditions if the next election were to be won by the opposition. The other half was asked the same questions without any information about the hypothetical winner of the election. I test the theory of self-enforcing patronage by estimating heterogeneous treatment effects across supporters and non-supporters. Based on the theory of patronage developed in this book, I expect supporters to be more likely to fear losing their jobs and experiencing negative changes in their working conditions if the opposition were elected, and the results of the survey experiments are consistent with this expectation. In contrast, the hypothetical questions about the opposition winning the election have no effect on the expectations of non-supporters. I corroborate these results using regression analysis. In line with the list experiment results (Chapters 4 and 5), I also use a direct question to show that supporters are disproportionally more likely to be partisan election monitors. In turn, the survey experiment results show that employees who monitor elections are more afraid of a change in the administration than those who do not monitor elections.

The remainder of this chapter is organized as follows. First, I describe the methodological approach and the survey experiments. I then present the results of the survey experiments and corroborate these results using regression analysis. Next, I use a direct question about monitoring elections to put the two pieces of the argument together, showing that public employees more involved in the provision of political services are those more afraid of a change in administration. Afterward, I discuss the main alternative explanations to the theory – threat of punishment and feelings of reciprocity. The last section presents the main results broken out by municipality.

6.1   EMPIRICAL STRATEGY: SURVEY EXPERIMENTS

Scholars studying public opinion in the United States have been using survey experiments for a while now.[2] The use of survey experiments in other

---

[2] See Gaines, Kuklinski, and Quirk (2007) for an overview of survey experiment research.

political science subfields is relatively more recent, but with the growing use of all types of experiments in the discipline, they have become an increasingly popular research tool (Druckman et al. 2006). This method provides a useful tool for testing the empirical implications of the theory of self-enforcing patronage. Like other experiments, survey experiments work by making treatment assignment exogenous to observed outcomes. This makes the technique extremely useful for identifying and isolating causal effects. Random assignment to either the treatment or the control group ensures that both groups of respondents are, on average, indistinguishable on both observable and unobservable characteristics. Therefore, any difference in average responses across groups can be attributed to the treatment. In this case, the technique enables identification of the causal effect of receiving information about the potential winner of the election on public employees' perceptions of job stability and change.

The survey experiments were embedded in the face-to-face survey of local public sector employees described in Chapter 3. Each of the survey experiments included two conditions, so two versions of the questionnaire were used in sequential order, assigning respondents alternately to either the treatment or the control group for both survey experiments.[3] Standard balance checks find that the groups are fairly equivalent on observable characteristics.[4] To identify the potential effects of a change in the administration on different types of public employees, I use two survey experiments. A randomly selected subset of respondents was asked to estimate the likelihood of losing their jobs and of suffering changes in working conditions if the opposition won the next election. The control group was asked the same questions but without providing any information about the hypothetical electoral outcome.[5]

---

[3] Since the start of the distribution was random, the generated groups are still, on average, indistinguishable on observable and unobservable characteristics. Ideally, in order to minimize potential spillover effects, respondents should have been randomly and independently assigned into each experimental condition for each survey experiment (Gaines, Kuklinski, and Quirk 2007), but this was logistically too complicated to implement with a pencil-and-paper questionnaire.

[4] Table A5 in Appendix A2 reports the average age, gender, and education of respondents for each condition. The balanced distribution of the variables across the two conditions suggests that the groups are fairly equivalent on observable characteristics. None of the differences between the control and treatment groups are statistically significant (at the 95 percent confidence level). Table A6 in Appendix A2 reports the number of surveys administrated by each enumerator by condition.

[5] Note that both experiments can only manipulate perceptions if respondents thought that there was some possibility of re-election. This seems likely considering that the reelection rates in the provinces studied here range from 40 to 47 percent (Micozzi 2009). Nevertheless, even if most employees thought that the mayor's reelection or the opposition winning were unlikely events, I would be underestimating the treatment effects.

In addition to the survey experiments, the survey instrument included other questions used in the following analysis. To identify support for the mayor or the party of the mayor, respondents were asked two different questions, as described in previous chapters.[6] The first asked them for whom they had voted in the last mayoral election. Responses were coded one if respondents said they had voted for the current mayor (*Mayor Voter*), and zero otherwise. Second, respondents were asked to report whether they identify themselves with a political party, and those who replied affirmatively were asked with which party they identified. This variable (*Mayor Party*) takes on the value of one if respondents identified themselves with the party of the mayor, and zero otherwise.[7] Respondents were also asked about their type of contract (*Tenure*); responses were coded one if employees reported having job security, and zero otherwise. Education (*College*) takes the value of one if employees reported having a college degree, and zero otherwise.[8]

6.2   SELF-ENFORCING PATRONAGE: SURVEY EXPERIMENT EVIDENCE

As mentioned earlier, one of the main advantages of experiments is that when properly implemented, control and treatment groups are, on average, equivalent on both observable and unobservable characteristics. Differences in average responses across groups can then be attributed to the additional information received by the treatment group. This allows me to use difference-in-means (*t*-tests) to analyze the results.[9] I also corroborate the main results with regression analyses. After focusing on the main treatment effects, I test the core of the argument by examining how support for the incumbent conditions the size of the treatment effects.

6.2.1   Perceptions of Job Stability

To measure public employees' perceptions of job stability, all respondents were asked to estimate the likelihood of keeping their jobs after the next election as follows: "On a scale from 0 to 10, where 0 means 'Not at all likely,' and 10 means 'Very likely,' how likely is it that you will continue working for the

---

[6] Recall that the political questions were asked in a separate questionnaire to increase response rates and to improve the accuracy of the responses. See Chapter 3 for a detailed description of the technique used.

[7] Missing values were coded as zero, but an alternative codification of this variable excluding missing values was also tried in all the analyses presented in this chapter; results were substantively identical.

[8] Summary statistics for all variables are provided in Table A7 in Appendix A3.

[9] All the difference-in-means tests reported here were calculated using Welch's approximation to account for potential unequal variances between the groups. The standard errors obtained with the Welch approximation differ only marginally from the ones obtained with a standard student *t*-test (which assumes equal variance across groups).

municipality next year, after the 2011 mayoral elections?" To facilitate the response, respondents were handed a card with the following picture:

Not at all likely					Likely					Very likely	DK
0	1	2	3	4	5	6	7	8	9	10	99

Half of the respondents, those selected into the treatment group, were shown the same card and asked the same question along with the following added statement: "if the incumbent mayor is not re-elected and the opposition wins?"[10] Public employees who were told this hypothetical about the incumbent losing and the opposition winning the next election responded differently from those who were not prompted to consider the hypothetical electoral outcome. Whereas the average response among the control group is 8.15, the figure drops to 7.75 among those who received the treatment. The average treatment effect is a significant 0.41 difference (at the 95 percent level).[11] In general, if the election were to be won by the opposition, public employees have more fear of losing their jobs afterward.[12]

Sabrina, a tenured employee from Santa Fe hired in 1985, described the fears associated with a change in administration: "In the municipal administration, I think that there is always something like a 'Sword of Damocles': Let's hope that they [the new administration] don't find out to whom I belong, that they don't have any political prejudice against me."[13] Indeed, the main empirical implication of the theory of self-enforcing patronage is that supporters of the

[10] I used a slightly different question in Salta because of the timing of the upcoming mayoral election. For political reasons beyond my control, the survey in Salta had to be postponed until after the local elections were held. Consequently, the surveys in Santa Fe and Tigre were conducted about a year before the next mayoral elections, whereas the survey in Salta was conducted right after local elections and almost four years before the next ones. The main issue with this was that many employees in Salta who did not have tenure at the time of the survey were expecting to get tenure in the next four years, and this expectation would affect their responses to the question about job stability. To get around this problem, another question was asked in Salta right after the one described above: "Now imagine that the next mayoral elections, instead of being in 2015, are next year. On this same scale (0 to 10), how likely is it that you keep on working for the municipality next year, after these hypothetical elections (*if the incumbent mayor is not re-elected and the opposition wins*)?" Both questions are highly correlated (0.8), but less so when restricting the sample to untenured employees (0.67) – those who may expect to receive job security. The results in this chapter are consistent across both measures. I decided to use the second question about "next year's" hypothetical election to keep it consistent with the questions in Tigre and Santa Fe.

[11] See Table 6.3 in the Chapter Appendix for more details on the *t*-test results.

[12] It is possible that the question is also capturing cases of employees who would resign. Yet, the comparison of the conditional average treatment effect for employees with and without job security (Figure 6.1) suggests that the question is most likely capturing the fear of being fired than resigning.

[13] Author interview, Santa Fe, August 16, 2011.

incumbent have more to fear from a change in the administration than non-supporters. I expect, then, that supporters would predict a higher likelihood of losing their jobs if the incumbent were to lose the upcoming election.

Employees without job security also have more to fear from a new administration. Tenured employees – who cannot be legally fired – should not fear losing their jobs regardless of the electoral outcome.[14] Valeria, a high-ranking employee from the Tigre personnel office, explained this clearly. When asked about the last change of administration, she explained: "After 20 years of the same administration [Tigre was governed by the same mayor between 1987 and 2006], things are complicated, people are afraid . . . the tenured employees are not, but the ones on temporary contracts are afraid." Interestingly – and in line with the expectations of the theory developed in this book – she then explained that in the end not that many people were fired, only those who were "very politically identified" with the previous administration.[15]

To examine supporters' reactions to the hypothetical electoral outcome, I estimate conditional average treatment effects (CATE). I do this by simply estimating causal effects separately for different subgroups of the population.[16] To identify support for the mayor, I used the same questions as outlined in previous chapters: respondents' self-identification with the mayor's party (*Mayor Party*) and vote for the mayor in the previous election (*Mayor Voter*). Results are presented graphically. For instance, the right plot in Figure 6.1 shows the effect of hearing the information about the incumbent mayor losing the election for those who identify themselves with the party of the mayor ("Yes") and those who do not ("No"). Because tenured employees cannot be fired, the figure presents the effects for the whole sample (black dots) and the effects for untenured employees (white dots) for each subgroup. The dashed line represents the quantity of greatest interest since a steeper slope indicates that hearing about the incumbent losing the election affects the subgroups differently. The number over the dashed line is the numeric value of the difference between the two. Vertical lines represent 95 percent confidence intervals.

Supporters given the hypothetical about an opposition candidate winning the election respond differently to the question about the likelihood of keeping their jobs than supporters not given the scenario. In contrast, hearing the hypothetical about the opposition winning has no effect (an effect not statistically distinguishable from zero) on the expectations of non-supporters about keeping their jobs in the municipal administration. The difference in effects between untenured employees (white dots) who reported having voted

---

[14] In the next section, I provide evidence that supporters with job security still fear things changing for the worse if the opposition gets into power.

[15] Author interview, Tigre, August 23, 2010.

[16] Table 6.4 in the Chapter Appendix shows the exact numeric effects within each subgroup. Section 6.3 presents the regression analysis of the survey experiments.

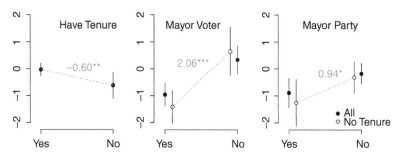

FIGURE 6.1 Perception of job stability, heterogeneous treatment effects
Note: Average treatment effects calculated as the difference between the treatment and the control group (*t*-test with unequal variance). Black circles indicate the treatment effect within each subgroup; white circles restrict the sample to untenured employees. Vertical lines represent 95 percent confidence intervals. $^{***} p < 0.01$, $^{**} p < 0.05$, $^{*} p < 0.1$.

for the incumbent and those who did not (middle plot) is a significant 2.06 (at the 99 percent level). Recall that the scale is 0 to 10, meaning that untenured employees who had voted for the current mayor feel, on average, 21 percent less confident about keeping their jobs if the opposition wins. Results are similar when using the alternative measure of support. The difference between untenured employees (white dots) who identified themselves with the party of the mayor and those who did not (right plot) is a significant 0.94 (at the 90 percent level), showing that untenured supporters of the mayor's party feel on average around 10 percent less secure about keeping their jobs if the opposition wins. As expected, the treatment effect is different for tenured and untenured employees (left plot) – a significant 0.60 difference (at the 95 percent level). Including only employees with no job security (white circles in the middle and right plots) makes all the effects stronger in the predicted direction.

6.2.2   Perceptions of Potential Job Changes

The fear of losing one's job if the opposition takes office is not the only mechanism that sustains patronage contracts; there are other incentives to stick to those contracts, especially for employees with job security. If an opposition politician wins the election, "disloyal" employees – the ones perceived as supporters of the old administration – may be transferred, sidelined, demoted, or assigned to different activities. Sabrina, the tenured employee from Santa Fe mentioned above, explained it clearly: "The fear [for a tenured employee] . . . is about changing jobs, changing the place of work; it is about being sent somewhere else, somewhere where one does not know how to do the job, or where one doesn't have much to do, or too far away from one's home, or with a different schedule, or without the extra monetary benefits that the current job allows one to earn . . . A lot of things can be changed." And, in fact, she continues, there were a few cases like this when the administration changed from the Peronists to the Radicals in 2007: "Old employees have been sidelined a little, their participation has been restricted. I know of people who had to ask to be transferred to another area because there was no room for them anymore where they used to work." She finished her description by adding: "I am not saying this happens, all I am saying is that one is afraid of it, it is *one's salary, one's livelihood* ... "[17]

The story of Jorge, another employee from Santa Fe, shows how the fears associated with a change in administration sometimes becomes real. I spoke with Jorge while I was fielding the survey pilot. He was sitting in an empty office by himself in the municipal Art Center with nothing but a desk and a couple of chairs; there was no computer, just some papers on the desk. When I inquired about his job, he asked whether the question was about his formal job or his "real" job, and I replied that I wanted to hear about both. Jorge said that, formally, he was the director of photography at the Art Center, but he was not doing that anymore because when the new administration arrived in 2007, it had appointed someone else to that position. Jorge had been hired in 1983, and at the time of the interview, he held the highest rank in the local civil service system. He had job security, so the administration could not fire him, and he was still getting his full salary as director of photography. When asked about what he was actually doing every day at the office, he replied "nothing." The new person was doing his old job and there was nothing for him to do. At the time of the interview, he was fifty years old.[18]

Laura, a tenured employee from Tigre hired in 1988, who sympathizes with the party that governed the municipality between 1987 and 2007, described the general atmosphere since the change in the administration in 2007. According to her, turnover was not widespread, but all the bosses changed, and "it was difficult at the beginning, sometimes politics gets mixed up with work." She said the new bosses were suspicious of the old employees (*había recelo*): they perceived them "almost as criminals."[19]

To establish whether public employees are in fact afraid of these types of negative changes should an opposition mayor be elected, I again use the hypothetical about the electoral outcome. All respondents were first asked how satisfied they were with their jobs, simply to frame the next question.[20] Then they were asked to estimate the likelihood of that level of satisfaction

---

[17] Author interview, Santa Fe, August 16, 2011. Emphasis added.
[18] Author interview, Santa Fe, July 22, 2010.
[19] Author interview, Tigre, January 6, 2011.
[20] The majority reported being satisfied (59 percent) and very satisfied (31 percent), while 8 percent reported being not very satisfied, and only eight respondents (0.7 percent) reported being not at all satisfied with their jobs. To understand the generally high level of satisfaction among public sector employees in Argentina, which is similar across municipalities, two characteristics of public employment are important. First, there is a wage premium for less-educated employees (Calvo and Murillo 2004, 2019). Second, many employees enjoy job security, a situation without equivalent in the private sector.

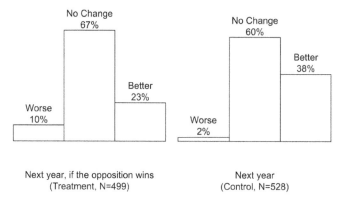

FIGURE 6.2 Perception of potential change, across treatment and control groups

changing after the next election: "On a scale from 0 to 10, where 0 means 'Not at all likely,' and 10 means 'Very likely,' how likely do you think it is that your level of satisfaction with your job will change next year, after the 2011 mayoral elections?" Respondents selected into the treatment group received the additional prompt about the outcome of the election: "if the incumbent mayor is not re-elected and the opposition wins?"[21] Immediately after this question, all respondents were asked: "Do you think that your situation will be better, the same, or worse?" Responses were coded 1 for better, 0 for no change expected, and −1 for worse.[22] Figure 6.2 shows the distribution of responses across treatment and control groups for this last question.

In line with the results from the first survey experiment, respondents who were given the hypothetical about the incumbent losing the election responded differently from those who did not receive that information. Whereas the average response among the control group was 0.36, the average for those who received the treatment was 0.13 – a significant 0.23 difference.[23] On average, public employees think that if the opposition were to win, their situation would worsen.[24]

---

[21] Respondents were assigned to either treatment or control for both survey experiment questions (perception of job stability and job change).

[22] Originally, these two questions were designed to be used together to get a 0–10 estimate of positive or negative change. But respondents found it difficult in the first question to give a 0–10 estimate, and there were numerous nonresponses. The second question, more straightforward, was easier to understand, and there were fewer nonresponses, so I decided to focus on it.

[23] Note that, regardless of the treatment, few respondents were expecting that working conditions would get worse. Because all three municipalities have rules that tie salary increases, promotions, and job security to years in the job, most employees think that, all else equal, working conditions will get better over time.

[24] Table 6.5 in the Chapter Appendix shows the *t*-test results.

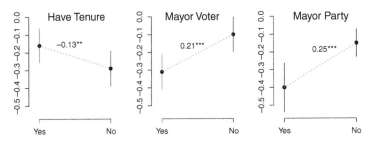

FIGURE 6.3 Likelihood of positive change, heterogeneous treatment effects
Note: Average treatment effects calculated as the difference between the treatment and the control group (*t*-test with unequal variance). Black circles indicate the treatment effect within each subgroup. Vertical lines represent 95 percent confidence intervals. *** $p < 0.01$, ** $p < 0.05$, * $p < 0.1$.

Figure 6.3 presents the differences in the size of the treatment effect across different subsets of employees – *Tenure, Mayor Voter,* and *Mayor Party.* As before, I expect the incumbent's supporters to be more likely to think that if the opposition wins, the change would be for the worse.[25] Although the theory of self-enforcing patronage does not provide a clear prediction in this case, employees with job security – those who, in general, have been in the job longer and may have already experienced a change in administration – may be less afraid of suffering negative changes.

As Figure 6.3 shows, the strength of the main treatment effect is conditional on the characteristic of the respondents predicted by the theory of self-enforcing patronage – support for the mayor. The mayor's supporters (both *Mayor Party* and *Mayor Voter*) who received the hypothetical about the opposition winning the election responded quite differently to the question about changes in working conditions than supporters who did not receive it. Hearing the hypothetical about the opposition winning has a significantly smaller effect on the expectations of non-supporters. The difference in effects between employees who reported having voted for the incumbent and those who did not (middle plot) is a significant 0.21 (at the 99 percent level). Given that the scale in this case is –1 to 1, 0.21 indicates that incumbent voters are, on average, 11 percent more likely to expect negative changes in working conditions if the opposition wins. The difference in effects between those who identify with the party of the mayor and those who do not (right plot) is a significant 0.25 (at the 99 percent level). Mayor party supporters are, on average, 13 percent more likely to expect negative changes if the opposition wins than non-mayor party supporters. Employees who have tenure also feel less afraid of the opposition assuming power than untenured ones

---

[25] Table 6.6 in the Chapter Appendix displays the exact numeric effects within each subgroup.

(left plot). The difference in effects between respondents with and without tenure is a significant 0.13 (at the 95 percent level).

6.3 REGRESSION ANALYSIS

This section corroborates the difference-in-means (*t*-test) results from the survey experiments using regression analysis, in which the experimental treatments are included as independent variables. Such analysis allows me to control for confounding factors, particularly the two main respondent characteristics that could condition the perception of risk associated with a change in administration: type of employment contract and level of education. I expect employees with job security to be less afraid of losing their jobs and suffering negative changes in their working conditions if an opposition candidate were to win the election. Conversely, I expect that employees with lower levels of education – and thus worse private sector labor market expectations – would be more afraid of a change in administration.

Table 6.1 presents a series of OLS regressions with interactions between the main characteristics of interest – *Mayor Party* and *Mayor Voter* – according to the theory of self-enforcing patronage, and the treatment assignment for both survey experiments, as well as controls for age (*Age*), gender (*Female*), education (*College*), time of hiring (*Current Mayor*), and type of contract (*Tenure*). The left panels present the results for the perception of job stability experiment, in which the dependent variable ranges from 0 to 10. The right panels present the results for the perception of job change experiment, in which the dependent variable ranges from –1 to 1.

The regression analyses are in line with the results obtained from the difference-in-means estimates in Section 6.2. Controlling for confounding factors, being a supporter (measured as *Mayor Voter* or *Mayor Party*) conditions the average treatment effect in the predicted directions. To illustrate, consider a male mayor voter from Tigre between the ages of forty-six and fifty-five, without a college degree, who was hired by the current administration and does not have job security. The estimation (from 0 to 10, with higher numbers indicating higher perception of stability) of his likelihood of keeping his job in the Tigre administration if the opposition wins is 6.52 [5.97, 7.07].[26] For a non-mayor voter with the same characteristics hired by the previous administration, the estimation increases to 8.06 [7.63, 8.48].[27] Using

---

[26] Ninety-five percent confidence intervals in square brackets.

[27] Predicted probabilities were calculated varying support for the mayor (*Mayor Party* and *Mayor Voter*) and *Current Mayor* at the same time while holding all categorical variables at their sample modes and all ordered variables at their sample medians. Since patronage jobs are disproportionally distributed to supporters (see Chapter 3), it is a more realistic scenario to compare mayor supporters hired by the current administration with non-supporters hired by the previous one. Holding time of hiring constant gives a predicted probability of 7.03 [6.49, 7.58] for the modal non-mayor voter hired by the current administration.

TABLE 6.1 *Perceptions of job stability and change – OLS regressions*

	Likelihood of staying in the job (0 to 10)		Change for better or worse (−1 to 1)	
Treatment* Mayor Voter	−1.08***		−0.21***	
	(0.27)		(0.07)	
Treatment* Mayor Party		−0.72**		−0.26***
		(0.29)		(0.08)
Treatment	0.30	−0.10	−0.10**	−0.15***
	(0.21)	(0.16)	(0.05)	(0.04)
Mayor Voter	0.57***		0.09*	
	(0.20)		(0.05)	
Mayor Party		0.49**		0.21***
		(0.20)		(0.05)
College	0.09	0.08	−0.13***	−0.10**
	(0.19)	(0.18)	(0.04)	(0.04)
Tenure	2.53***	2.47***	−0.05	−0.06
	(0.21)	(0.20)	(0.05)	(0.05)
Current Mayor	−1.03***	−0.98***	0.05	−0.00
	(0.19)	(0.18)	(0.05)	(0.05)
Constant	7.44***	7.60***	0.29***	0.31***
	(0.34)	(0.31)	(0.08)	(0.07)
Observations	1,059	1,125	966	1,021
R-squared	0.36	0.34	0.08	0.09

Note: Left panels present the results for the perception of job stability experiment (0 to 10 scale); right panels present the results for the perception of change experiment (−1 to 1 scale). Results were substantively equivalent when using ordered probit. All models also include controls for age, gender, and municipality (not reported). Robust standard errors in parentheses. *** $p < 0.01$, ** $p < 0.05$, * $p < 0.1$.

Mayor Party as a measure of support yields similar results.[28] Regarding the likelihood of change, consider again the same modal supporter: a 46- to 55-year -old male mayor voter from Tigre, without a college degree, hired by the current administration, and without job security. On a −1 to 1 scale, in which 1 means "better," the estimation of the likelihood of change if the opposition wins is 0.06 [−0.06, 0.18]. For a non-mayor voter with the same characteristics hired by

[28] Indeed, 6.63 [6.04, 7.21] for a mayor party supporter with the same characteristics as the modal voter above hired by the current administration versus 7.84 [7.44, 8.23] for a non-supporter with the same characteristics hired by the previous administration.

the previous administration, the estimation increases to 0.14 [0.03–0.26]. Again, results using *Mayor Party* to measure support are similar.[29]

Both the difference-in-means and the regression analysis of the survey experiments show that on average, public sector employees affiliated with the incumbent mayor (*Mayor Voter* and *Mayor Party*) have strong incentives to try to keep the mayor in power. The results show that employees whom a new administration could perceive as supporters of the previous administration (those more closely connected to the mayor's network) are afraid they will lose their jobs or suffer a decline in work conditions if the opposition wins the election. This is a strong incentive for them to provide the political services that could help keep the incumbent in office.

6.4 PUTTING THE PIECES TOGETHER

The evidence presented so far shows that supporters are more involved than other employees in the provision of political services (Chapters 4 and 5) and that supporters believe that their jobs and working conditions could change for the worse with a new administration (Sections 6.2 and 6.3 above). According to the theory of self-enforcing patronage, the latter belief is the main reason why supporters provide more political services. To try to keep the incumbent in office and avoid those potential negative changes, supporters are willing to contribute to the electoral effort by doing political work. Are employees who are more afraid of a change in the administration actually the ones providing more political services? In this section, I put both pieces of the argument together and show that, at least for one political service – monitoring elections – this is indeed the case.

As outlined above, interviewers used two different questionnaires in sequential order to create groups for the survey and list experiments, alternating the assignment of respondents to either the treatment or the control groups. Ideally, respondents would have been randomly and independently assigned to an experimental condition for each experiment (Gaines, Kuklinski, and Quirk 2007). However, the survey included four list experiments and two survey experiments, and it was conducted with a pencil-and-paper questionnaire, so this was logistically too complicated to implement. As a consequence, there is complete overlap between treatment and control conditions for both the list and survey experiments, making it impossible to combine them to show that those providing the most political services are indeed the ones more afraid of a change in administration.

---

[29] For a mayor party supporter with the same characteristics as the modal voter above hired by the current administration, the estimation of the likelihood of change is 0.04 [–0.09, 0.18], versus 0.09 [–0.01, 0.20] for a non-supporter hired by the previous administration.

To get around this issue, the survey included a direct question about one of the political services – monitoring elections (*Monitor*).[30] All respondents were asked if they had participated as partisan election monitors (party poll watchers) in the last election. Importantly, this question was included in the protected section of the survey instrument (Part B).[31] When asked directly, a proportion of 0.16 [0.14, 0.19] of respondents replied that they acted as partisan election monitors in the previous election.[32] When the question was asked with a list experiment, the estimated proportion of those who acted as partisan monitors was 0.12 [0.04, 0.21] (Chapter 4). In this case, the direct question returned an estimate that is statistically indistinguishable from that produced by the list experiment. Because the direct question was asked in the protected part of the survey, the fact that the direct question and the list experiment yielded roughly the same estimates does not necessarily mean that the question about monitoring elections was not sensitive.[33]

The direct question allows me to put the two pieces of the argument together. Are employees who act as partisan poll monitors more afraid of a change in the administration? To answer this question, I first replicate the analysis from Chapter 4 using the direct question to show that supporters are more involved in the provision of political services (monitoring elections, in this case) than non-supporters. In line with the results from the list experiment, Figure 6.4 below shows that the mayor's supporters are significantly more likely than non-supporters to report being partisan election monitors.[34]

As expected, and in line with the list experiment estimates from Chapter 4, the mayor's supporters are disproportionally more involved in the partisan monitoring of elections than non-supporters. Among the subgroup who reported voting for the incumbent (left plot), 22 percent acted as monitors, while the percentage among non-mayor voters drops to 9 percent. The 14 percentage-point difference is significant at the 99 percent level. The pattern is similar when the mayor's support is measured with party identification (right plot). Among the subgroup who self-identified with the

---

[30] The reason I chose to ask directly only about one political service and not about all of them was twofold. First, the survey had to be approved by the local authorities, and I was afraid that too many direct political questions would jeopardize my chances of getting this approval. Second, I was also concerned about public employees' reaction to a survey with too many political questions.

[31] See Chapter 3 for a description of the measures taken to minimize bias and non-responses on Part B of the questionnaire.

[32] In the Tigre and Santa Fe cases, the question referred to the 2009 election; in case of Salta, it was about the 2011 election. Ninety-five percent confidence intervals in square brackets.

[33] Indeed, other applications to similar topics have found that direct questions underestimate the prevalence of sensitive behaviors relative to list experiments (e.g., González-Ocantos et al. 2012; González-Ocantos, Kiewiet de Jonge, and Nickerson 2015; Oliveros 2019). See Chapter 3 for a test of the effectiveness of the protected questionnaire.

[34] Table 6.7 in the Chapter Appendix shows the numeric values in the figure as well as the list experiment estimates for comparison.

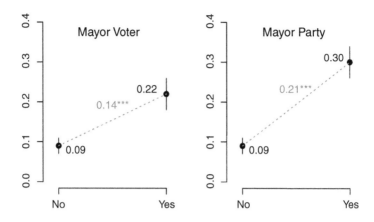

FIGURE 6.4 Partisan election monitors (direct question), by support for the mayor
Note: Black circles indicate the proportion of employees in each subgroup who reported being partisan election monitors in the previous election. Vertical lines represent 95 percent confidence intervals. *** $p < 0.01$, ** $p < 0.05$, * $p < 0.1$.

mayor's party, 30 percent reported acting as election monitors in the previous election, while only 9 percent of those who did not self-identify with the mayor's party did so. The 21 percentage-point difference between these groups is significant at the 99 percent level.[35]

Are employees who reported acting as partisan monitors also more afraid of a change in the administration? To answer this question, I once again estimate conditional average treatment effects (CATE) across subgroups to examine heterogeneous reactions to the hypothetical electoral outcome. The results, also corroborated with regression analysis, are shown in Figure 6.5.[36] Again, because tenured employees cannot be fired, results for the perception of job stability experiment (left plot) are presented for the whole sample (black dots) and for untenured employees (white dots).

In line with previous results, in both survey experiments, partisan monitors who receive the hypothetical about the opposition winning the election respond differently than monitors who do not hear the hypothetical. In contrast, hearing the hypothetical about the opposition winning has no effect on non-monitors' expectations about job stability, and only a small effect on their expectations about the likelihood of change.

---

[35] For comparison, the list experiment estimates yield an 18 percentage-point difference between mayor voters and non-mayor voters (significant at the 95 percent level) and a 21 percentage-point difference between mayor party supporters and non-mayor party supporters (significant at the 95 percent level).

[36] Table 6.8 in the Chapter Appendix shows the numeric effects within each subgroup.

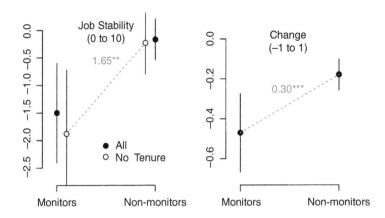

FIGURE 6.5 Perceptions of job stability and change, heterogeneous treatment effects across monitors and non-monitors
Note: Average treatment effects calculated as the difference between the treatment and the control group (*t*-test with unequal variance). Black circles indicate the treatment effect within each subgroup; white circles restrict the sample to untenured employees. Vertical lines represent 95 percent confidence intervals. *** $p < 0.01$, ** $p < 0.05$, * $p < 0.1$.

The difference in effects between untenured employees who acted as monitors and non-monitors (left plot, white circles), is a significant 1.65 (at the 95 percent level). Since the outcome was measured on a 0 to 10 scale this means that untenured employees who acted as election monitors are, on average, 17 percent less confident about keeping their jobs if the opposition wins. On the question about working conditions, hearing the hypothetical about the opposition winning yields a significant (at the 99 percent level) 0.30 difference in effects between monitors and non-monitors (right plot). Given the −1 to 1 scale in this case, 0.30 indicates that on average, monitors are 15 percent more likely than non-monitors to expect negative changes in working conditions with the opposition in power.

Similar results are obtained using regression analysis. Table 6.2 presents OLS regressions with interactions between the treatment assignments for both survey experiments and election monitoring (*Monitor*), as well as controls for age, gender, education, time of hiring, type of contract, and municipality. The left panel presents the results for the perception of job stability experiment, in which the dependent variable ranges from 0 to 10. The right panel presents the results for the perception of change experiment, in which the dependent variable ranges from −1 to 1.

TABLE 6.2 *Perceptions of job stability and change, by monitors and non-monitors – OLS regressions*

	Likelihood of staying in the job	Change for better or worse
Treatment*Monitor	−1.02**	−0.31***
	(0.43)	(0.10)
Treatment	−0.12	−0.18***
	(0.15)	(0.04)
Monitor	0.42	0.06
	(0.26)	(0.07)
College	0.03	−0.12***
	(0.19)	(0.05)
Tenure	2.67***	−0.02
	(0.20)	(0.05)
Current Mayor	−0.90***	0.04
	(0.19)	(0.05)
Constant	7.71***	0.33***
	(0.33)	(0.08)
Observations	1,016	923
R-squared	0.35	0.08

Note: Left panel presents the results for the perception of job stability experiment (0 to 10 scale); right panel presents the results for the perception of change experiment (−1 to 1 scale). Results were substantively equivalent when using ordered probit. All models also include controls for age, gender, and municipality (not reported). Robust standard errors in parentheses. *** $p < 0.01$, ** $p < 0.05$, * $p < 0.1$.

The regression analyses corroborate the difference-in-means results. Controlling for confounding factors, being a partisan election monitor conditions the average treatment effect in the direction predicted by the theory of self-enforcing patronage. To illustrate, consider again a modal respondent: a 46- to 55-year-old male partisan monitor from Tigre, without a college degree, who was hired by the current administration and does not have tenure. The estimation (0–10, with higher numbers indicating higher perception of stability) of the likelihood of keeping his job with a new administration is 6.25 [5.45, 7.05]. The estimation of a non-monitor hired by the previous administration, with otherwise the same characteristics, increases to 7.75 [7.35, 8.16].[37] In terms of the likelihood of change, for the same modal partisan monitor hired by the current administration

---

[37] Ninety-five percent confidence intervals in square brackets. As in the previous section, predicted probabilities are calculated varying *Monitor* and *Current Mayor* at the same time while holding all categorical variables at their sample modes and all ordered variables at their sample medians.

(male, 46–55, from Tigre, no college degree, and untenured), the estimation of the likelihood of change (on a −1 to 1 scale, in which 1 means better) is −0.11 [−0.29, 0.06]. For a non-monitor hired by the previous administration with otherwise the same characteristics, the estimation becomes positive and increases to 0.11 [0.00, 0.21].

Both the regression analysis and the difference-in-means analysis of the survey experiments show that employees who help with the electoral effort (in this case, as partisan election monitors) are more afraid of a change in the administration than their coworkers who do not help with the electoral effort. Putting together both parts of the argument, this section shows that supporters are more involved in the provision of services because they have more to lose from a change in the administration.

6.5   ALTERNATIVE EXPLANATIONS

Consistent with the theory of self-enforcing patronage developed in this book, this chapter shows that supporters have strong incentives to help the incumbent stay in power. Because they believe that an opposition politician could have them fired or sidelined, helping the incumbent remain in power is perfectly aligned with their own interests. As long as their personal interests are aligned with those of the incumbent, the incumbent does not need to use any type of incentive to encourage or pressure supporters to provide political services. Other employees, however, may be in a different situation; some do not fear losing their jobs or may even think that their situation would improve with an opposition politician in power. Yet, at least some of these employees sometimes provide political services as well (see Chapters 4 and 5). For these employees, the type of incentive alignment upon which the theory of self-enforcing patronage is constructed may not exist.

The theory presents a solution to the commitment problem that arises in clientelistic agreements because of the sequenced nature of the exchange (see Chapter 2). Other scholars have pointed to the threat of punishment and feelings of reciprocity as explanations for the behavior of clients – patronage employees here. In this and previous chapters, I provide evidence that for patronage employees it is neither reciprocity nor the threat of punishment that ensures that they uphold their part of the deal, but rather that their fates are tied to the political fate of their patron. Support for the incumbent indeed is the main predictor for the provision of services, even after controlling for these two alternative explanations. In this theory of patronage, clients' compliance with clientelistic agreements is ensured by their incentives being aligned with those of their patrons: Both the patron and client will benefit from the patron's success. Certainly, threat of punishment or feelings of reciprocity may also be present or possible in patronage arrangements; neither of these two factors, however, are *necessary* characteristics of such arrangements.

The theory developed in this book provides a novel alternative to existing explanations, but it is possible that different logics coexist, albeit to a different degree. This section presents some anecdotal evidence for the theory of punishment (among certain types of employees) but no evidence for the theory of reciprocity.

6.5.1   Punishment

The story of Laura exemplifies the type of employees that may require a different type of "incentive" in order to contribute to the electoral mobilization. Laura, a tenured administrative employee from Tigre, describes the electoral activities that employees usually conduct. Among other things, she says, they are in charge of the organization and mobilization for different campaign events; at election time, public employees often have to attend those events on weekends. "Some of us go. Sometimes they tell you, 'You have to go,' especially if it is in the area ... It is up to you whether you go or not, but if you need something later on ... if you have children and you need to be absent some other day ... " Political work on weekends was a common practice during the previous administration; as Laura says, "the employees already know."[38]

Besides helping organize campaign events, employees also help before and during Election Day – always a Sunday in Argentina. In the two weeks prior to the 2009 election, Laura and her coworkers were asked by their boss to take turns at the local Peronist office helping citizens with questions about the electoral register; most typically, they were seeking the addresses of their assigned polling places. On Election Day, some employees worked as partisan election monitors while others – like Laura – helped by delivering lunch to the monitors. Laura had been hired in 1988 during the previous opposition administration, thanks to her brother who was then a councilman for the Radical party. She herself joined the party in 1984, and she was still party affiliated and voted in the (non-mandatory) Radical primary in 2010, the year before the interview. Like most people in her office, however, she contributes to the Peronist party campaign.[39]

Due to the tenure system, when a new mayor takes office many employees in the public administration cannot be fired. What about public employees who, like Laura, were hired by the previous administration and remained in their jobs when a different party took over? What about employees who – again like Laura – were hired by the previous administration because of their political connections? What about employees who identify with the opposition? The list experiment estimates presented in Chapters 4 and 5 show that some of them, like Laura, do in fact provide political services (albeit to a much lesser extent than supporters).[40] But there is no reason for them to be afraid of a change in

---

[38] Author interview, Tigre, January 6, 2011.

[39] Author interview, Tigre, January 6, 2011.

[40] Recall that the questions about political services did not ask for which party these services were provided so it is possible that a few employees were providing services for the opposition. The estimates presented throughout the book are thus conservative.

administration. They are less likely to be supporters of the incumbent and, thus, less likely to be seen as "disloyal" by a new mayor, and more likely to have tenure because they have been in the job longer. They are also less likely to believe that things would be worse with a new administration from a different party.[41] Employees retained from prior administrations may even support the opposition, as Laura does.[42] It is thus difficult to argue that the incentives of these types of employees are aligned with the incentives of the incumbent and that the theory of self-enforcing patronage can explain their behavior. Why do public employees like Laura provide political services?

To convince these types of employees – those whose incentives are not aligned with the incentives of the incumbent – to collaborate and provide political services, other mechanisms may be in place. At least some of the employees who had been appointed by previous administrations might be subjected to the kind of "encouragement," either positive or negative, that the theory of punishment predicts. To make non-supporters help with the provision of political services, in particular, some inducement may be necessary. Indeed, these types of employees appear to be sometimes motivated by the threat of punishment or more subtly, as in the case of Laura, by the loss of benefits that comes with not doing what the boss asks – even when it is not part of the formal job.

Not all political services are equal in this regard. The contribution of supporters and non-supporters varies across the different political services (see Chapters 4 and 5). Among those who did not identify with the mayor's party, the list experiments estimate that 16 percent helped with electoral campaigns (versus 34 percent for supporters), 20 percent attended rallies (versus 28 percent for supporters), and 37 percent provided favors in the previous week (versus 57 percent for supporters). In contrast, the percentage of non-supporters acting as election monitors was not statistically distinguishable from zero (versus 27 percent for supporters).[43] Attending rallies is the activity with the smallest difference between supporters and non-supporters. This is consistent with what we know from the existing literature; ethnographic work shows that public employees and beneficiaries of social welfare programs are often expected to turn out to rallies (e.g., Auyero 2001; Quirós 2006; Szwarcberg 2015; Vommaro and Quirós 2011; Zarazaga 2014). How these "expectations" translate into people

---

[41] For the job stability experiment, the difference between employees hired by the current administration and employees hired by previous administrations is a significant 0.53 (at the 90 percent level). For the likelihood of change experiment, the 0.08 difference is not significant. See Table 6.9 in the Chapter Appendix.

[42] Of course, not all employees hired by previous administrations were hired through political connections, nor are they all supporters of the opposition. The example of Laura was chosen purposely to illustrate an extreme case.

[43] When measured with the direct question, the reported percentage of non-supporters acting as election monitors was 9 percent (versus 30 percent for supporters).

actually attending a political rally may vary. As Auyero points out, sometimes "'gratitude' goes without saying because it almost always comes without asking ... On a few occasions, attendance is explicitly required. Yet such requests are seldom phrased as orders, obligations; rather, they are usually phrased as invitations" (2001, 161). On other occasions, attendance at rallies is monitored. According to Szwarcberg, brokers use lists with the names of "machine members, beneficiaries of welfare programs, public employees, neighborhood community organizers, and party activists whose problems they have solved, are solving, or are thinking about solving in the future. Everyone who had come to ask for help or who had been offered assistance without asking is on these lists and is expected to be at the rally" (2009, 15).

Attending rallies does not require an ideological commitment and, if the rallies take place during working hours, attendance also entails a relatively low cost for employees. My own research also suggests that public employees are sometimes "taken" to rallies by local authorities during and after their working hours. A Salta telephone operator recalled that the last time she attended a rally was when a councilman from the mayor's party took office: "They brought us from here (the municipality) ... they told us we had to support him."[44] Often, the choice is not between attending a rally or staying home, but between attending a rally or staying at the place of work. Among the 280 respondents who reported attending a rally in the previous three months, 41 percent reported attending it with coworkers.[45] Additionally, even if employees have to be "encouraged" to attend, what counts is that they actually turn out. The sincerity of their support for the mayor is irrelevant to whether their presence contributes to making the rally a success. At the same time, if encouragement is "needed," it might also matter that attendance at rallies is easy to monitor.

On the opposite side of the spectrum, non-supporters are generally not asked to act as partisan election monitors. In Argentina, monitoring elections is considered a crucial and very sensitive activity, one that requires someone who would be willing to defend the interest of the party if needed.[46] While being an election monitor is a very visible activity, and therefore potentially easy to monitor, monitoring actual behavior inside each polling place – which is what matters in this case – is not. Because only one partisan monitor by party is allowed outside each room where voting occurs, monitoring the behavior of the monitors is, at the very least, difficult and probably impossible. It is not surprising then that politicians choose only those they fully trust as monitors. Illustrative of this point is the fact that Laura – the employee from the opposition whose participation in political

---

[44] Author interview (Josefina), Salta, June 15, 2011.

[45] Recall that the survey instrument had to be approved by the local authorities, so a direct question about whether employees were "forced" into attending rallies was not possible.

[46] See Chapter 3 for a description of partisan monitors' duties and their importance in Argentinean elections.

activities was described at the beginning of this section – delivered lunch to the monitors during the 2009 election but did not act as an election monitor herself.

In other cases, employees may participate in political activities that are not necessarily or obviously linked to the survival of the incumbent in office. In those cases, the theory of self-enforcing patronage does not provide any analytical leverage to explain public employees' behavior. One such situation happened in Salta during a non-mandatory local primary election in January 2011. The mayor's race was virtually uncontested (he won the primary election with 90 percent of the vote), but the race for City Council candidacies was strongly competitive (while all factions still support the mayor). Soledad, an untenured architect, described the primary: "Your boss comes over with a paper ballot and tells you where you are voting; he asks you if you will need transportation on Election Day; and he gives you the party list that you have to vote for ... Everyone under a temporary contract has to go vote ... They don't tell you directly, but the understanding is that voting is a requirement for the renewal of your contract." According to her, everyone votes in primaries. She does too, but always submits a blank ballot.[47] Another employee corroborated that untenured employees are "required" (*obligados*) to vote when asked. The day of the 2011 primary, she got a phone call to "remind" her that there was only one hour left before the polls closed and that they were "expecting her"; she went and submitted a blank ballot.[48] A few other employees recounted being asked to vote in this primary, with their bosses giving party leaders lists with their names. On Election Day, those lists were used to control turnout.[49] The strategy proved successful in terms of turnout: 53 percent of the Salta survey respondents reported voting in the 2011 primaries, compared to only 12 percent turnout of the general population.

6.5.2 Reciprocity

In contrast to the theories of self-enforcing patronage and of punishment, other theories argue that clientelism is sustained on norms of reciprocity (e.g., Finan and Schechter 2012; Lawson and Greene 2014; Scott 1972). From this perspective, clients behave according to their patrons' wishes out of a sense of gratitude. In the particular case under study here, this would mean that public employees provide political services to the incumbent out of gratitude for their jobs. According to this theory, therefore, employees who believe in norms of reciprocity and who owe their jobs to the incumbent politician should be more involved in the provision of political services.

---

[47] Author interview, Salta, August 3, 2011.
[48] Author interview (Paulina), Salta, June 8, 2011.
[49] Various interviews with the author, Salta, June and August 2011.

Interviews with public employees did not reveal the presence of feelings of reciprocity. Of course, this does not mean that those feelings are not present; it is entirely possible that they are just not that easy to verbalize and discuss openly. Measuring attitudes toward reciprocity is also challenging.[50] Because the survey was conducted with a pencil-and-paper questionnaire and already contained other experiments, I opted to measure the norm of reciprocity by using respondents' level of agreement with the following statement: "We always have to return the favors that people have done for us."[51] The distribution of responses was: 66 percent strongly agree, 20 percent agree more than disagree, 8 percent disagree more than agree, and 6 percent strongly disagree. Those who answered "strongly agree" or "agree" are coded as being subject to a norm of reciprocity (coded 1), with the rest coded as zero.

To study whether the provision of services is conditional on respondents' attitudes toward reciprocity, Figure 6.6 compares the political services list experiment estimates (Chapters 4 and 5) across reciprocal and nonreciprocal groups of individuals for employees hired during the current administration and those hired by previous administrations.[52] If the theory of reciprocity were correct, employees hired by the current administration and who believe in norms of reciprocity should be more involved in the provision of political services.

Figure 6.6 presents conflicting results across services, results that do not seem to provide evidence in favor of the theory of reciprocity.[53] For two activities – providing favors and monitoring elections (plots on the right) – employees hired by the current administration who agree with the reciprocity statement seem to be less involved in the provision of services (although the differences are not significant). For the other two services – helping with the electoral campaign and attending political rallies – employees hired by the current administration who agree with the reciprocity statement seem to be more involved than those who do not agree with it. Only for the case of attending rallies, however, is the difference significant.[54]

---

[50] Finan and Schechter (2012) use trust games to measure levels of reciprocity among voters; the implementation of such games was simply impossible in the context of the research conducted for this book. Baldwin (2013, 2015) and Lawson and Greene (2014), in turn, opted to use survey experiments with hypothetical third persons to diminish social desirability bias.

[51] González-Ocantos, Kiewiet de Jonge, and Nickerson (2015) and González-Ocantos, Kiewiet de Jonge, and Meseguer (2018) use a similar question.

[52] Table 6.10 in the Chapter Appendix provides the numerical values represented in the figure.

[53] These results are consistent with those presented in Chapter 4, where Table 4.2 shows the results of a multivariate analysis in which all the models are ordinary least squares regressions with the list experiment counts for political services as dependent variables. Among other covariates, the regressions include an interaction between believing in norms of reciprocity (coded as described above) and being appointed by the current mayor. As in the analysis here, the coefficient for this interaction is only significant for attending rallies.

[54] An alternative coding for the reciprocity variable, in which those who strongly agree with the statement were coded 1 and the rest were coded 0 yields results that are still not supportive of the

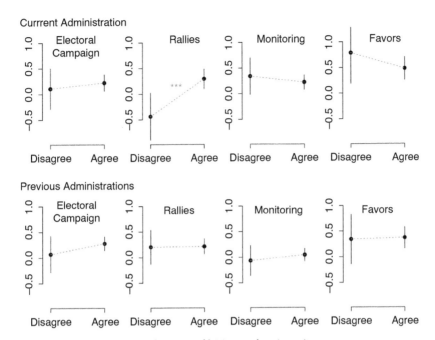

FIGURE 6.6 Political services by time of hiring and reciprocity
Note: Black circles indicate the proportion of employees in each subgroup (those who agree with the reciprocity statement and those who do not) who performed each of the political services, calculated as the difference between the treatment and the control group (*t*-test with unequal variance). Vertical lines represent 95 percent confidence intervals. *** $p < 0.01$, ** $p < 0.05$, * $p < 0.1$.

The quite imperfect measure of reciprocity used in this analysis means that these results should by no means be understood as a rejection of the reciprocity theory. Besides the problematic measure and the small sample size in some of the subgroups, which makes the estimation more difficult, feelings of gratitude can coexist with the pursuit of a more strategic interest – as predicted by the theory of self-enforcing patronage. More research is needed to determine the importance of feelings of reciprocity in patronage exchanges. Nonetheless, in this book, I do not find qualitative or quantitative evidence that feelings of reciprocity affect the behavior of public employees. More reciprocal employees do not seem to reciprocate for their jobs in the administration by providing more political services than non-reciprocal employees.

theory of reciprocity. Attending political rallies is again the only political service that seems to support the theory of reciprocity.

6.6 ROBUSTNESS TEST

As with any other project with a limited geographic scope, there is a question as to whether these results would apply to other settings. The three municipalities studied in this book are very different both politically and economically, however, making it more likely that a theory that applies in all three municipalities would also apply to other places. Figure 6.7 presents once again the results for the two survey experiments analyzed in this chapter,

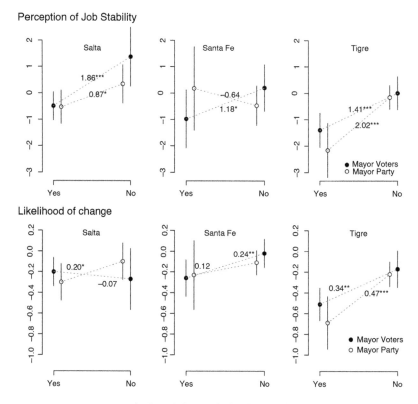

FIGURE 6.7 Perceptions of job stability and likelihood of change across municipalities, heterogeneous treatment effects

Note: Average treatment effects calculated as the difference between the treatment and the control group (*t*-test with unequal variance). Black circles indicate the treatment effect for mayor voters and non-mayor voters; white circles indicate the treatment effect for mayor party and non-mayor party. Vertical lines represent 95 percent confidence intervals. *** $p < 0.01$, ** $p < 0.05$, * $p < 0.1$.

showing the results for mayor voters and supporters of the mayor's party in each municipality.[55]

The results by municipality presented in Figure 6.7 are broadly consistent with the ones obtained by grouping the three municipalities together. Two partial exceptions are *Mayor Party* in the job stability experiment in Santa Fe and *Mayor Voter* in the likelihood of change experiment in Salta. In both of these cases, the coefficient for the difference-in-effects estimation has the opposite sign (albeit not significant) from what the theory predicts and what is obtained from the whole sample. In both cases, the small sample sizes resulting from the limited number of employees from the mayor's party in Santa Fe (65 respondents) and from Salta employees who reported not voting for the mayor (57 respondents) make the estimation more difficult. Finally, when measuring support for the mayor with the *Mayor Party* variable in the likelihood of change experiment in Santa Fe, the result is not significant (although the sign of the coefficient is as expected). Despite these caveats, the main expectations of the theory of self-enforcing patronage tested with the survey experiments outlined in this chapter generally hold when the sample is divided by municipality.

6.7 SUMMARY

This book proposes a novel explanation for the sustainability of patronage contracts. By treating both patrons and clients – in this case, public employees – as active agents with clear individual interests, it departs from existing explanations that are based on either feelings of reciprocity or threat of punishment. According to the theory of self-enforcing patronage, patronage employees provide political services to the incumbent because they believe that it is in their best interest to keep the incumbent in power. In this way, the commitment problem that arises in patronage contracts because of the sequenced nature of the exchange of public jobs for political services disappears because of the alignment of interests between politicians and patronage employees.

In this chapter, I used two survey experiments embedded in a survey of local public employees as well as interviews with public employees, brokers, and politicians to test the main empirical predictions of this theory. The empirical evidence strongly supports the theory of self-enforcing patronage and draws attention to the interests and strategic behavior of clients, rather than treating them as nonstrategic actors who are primarily driven by short-term responses to patrons' actions. Public

---

[55] Table 6.11 in the Chapter Appendix presents the values displayed in the figure.

employees who support the mayor are more afraid of losing their jobs or of things changing for the worse if an opposition mayor is elected than employees who do not support the mayor.

Once the alignment of incentives predicted by the theory is taken into account, the role of monitoring and punishment becomes very limited, although it might still affect the behavior of certain types of employees and certain types of services under certain conditions. For example, employees hired by previous administrations, sometimes from a different party than the incumbent mayor, have no fear of losing their jobs or experiencing worsening job conditions if the opposition wins the election. For these types of employees, it is hard to find the alignment of incentives upon which the theory of self-enforcing patronage relies. However, some of these employees still provide certain political services. In this chapter, I provide some anecdotal evidence that their behavior could be explained by threat of punishment, particularly for those services that are low cost, low commitment, and highly visible, such as attending rallies. I find no evidence to support the theory that employees provide political services because of a norm of reciprocity or deference.

6.8 CHAPTER APPENDIX: ADDITIONAL TABLES

TABLE 6.3 *Perception of job stability, survey experiment estimates*

. . . if the incumbent mayor is not re-elected and the opposition wins? (treatment)	7.75
	(0.12)
	N=563
. . . ? (control)	8.15
	(0.11)
	N=568
Treatment effect	−0.41**
	(0.16)
	N=1,131

Note: Two-sample t-test with unequal variance. Standard errors in parentheses. *** $p < 0.01$, ** $p < 0.05$, * $p < 0.1$.

TABLE 6.4 *Perception of job stability, heterogeneous treatment effects*

| Characteristic | Whole Sample | | | Employees without Tenure | | |
	No	Yes	Difference in Effects	No	Yes	Difference in Effects
Tenure	−0.62**	−0.03	−0.60**			
	(0.25)	(0.12)	(0.28)			
	N=572	N=559	N=1,131			
Mayor Voter	0.34	−0.96***	1.30***	0.65	−1.41***	2.06***
	(0.27)	(0.21)	(0.35)	(0.46)	(0.31)	(0.55)
	N=417	N=647	N=1,064	N=184	N=348	N=532
Mayor Party	−0.18	−0.89***	0.71**	−0.32	−1.26***	0.94*
	(0.20)	(0.28)	(0.35)	(0.30)	(0.44)	(0.53)
	N=764	N=367	N=1,131	N=378	N=194	N=572

Note: In each panel, the first two columns show the average treatment effects, calculated as the difference between the treatment and the control group (*t*-test with unequal variance) across respondents with and without each characteristic. The third column shows the difference in effects. Values in the left panel refer to the whole sample. Values in the right panel refer to employees without tenure. Standard errors in parentheses. *** $p < 0.01$, ** $p < 0.05$, * $p < 0.1$.

TABLE 6.5 *Do you think that your situation would be better, the same, or worse?*

. . . if the incumbent mayor is not re-elected and the opposition wins? (treatment)	0.13
	(0.03)
	N=499
. . . ? (control)	0.36
	(0.02)
	N=528
Treatment effect	−0.23***
	(0.03)
	N=1,027

Note: Two-sample *t*-test with unequal variance. Standard errors in parentheses. *** $p < 0.01$, ** $p < 0.05$, * $p < 0.1$.

TABLE 6.6 *Likelihood of positive change, heterogeneous treatment effects*

Characteristic	No	Yes	Difference in Effect
Have Tenure	−0.29***	−0.16***	−0.13**
	(0.05)	(0.05)	(0.07)
	N=521	N=505	N=1,026
Mayor Voter	−0.10**	−0.31***	0.21***
	(0.05)	(0.05)	(0.07)
	N=381	N=590	N=971
Mayor Party	−0.15***	−0.40***	0.25***
	(0.04)	(0.07)	(0.07)
	N=701	N=326	N=1,027

Note: The first two columns show the average treatment effects calculated as the difference between the treatment and the control group (*t*-test with unequal variance) across respondents with and without each characteristic. The last column shows the difference in effects. Robust standard errors in parentheses. *** $p < 0.01$, ** $p < 0.05$, * $p < 0.1$.

TABLE 6.7 *Partisan election monitors, by support for the mayor*

	Mayor Party Supporter			Mayor Voter	
	Direct Question	List experiment		Direct Question	List experiment
Yes	0.30***	0.27***	Yes	0.22***	0.20***
	(0.02)	(0.08)		(0.02)	(0.06)
	N=354	N=381		N=625	N=679
No	0.09***	0.06	No	0.09***	0.02
	(0.01)	(0.05)		(0.01)	(0.07)
	N=711	N=791		N=373	N=424
Difference in means	0.21***	0.21**	Difference in means	0.14***	0.18**
	(0.02)	(0.09)		(0.02)	(0.09)
	N=1,065	N=1,172		N=998	N=1,103

Note: In each panel, the column on the left presents the responses to the direct question (included in Part B of the questionnaire); the column on the right shows the list experiment estimates. Standard errors in parentheses calculated with unequal variance. *** $p < 0.01$, ** $p < 0.05$, * $p < 0.1$.

TABLE 6.8 *Perception of stability and likelihood of change, by monitors and non-monitors*

	Monitors	Non-monitors	Difference in Effects
Perception of job stability, heterogeneous treatment effects			
All employees	−1.50***	−0.17	−1.33***
	(0.46)	(0.19)	(0.47)
	N=166	N=856	N=1,022
Non-tenured	−1.88***	−0.23	−1.65**
employees	(0.59)	(0.29)	(0.65)
	N=110	N=426	N=536
Likelihood of change for better or worse, heterogeneous treatment effects			
All employees	−0.47***	−0.18***	−0.30***
	(0.10)	(0.04)	(0.10)
	N=149	N=780	N=929

Note: The first two columns show the average treatment effects calculated as the difference between the treatment and the control group (*t*-test with unequal variance) across monitors and non-monitors. The last column shows the difference in effects. Standard errors in parentheses. *** $p <$ 0.01, ** $p < 0.05$, * $p < 0.1$.

TABLE 6.9 *Perception of stability and likelihood of change, by time of hiring*

	Perception of Job Stability			Likelihood of Change		
Characteristic	No	Yes	Difference in Effects	No	Yes	Difference in Effects
Hired by	−0.12	−0.65**	0.53*	−0.19***	−0.27***	0.08
current	(0.14)	(0.28)	(0.29)	(0.05)	(0.05)	(0.07)
mayor	N=614	N=514	N=1,128	N=557	N=468	N=1,025

Note: In each panel, the first two columns show the average treatment effects calculated as the difference between the treatment and the control group (*t*-test with unequal variance) across respondents hired by previous administrations and those hired by the current one. The last column shows the difference in effects. Standard errors in parentheses. *** $p < 0.01$, ** $p < 0.05$, * $p < 0.1$.

TABLE 6.10 *Political services by time of hiring and reciprocity*

	Hired by Current Administration			Hired by Previous Administrations		
	Disagree	Agree	Difference	Disagree	Agree	Difference
Electoral Campaign	0.11	0.22***	0.11	0.07	0.28***	0.21
	(0.20)	(0.08)	(0.23)	(0.18)	(0.07)	(0.18)
	N=68	N=459	N=527	N=91	N=540	N=631
Political Rallies	−0.44*	0.29***	0.73***	0.20	0.22***	0.01
	(0.23)	(0.10)	(0.28)	(0.17)	(0.08)	(0.20)
	N=68	N=461	N=529	N=91	N=540	N=631
Election Monitors	0.34*	0.22***	0.12	−0.06	0.04	0.11
	(0.18)	(0.07)	(0.21)	(0.15)	(0.06)	(0.16)
	N=68	N=461	N=529	N=91	N=541	N=632
Favors	0.79***	0.48***	0.30	0.34	0.37***	0.03
	(0.30)	(0.11)	(0.33)	(0.25)	(0.11)	(0.28)
	N=68	N=465	N=533	N=92	N=545	N=637

Note: Table displays respondents' level of agreement with the following statement: "We always have to return the favors that people have done for us." In each panel, the first two columns indicate the proportion of respondents in each subgroup (those who agree with the reciprocity statement and those who do not) who performed each of the political services, calculated as the difference between the treatment and the control group (*t*-test with unequal variance). The last column shows the difference in proportions. Standard errors in parentheses. *** $p < 0.01$, ** $p < 0.05$, * $p < 0.1$.

TABLE 6.11 *Perceptions of job stability and likelihood of change by municipality, heterogeneous treatment effects*

		Perception of job stability			Likelihood of change		
		No	Yes	Difference in Effects	No	Yes	Difference in Effects
Salta	Mayor voters	1.37**	−0.49*	1.86***	−0.27*	−0.20**	−0.07
		(0.57)	(0.27)	(0.64)	(0.15)	(0.07)	(0.16)
		N=65	N=278	N=343	N=57	N=261	N=318
	Mayor Party	0.34	−0.53	0.87*	−0.10	−0.30***	0.20*
		(0.37)	(0.32)	(0.49)	(0.09)	(0.09)	(0.12)
		N=163	N=192	N=355	N=156	N=171	N=327
Santa Fe	Mayor voters	0.20	−0.98*	1.18*	−0.02	−0.26**	0.24**
		(0.45)	(0.56)	(0.71)	(0.07)	(0.09)	(0.11)
		N=219	N=164	N=383	N=202	N=148	N=350
	Mayor Party	−0.47	0.18	−0.64	−0.11*	−0.23	0.12
		(0.38)	(0.81)	(0.93)	(0.06)	(0.17)	(0.15)
		N=326	N=65	N=391	N=296	N=61	N=357
Tigre	Mayor voters	0.01	−1.40***	1.41***	−0.17*	−0.51***	0.34**
		(0.32)	(0.33)	(0.49)	(0.09)	(0.08)	(0.12)
		N=133	N=205	N=338	N=122	N=181	N=303
	Mayor Party	−0.15	−2.16***	2.02***	−0.22***	−0.69***	0.47***
		(0.23)	(0.52)	(0.49)	(0.06)	(0.13)	(0.13)
		N=275	N=110	N=385	N=249	N=94	N=343

Note: In each panel, the first two columns show the average treatment effects calculated as the difference between the treatment and the control group (*t*-test with unequal variance) across respondents with and without each characteristic. The last column shows the difference in effects. Standard errors in parentheses. *** $p < 0.01$, ** $p < 0.05$, * $p < 0.1$.

7

Beyond the Argentine Case

Based on data collected from local administrations in Argentina, Chapters 3 to 6 provide strong evidence in support of the theory of self-enforcing patronage. Can this theory help explain the functioning of patronage employment in other places? While the data to test the theory systematically in other countries is not available,[1] this chapter presents additional evidence from Latin America as an out-of-sample test of the theory, providing more confidence about the external validity of the argument. I draw attention to a series of patterns found in other Latin American countries that is consistent with the theory of self-enforcing patronage, increasing the likelihood that the theory and the findings of this book are portable to other contexts. In this chapter, I describe the remarkably weak Latin American civil service systems and provide evidence in line with the empirical implications of the theory: that public employees are more involved in the provision of political services than non-public employees are, that there is political bias in hiring decisions, and that patronage employees have good reasons to fear losing their jobs or suffering negative changes in their working conditions under a new administration. The first section in this chapter discusses Latin American civil service systems and their characteristics in order to assess whether the theory of self-enforcing patronage fits the general patterns found across the region. The second section considers three particular cases in more detail – Argentina (beyond the three municipalities analyzed before), Bolivia, and Chile.

7.1 PATRONAGE IN LATIN AMERICA

Patronage is a widespread phenomenon that has been reported in countries all over the world. Scholars have studied patronage appointments in Africa (e.g.,

---

[1] See the Introduction for a discussion on the difficulties of measuring patronage on a large scale.

Brierley 2021; Driscoll 2018; Kopecký 2011), Asia (e.g., Iyer and Mani 2012; Pierskalla and Sacks 2020), Europe (e.g., Chubb 1981, 1982; Golden 2003; Kopecký, Mair, and Spirova 2012), and the United States (e.g., Banfield and Wilson 1963; Folke, Hirano, and Snyder 2011; Johnston 1979; Wolfinger 1972). According to expert surveys, political criteria outweigh merit criteria in hiring in 64 percent of non-OECD countries (Schuster 2017, calculated from Dahlberg et al. 2013). In a survey of 23,000 civil servants across ten developing countries in Africa, Asia, Eastern Europe, and Latin America, a significant number of respondents in all countries report that personal and political connections matter for recruitment, promotion, and salaries (Meyer-Sahling, Schuster, and Mikkelsen 2020). However, the mere fact that patronage exists beyond Argentina is not evidence that the theory developed in this book helps us understand how patronage actually *works* in those places. While the data to directly test the theory of self-enforcing patronage in other Latin American countries – let alone beyond Latin America – is not available, this chapter describes a series of characteristics of the functioning of Latin American public administrations that are consistent with the theory. The goal of this chapter is to provide evidence that the empirical implications of the theory of self-enforcing patronage are consistent with patterns observed beyond the three municipalities studied in the previous chapters.

According to the argument advanced in this book, patronage jobs are disproportionally distributed to (perceived) supporters because only they can credibly commit to providing political support. Their fates are tied to the political fate of the politician who hired them. Patronage employees believe that their jobs and working conditions will be maintained by the incumbent but not by a competing politician, because – as perceived supporters of the incumbent – they cannot credibly commit to provide political services to an opponent. Supporters thus have large incentives to provide political services to help the incumbent stay in power, which makes their original commitment to provide political services credible. Even supporters with job security (tenure), who cannot easily be fired, believe that they may suffer negative changes in their working conditions with a new administration.

A weak civil service system is a precondition for any theory of patronage. The theory developed here addresses the commitment issues associated with patronage contracts, and such contracts are only possible where civil service systems are weak or nonexistent – the case in most Latin American countries. The theory does not carry much explanatory power in contexts with strict regulations about hiring and firing, where appointments to public jobs are completely based on merit and dismissals are only a product of bad performance. However, the absence of a strong civil service system does not in itself imply that, as predicted by the theory of self-enforcing patronage, there is political bias in the distribution of jobs, an understanding that those jobs are distributed in exchange for political services, or that patronage employees are afraid of losing their jobs or suffering negative changes in working conditions with a new administration.

Beyond the precondition of a weak civil service system, three other practices commonly found in Latin American public administrations are consistent with the main empirical implications of the theory: the provision of political services by public employees, political bias in hiring decisions, and fear of negative changes or firing under a new administration. After providing a general description of Latin American civil service systems, I rely on secondary literature and survey data to show that public employees are indeed disproportionally involved in the provision of political services, that political hiring is common practice, and that Latin American public employees have good reasons to fear a change in the administration.

Irrespective of the type of civil service and its politicization, a key assumption of the theory of self-enforcing patronage is that public employees in particular care about retaining their jobs and working conditions. The theory only has explanatory power in contexts in which keeping a public sector position is enough of an incentive to encourage patronage employees to provide political services. Public sector jobs are indeed highly valued in Latin America. In 2012, the average public employee in Latin America earned 38 percent more than a formal private employee and twice as much as an informal worker. Moreover, the salary of the average public employee in Latin America increased 40 percent between 1992 and 2012, compared to only 19 percent for formal workers in the private sector and 8 percent for informal ones. As in the Argentinean case, the wage gap generally favors less-educated employees (Arcidiácono et al. 2014, 32–33).[2]

At the same time, labor benefits are considerably more generous in the public sector than in the private sector. In 2011–12, 84 percent of public sector employees in Latin America had retirement plans associated with their jobs, compared to 66 percent among formal workers in the private sector.[3] Similar differences exist in terms of health insurance. While 83 percent of public employees had health insurance associated with their jobs, the proportion decreased to 67 percent for formal private employees.[4] Public employees, on average, also report working

---

[2] Data based on the analysis of household surveys in fifteen Latin American countries: Argentina, Bolivia, Brazil, Chile, Colombia, Costa Rica, Ecuador, El Salvador, Honduras, Mexico, Panama, Paraguay, Peru, Uruguay, and Venezuela (Arcidiácono et al. 2014).

[3] There is significant variation across countries in this regard. At one extreme, in Uruguay 100 percent of public employees have retirement benefits (versus 93 percent in the formal private sector). At the opposite extreme, in Honduras only 22 percent of public employees enjoy retirement benefits (versus 4 percent in the formal private sector). The countries examined in this chapter are in the middle: Argentina with 90 percent in the public sector and 79 percent in the private sector, Chile with 91 percent in the public sector and 88 percent in the private sector, and Bolivia with 82 percent in the public sector and 43 percent in the private sector (Arcidiácono et al. 2014, 68).

[4] There is also significant variation across countries regarding health insurance. In Argentina, the percentage of public employees with health insurance is 91 percent (versus 79 for private employees), in Chile it is 89 percent (versus 85), and in Bolivia it is 77 percent (versus 40 percent) (Arcidiácono et al. 2014, 68).

fewer hours per week than workers in the formal private sector: 42 hours versus 47 (Arcidiácono et al. 2014, 27). Finally, the possibility of having job security (a tenured contract) is virtually nonexistent outside the public sector.

7.1.1   Weak Civil Service Systems

All Latin American countries have constitutionally recognized civil services systems (Iacoviello 2006). These systems recognize the legitimacy of political appointments for some high-level positions, often institute tenure rights for the rest of their employees, and in many cases also mandate the selection of nonpolitical employees on the basis of merit. Many countries in the region have introduced rules about merit-based competition for recruitment of new employees, although implementation has been haphazard in most cases (Iacoviello 2006; Longo 2006a; Zuvanic, Iacoviello, and Gusta 2010). Civil service systems in most Latin American countries, however, coexist with political criteria for hiring, firing, and promotions (Cortázar Velarde, Lafuente, and Sanginés 2014; Grindle 2012; Iacoviello 2006). Indeed, cross-national analysis of 117 countries shows that countries with and without legal merit requirements exhibit similar levels of meritocracy in practice (Schuster 2017).

Civil service systems in Latin American countries can be classified into three main groups based on their level of professionalization, as evaluated by the Inter-American Development Bank (IDB) (Echebarría 2006). Figure 7.1 reproduces the IDB study's findings on merit criteria. It is based on an index that measures the extent to which "objective, technical, and professional procedures exist and are followed to recruit, select, promote, compensate and dismiss employees" (Zuvanic, Iacoviello, and Gusta 2010, 152). Low values on the 0 to 100 scale indicate the absence of merit criteria, while high values indicate the use of these criteria. In some Latin American countries, particularly in Central America (with the exception of Costa Rica), hiring occurs only through political connections. Partisan bias in recruitment is so

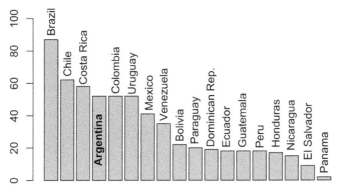

FIGURE 7.1   Merit index in Latin American countries (2004)
Source: Echebarría 2006

widespread in some of the countries in this group that it is possible to predict the partisan affiliation of public employees based on the year they were hired (Iacoviello 2006). In others – Argentina among them – some formal criteria for the selection and promotion of employees based on merit exist, but they are poorly implemented and coexist with political criteria. Finally, Brazil, Chile, and Costa Rica have solid merit systems for the recruitment and promotion of public employees (Iacoviello 2006; Zuvanic, Iacoviello, and Gusta 2010).[5]

As Figure 7.1 shows, the institutionalized use of merit criteria for selection, promotion, and dismissal of Latin American public sector employees is rare. The average for the region is 33 points (out of 100), ranging from 2 points for Panama to 87 points for Brazil. Argentina, with 52 points, is considered to be among the countries with intermediate civil service development (together with Colombia, Uruguay, Mexico, and Venezuela), where merit-based practices coexist with political patronage (Iacoviello 2006; Zuvanic, Iacoviello, and Gusta 2010). Importantly for the generalizability of this book's findings, Argentina is not an outlier among Latin American countries in terms of meritocracy in the public administration. If anything, Argentina is actually closer to the meritocratic cases of Brazil, Chile, and Costa Rica than to the ones where discretionary hiring is the norm.

The IDB repeated the study in 2014 but unfortunately did not include Argentina (or Venezuela). Figure 7.2 presents the new indexes by country

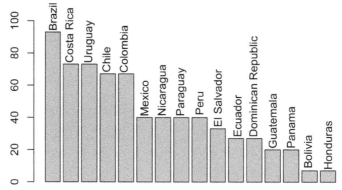

FIGURE 7.2 Merit index in Latin American countries (2011–13)
Source: Cortázar Velarde, Lafuente, Sanginés (2014)

---

[5] The mechanisms for hiring and firing (whether meritocratic or politicized) are not the only characteristics of civil service systems that are important for establishing the professionalization of the public administration and the strength of the civil service system. Other characteristics, such as functional capacity or flexibility, are also important. For a theory of patronage, however, the presence or absence of merit criteria for hiring and firing is the most important characteristic of civil service systems.

using a similar methodology.[6] The average for the region increased from thirty-three to forty-two points. Almost all countries, except Mexico and Bolivia, show some improvement. Competitive hiring is well established in Costa Rica and Brazil and was significantly reinforced in Chile, Colombia, and Uruguay during the intervening ten years. In Bolivia and Honduras, by contrast, competitive hiring is extremely rare. In the rest of Latin America, although there are some meritocratic systems, discretionary appointments are still the norm (Cortázar Velarde, Lafuente, and Sanginés 2014).

Several common practices explain the gap between the legal status of civil service systems in all Latin American countries and the reality described by the IDB index. In some cases, meritocratic reforms are relatively recent: Nicaragua in 2007, Paraguay in 2008, Peru in 2008, and Ecuador in 2010 (Cortázar Velarde, Lafuente, and Sanginés 2014). That said, the most obvious way to maintain the patronage system is "simple failure to observe laws and regulations" (Grindle 2012, 150). Getting around the law has been accomplished through two main mechanisms – delaying the process of implementation and hiring outside the system with the use of temporary contracts.

In El Salvador, for instance, the civil service law (1961) was modified several times, but the regulatory framework was never established (Iacoviello and Chudnovsky 2015). In Peru, Congress approved the Public Employment Law in 2004, but the specific regulations needed to make the law effective were not approved; in 2008 a new (more limited) reform was approved and implemented (Cortázar Velarde, Lafuente, and Sanginés 2014). In Guatemala, the civil service law was passed in 1968, but its regulatory framework was only put in place in 1998 (Iacoviello and Chudnovsky 2015). In the Dominican Republic, a new public sector law was passed in 2008, and the 2010 Constitution restricted presidential discretionary appointments to top-level positions and established merit requirements for hiring by the administration. Even so, very few examinations took place, and when they did, they were often manipulated – information on vacancies was not made publicly available, job descriptions were tailored to fit preferred candidates, applications were "lost," and exams leaked (Schuster 2017).

Besides delay, another common mechanism used to maintain discretion in hiring – in this case, without contravening the civil service laws and regulations – is the widespread use of temporary appointments. The systematic use of these appointments allows governments to avoid restrictions on recruitment and the tenure system, which gives politicians more autonomy for both hiring and firing. Of course, these temporary employees have more to

---

[6] Because of changes in the methodology, the indexes reported in Figure 7.2 are not immediately comparable to the Argentinean case. The report does provide the adjusted measures for the 2004 indexes, but only for the countries included in the new report. Figure 7.2 still allows for cross-country comparisons.

fear with a new administration. Tenured employees might be afraid of negative changes in working conditions when administrations turn over, but temporary employees could lose their jobs. One of the empirical implications of the theory developed in this book is that temporary employees who support the politician in power will be more enthusiastic collaborators than those who enjoy tenure rights. Having so much to lose works as a strong incentive to try to keep their patrons in office. As the examples below show, the use of flexible short-term contracts is a very popular practice among Latin American administrations.

In Peru, for instance, about 40 percent of public sector employees work under temporary contracts (Iacoviello 2006). In El Salvador, the only reform to the Civil Service Law (1961) was introduced in the 1990s to address the situation of temporary employees, who constituted 40 percent of total personnel at that time (Longo 2006a).[7] By 2012, the number of temporary contracts in the national administration had been reduced to 21 percent, but in public enterprises and decentralized agencies 38 percent of employees were still working under such contracts (Iturburu 2012a). In Ecuador, temporary contracts are supposed to be used to cover the short-term absences of career civil servants; in practice such contracts can last several years (Brassiolo, Estrada, and Fajardo 2020). In the Dominican Republic, the 2008 law required competitive entrance exams only for career positions; in response, politicians opted to place recruits in temporary positions or positions below the career level (Schuster 2017).[8]

The merit index discussed above is based on a general assessment of national civil service systems, but there is significant variation across different agencies and levels of government. In fact, different types of bureaucracies can coexist within the same country (Gingerich 2013b; Zuvanic, Iacoviello, and Gusta 2010). In Uruguay, the proportion of temporary employees is about 15 percent, but there is significant variation across agencies. Uruguay's Ministry of Transportation, for instance, had 85 percent of its employees under temporary contracts in 2004, while the Ministry of Tourism had 50 percent (Iacoviello 2006). All Latin American countries, even the ones with the weakest meritocratic systems, have areas of the administration that are more professionalized. For instance, the Customs Office in Bolivia, and the Secretary of Labor, the Administration and Personnel National Office (ONAP), the Comptroller General's Office, and the Supreme Court in the Dominican Republic (Longo 2006a).[9]

---

[7] Since 2004, when the research for the IDB report was conducted, the Salvadorian Civil Service Law has been modified many more times, but no regulatory framework legislation has yet been passed (Iturburu 2012a).

[8] See Grindle (2012, 227–239) for more examples of practices to bypass civil service regulations.

[9] See also Gingerich (2013b) for more examples and evidence of within-country variation in the cases of Bolivia, Brazil, and Chile.

At the same time, lower levels of the administration tend to have more employees under flexible short-term contracts and are usually more politicized than their national counterparts. Even in Brazil, with one of the most professional and meritocratic civil service systems at the federal level, mayors have significantly more discretion over the distribution of short-term contracts (Sells 2020). Indeed, around one third of public employees at the municipal level in Brazil are hired on temporary contracts (Toral 2020) compared to only 13 percent at the federal level, according to official data.[10] Chile, a country that, like Brazil, ranks high for its use of meritocratic criteria in hiring at the national level, also includes local administrations where discretionary criteria are more pronounced (Leyton Navarro 2006). In 2014, 50 percent of Chilean municipal public employees worked under freelance contracts (*a honorarios*), compared to 17 percent of personnel working under such contracts in the central administration (Valdebenito Pedrero 2017, 49).

7.1.2 Political Bias in Hiring and Firing

A quote from Grindle (2012, 151–52) vividly illustrates the functioning of at least some Latin American administrations:

Many of the patronage systems in Latin America resembled the kind of electoral partisanship and rotation in office found in the United States in the nineteenth century. With each election, even when the same party was returned to office, jobs were lost, shifted, and allocated to party stalwarts who had been helpful in winning the election. Frequently, the first year of a new administration was one in which little was accomplished other than recruiting personnel and making plans for new initiatives. Similarly, the final year of an administration, taking place in an election year, was often a time of poor performance as officials engaged widely in electoral mobilization or worked to establish alliances to ensure they could find jobs after the election.

Finding direct evidence of political bias in hiring and firing decisions is not an easy task. Nevertheless, some Latin American administrations are so politicized that there is little doubt about the existence of political bias. For instance, according to a survey conducted in 2008 in the Dominican Republic's public administration, 70 percent of hires were made based on recommendations and political influence (Iacoviello 2009b). While some progress has been made in terms of merit examinations and tenure protection since then, the fact that the institutions in charge of enforcing these protections – such as audit institutions and the judiciary – remain politicized means that progress has been limited, and salaries, transfers, and promotions are still at the discretion of political patrons (Oliveros and Schuster 2018). Such a politicized bureaucracy explains why employees appointed to their positions, with no job stability, are perceived to

---

[10] 878,611 on regular contracts (*cargo efetivo*) out of 1,015,811 total active federal public employees (*vínculos dos servidores ativos*). Source: www.portaltransparencia.gov.br/servidores (last accessed January 2020).

be easier to mobilize for electoral campaigns than those with job security hired after passing examinations (Oliveros and Schuster 2018). In Panama, only 18 percent of national employees are considered to be formally part of the public administration (*acreditados*); the rest are subject to discretionary appointments and dismissal (Longo 2006b). In Ecuador, political connections to the mayor increase the likelihood of an applicant obtaining a job in the local administration, particularly for low-skilled positions (Brassiolo, Estrada, and Fajardo 2020).

Even in Brazil, the Latin American country with the highest meritocratic score, according to the 2006 and 2014 IDB reports (Cortázar Velarde, Lafuente, and Sanginés 2014; Echebarría 2006), recent work shows partisan bias in hiring decisions at the municipal level. Using a regression discontinuity design in close mayoral elections, Brollo, Forquesato, and Gozzi (2017) show that winning a mayoral election has a significant positive effect on that party's members gaining jobs in the local public administration. In particular, they find that the proportion of members of the winning party employed by the municipal administration is 35 to 41 percent higher than that of members of the runner-up party. Although employment of party members is higher for senior positions, partisan appointments happen at all levels of the administration. Using a similar methodology, Colonnelli, Prem, and Teso (2018) show that being a supporter of the party in power – measured as being either a candidate for a seat in the local council or a campaign donor – increases the probability of having a public sector job in the local administration by 11 percentage points relative to the probability of employment for supporters of the runner-up party. The study also finds this partisan bias in hiring across all levels of the local administration, not just at the top of the bureaucracy. Personal and political connections seem to matter for hiring at the federal level as well. In a survey of federal civil servants, around 10 percent attributed at least some importance to political connections for recruitment, promotion, and payment; while around 25 percent reported the same for personal connections (Meyer-Sahling, Schuster, and Mikkelsen 2020).

The politicization of hiring decisions generates strong incentives for new incumbents to hire new, more loyal employees. Each new administration has "reasons to have no confidence in the competence and loyalty of employees appointed by previous administrations," which in turn motivates the appointment of new bureaucrats (Iacoviello 2006, 544). Where employees can be easily fired, this search for loyal employees might translate into high rates of turnover with each change in the administration. Because many Latin American countries guarantee job stability for public employees, the distrust of old employees who cannot be fired often ends up generating parallel bureaucracies of new, more responsive employees. As a result of this practice of sidelining those hired by previous administrations, working conditions for the old employees may suffer.

   The fear of suffering negative changes or even losing their jobs with a new administration seems to be justifiable in many Latin American countries. In Ecuador, Guatemala, Honduras, Nicaragua, Panama, and Peru, there is mass replacement of public employees with each change of administration (Iacoviello 2006; Zuvanic, Iacoviello, and Gusta 2010). In Panama, during Mireya Moscoso's administration (1999–2004), about 25,000 public employees were fired and replaced with supporters (Longo 2006b). This was not unusual; high instability and turnover with each change in administration have been routine in Panama for a long time (Strazza 2012). In the Dominican Republic, about 3,000 civil servants (*funcionarios de la Carrera Administrativa*) who were supposed to be protected by the tenure system lost their jobs in 2004 as a result of a change in the administration (Longo 2006b). In Guatemala, labor unions and NGOs estimate that mass layoffs (*barridas*) with changes in administration affect between 20 and 30 percent of public employees (Iturburu 2012b). Even in Brazil, the electoral defeat of an incumbent mayor generates both an increase in the dismissal of temporary workers and an increase in the hiring of civil servants by the outgoing mayor; when the new mayor takes office, there is also an increase in the hiring of temporary workers (Toral 2020).

   I am certainly not claiming that the turnover of public personnel is something that happens with every change in administration, or to the majority of workers. However, the fact that it does occur sometimes may be enough to affect the behavior of employees. To the extent that being fired is a plausible expectation, it does not need to happen to many public employees or too often. The mere possibility of losing the job or suffering negative changes in working conditions with a new administration may be enough to affect the behavior of patronage employees.

7.1.3   Political Services

In Latin American bureaucracies, the politicization of civil service regulations, the political bias in hiring and firing, and the fear employees have of job loss or downgraded working conditions, come hand-in-hand with the provision of political services by public sector employees. Indeed, on average, Latin American public employees are more involved in political activities and the provision of political services than non-public employees. According to cross-national survey data from the AmericasBarometer, Latin American public employees are more likely to participate in demonstrations and protests, to work for electoral campaigns, to participate in political meetings, to identify with a political party, and to vote than other workers.

   To compare the level of involvement in political activities and political services by public and non-public employees, I employ data from 135 AmericasBarometer surveys conducted in 2004, 2006/07, 2008, 2010, 2012, 2014, 2016/17, 2018/19 across eighteen Latin American countries (see

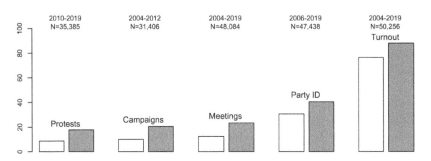

FIGURE 7.3 Political services by public and private sector employees in eighteen Latin American countries (2004–19)
Note: Public employees are those working for any level of the administration or a public-owned company (grey bars); salaried private employees are those employed in the private sector (white bars). Years and number of observations for each activity reported on top. Unweighted sample. Source: AmericasBarometer 2004–19.

Table 7.2 in the Chapter Appendix). Figure 7.3 plots the unweighted percentages of AmericasBarometer (2004–19) survey respondents who were employed in the public and private sector with a regular salary (*asalariados*) at the time of the survey and provided an affirmative answer when inquired about these political activities. Grey bars show the responses of public sector employees; white bars show the responses of salaried private sector employees.[11]

Figure 7.3 shows that public sector employees (grey bars) are more involved in political activities and political services than salaried private sector employees (white bars). While 18 percent of public employees reported having participated in a protest or demonstration in the last twelve months, the percentage drops to 9 percent for salaried private employees, a significant 9 percentage-point difference.[12] About 21 percent of public employees reported working for political parties or candidates in the last election, compared to 10 percent of private employees, a 10 percentage-point difference. In regard to attending the meetings of a political party or a political organization, the difference between

---

[11] See the Chapter Appendix for question wording, coding, descriptive statistics, and countries included (Tables 7.1 and 7.2). Public employees are state workers or workers at a state company; salaried private employees are those employed in the private sector getting a regular salary (*asalariados*). About half of all respondents in the sample reported having some type of job. Those who reported having a job also included business owners or partners, the self-employed, and unpaid workers. Comparing public employees to this broader group of workers yields very similar, albeit slightly smaller, differences in means. See Tables 7.3 and 7.4 in the Chapter Appendix.

[12] Differences for all activities are significant at the 99 percent level. See Table 7.3 in the Chapter Appendix for exact numeric values.

public employees (23 percent) and private employees (12 percent) is 11 percentage points. Public sector employees are also 10 percentage points more likely to identify themselves with a political party (40 percent) than private sector employees (31 percent). Finally, while 88 percent of public employees reported having voted in the last presidential election, the percentage drops to 76 percent for private employees, a 12 percentage-point difference.

Of course, public employees may be different from other workers in ways that are correlated with the likelihood of participating in these political activities. To control for some of these characteristics, I run a series of OLS and logistic regressions in which the dichotomous outcome variables are whether the respondent participates (1) or not (0) in each of the political activities. Each regression includes controls for age, gender, education, and dummy variables for year and country. The results are broadly consistent with the ones reported on Figure 7.3 (see Tables 7.5 and 7.6 in the Chapter Appendix).

7.2 A CLOSER LOOK AT THREE CASES

Can the theory of self-enforcing patronage explain patronage contracts in other countries in Latin America? In this section, I draw on three case studies to show in more detail that the patterns found in the three municipalities studied in the previous chapters are also present in other settings. For each case, I describe the strengths and weaknesses of the civil service system and provide evidence that, in line with the empirical implications of the theory of self-enforcing patronage, public employees are involved in political activities; there is partisan bias in hiring decisions; and patronage employees have good reasons to fear losing their jobs or suffering negative changes in their working conditions with a new administration. I first present evidence from Argentina to show that the three municipalities chosen were not outliers but representative of the patterns found in the rest of the country at different levels of the public administration. Then I focus on two other countries, one with a widely politicized bureaucracy – Bolivia – and one with a bureaucracy closer to the meritocratic Weberian ideal – Chile.

7.2.1 Argentina

At the outset of the 1990s, most Argentinean national public sector employees were discretionally appointed and obtained tenure after one year of service (Grindle 2012). There was no meritocratic system of recruitment in place, but job stability for public employees had been constitutionally guaranteed in 1949, which limited the extent of personnel turnover when administrations changed.[13] As a result,

---

[13] The 1949 Constitution – passed during Juan Domingo Perón's presidency – was largely ignored during the 1957 constitutional reform, which was based on the 1853 Constitution. The one notable exception was Article 14bis, guaranteeing (among other things) job stability for public sector employees.

many employees brought into the system through patronage remained in the public sector thanks to the tenure system (Grindle 2012). In 1991, a new civil service career system was introduced: SINAPA (*Sistema Nacional de la Profesión Administrativa*). Among the main characteristics of the reform was the introduction of meritocratic criteria and open competitions for hiring and promotions.[14] The system had a good start: by 1999, 25 percent of the total national administration had been recruited under the new rules (Ferraro 2011).

However, the new civil service system introduced in 1991 was not an obstacle to "massive political appointments a few years thereafter" (Ferraro 2011, 172). By 2007, the percentage of SINAPA employees in the national administration was reduced to 17 percent (Ferraro 2011, 170), and the system "had been largely pushed to the margin" by a resurgence of patronage appointments (Grindle 2012, 215; Iacoviello and Zuvanic 2006a).[15] Moreover, the establishment of SINAPA took place simultaneously with a process of decentralization (particularly in health and education) and the consequent growth of local administrations to which SINAPA did not apply. In 2008, SINAPA was replaced by SINEP (*Sistema Nacional de Empleo Público*), with one of the main differences between the systems being that while the older system gave priority to internal candidates, SINEP facilitates the entrance of personnel from outside the public administration. By 2012, however, only 12 percent of the national public administration operated under SINEP regulations (Pomares, Gasparin, and Deleersnyder 2013).

To avoid civil service regulations around hiring and firing, incumbents at all levels of the Argentinean government have come to use flexible short-term contracts (*contratados*), creating a parallel bureaucracy of temporary employees (Ferraro 2011; Grindle 2012; Iacoviello and Llano 2017; Scherlis 2013). The use of these type of contracts has increased significantly in the last two decades. Between 2003 and 2012, national public employment increased by 71 percent. During the same period, temporary personnel on short-term contracts (often hired as self-employed workers) increased by 224 percent, while personnel with regular contracts (both tenured and untenured, *de planta permanente y transitoria*) increased by 43 percent (Pomares, Gasparin, and Deleersnyder 2013). The participation of temporary employees on short-term contracts in the national public administration went from 17 percent in 2004 to 36 percent in 2014 (author's calculations based on

---

[14] Together with the civil service reform and other market-oriented reforms introduced in the 1990s, the national administration was downsized massively, reducing the number of public employees from 347,000 to 200,000 (Grindle 2012, 187). Provincial employment levels, in contrast, remained largely intact (Gibson and Calvo 2000). At the same time, about 300,000 public jobs at the national level disappeared as a result of the privatization of state companies and about 200,000 jobs (mainly in health and education) were transferred to provincial public sectors (Gibson and Calvo 2000).

[15] See Grindle (2012, 215–16) for a description of the variety of mechanisms used to bypass the civil service system.

Iacoviello and Llano 2017, 96).[16] And these numbers hide significant variation across agencies. For instance, in 2014, while 87 percent of the 10,008 employees at the Ministry of Welfare worked under flexible short-term contracts, only 1 percent of the 22,099 employees at AFIP, the agency responsible for tax collection, had these type of contracts (author's calculations based Iacoviello and Llano 2017, 97). Regardless of their initial contracts, many employees are eligible for tenure after serving for some time, resulting in a system that eventually bestows job security (*pase a planta*) to those appointed outside the system (Grindle 2012; Scherlis 2013).[17]

The flexibility in hiring and firing opens the door for political appointments. According to the experts and key informants interviewed by Panizza, Ramos Larraburu, and Scherlis (2018), patronage appointments can be found at all levels of the Argentinean national administration.[18] All the experts considered most appointments at the top level of the administration (just below positions such as ministers) to be political appointments, with 89 percent of experts estimating the proportion to be between 80 and 100 percent, while 11 percent put it in the 50–79 percent range. For middle levels of the administration – positions civil service regulations prescribed to be filled with career civil servants – 64 percent of experts estimated that more than 50 percent of appointments were political; 32 percent estimated the percentage to be between 10 and 49 percent; and only 4 percent of experts estimated that political appointments at this level were less than 10 percent. For lower levels of the administration, 21 percent of experts estimated the scope of political appointment to be on the 50–100 percent range, 32 percent estimated it to be in the 10–49 percent range, and 46 percent estimated that only a few (less than 10 percent) political appointments were made at this level (Panizza, Ramos Larraburu, and Scherlis 2018, 74). Besides political appointments, personal connections also matter when applying for a job in the Argentinean public administration. Indeed, the appointment of the relatives, friends, and acquaintances of public employees and politicians is a widespread practice, particularly at lower levels of the administration where strictly partisan appointments are less relevant (Scherlis 2013).

---

[16] Excluding police and military forces.

[17] Since 1992, public sector labor legislation stipulates annual negotiations with the unions over salaries and benefits. These annual meetings provide the setting for the unions to bargain over contracts, which make tenure rights more likely for many workers hired under short-term contracts that did not originally entitle them to tenure (Grindle 2012; see also, Scherlis 2013). This pressure from the unions to secure tenure contracts for their affiliates was mentioned in interviews in Salta and Santa Fe. In fact, a relatively high-rank political appointee in Santa Fe's provincial administration explained that there was an agreement between the municipality and the unions to give tenure to 10 to 12 local public employees per month (Author interview, Santa Fe, 7 June, 2010).

[18] The survey focuses on four ministries: Ministry of Agroindustry, Ministry of Social Development, Ministry of Foreign Affairs, and Ministry of the Economy.

As with the flexible short-term contracts described above, these estimations of the proportion of political appointments also hide significant variation in the degree of politicization across different agencies and policy sectors. For instance, political appointments have been traditionally common in welfare and public media, while foreign affairs and finance as well as the tax collection agency (AFIP) and the Central Bank are generally less politicized (Scherlis 2013). During the Kirchners' administrations (2003–15), three sectors became highly politicized: Telam, the national news agency, the Ministry of Welfare, and the National Institute of Statistics (INDEC) (Scherlis 2010, 139–43). The most infamous example of politicization happened at INDEC, where the government took over an institution largely considered professional and independent in order to manipulate inflation data (Boräng et al. 2018).

The perception of politicization and bias in hiring decisions that the experts interviewed by Panizza, Ramos Larraburu, and Scherlis (2018) described is corroborated by voter survey data. Using a novel methodology to measure the size of partisan networks and the proximity of individual voters to those networks, Calvo and Murillo (2013, 2019) show that voters' perceptions of the likelihood of being offered a public sector job increases with their proximity to party activists and candidates. In particular, proximity to the Peronist network (i.e., knowing more Peronist activists and candidates) is a statistically significant predictor of Peronist voters' expectations of receiving a public sector job from that party; while proximity to the Radical network increases the expectations of receiving a job from that party among Radical voters.[19] These results, they argue, suggest that jobs are likely going to core supporters "who serve as brokers getting votes for the party" (Calvo and Murillo 2013, 873).[20] Indeed, in the words of a Peronist politician: "where the party is the incumbent, the structure of the state is usually at the service of incumbent candidates . . . where the mayor was Peronist [in the province of Buenos Aires] there was a strong mobilization of what is called the 'municipal machine'" (cited by Calvo and Murillo 2019, 91).

Mass layoffs for political reasons with changes in the administration have not been common (Iacoviello and Zuvanic 2006a; Scherlis 2013), but individual cases still occur, especially in local administrations that are generally more politicized than the national one. When the Peronist Raúl Othacehé took office in 1989 as the new mayor of Merlo (Buenos Aires province), for instance, 1,200 supporters of the old mayor were fired. The previous mayor, Gustavo Green, also a Peronist, used to be on good terms with Othacehé. So much so that, following a request from Othacehé, Green had hired Othacehé's supporters in the local administration in order to finance their work during the

---

[19] The authors also find that proximity to partisan networks increases voters' perceptions of obtaining handouts and public works for their communities.

[20] For the perspective of the most politically active patronage employees (*militantes*) on how they reconcile their political work with their formal jobs in Argentina (and Brazil), see Rocca Rivarola (2019).

electoral campaign. When Othacehé fired Green's supporters, Green made public the letter in which Othacehé had asked him to distribute patronage jobs to "people who are with us, who work for the Peronist cause" (*gente que está con nosotros, que trabaja por la causa justicialista*) (M. O'Donnell 2005, 165). Another peculiar example is described by Stokes et al. (2013, 121). In this case, the turnover of public employees was not caused by a lost election but by a divorce. In the province of Córdoba, the Peronist Juan Manuel de la Sota was elected governor in 1999 and reelected in 2003; his wife Olga Riutort was put in charge of the Secretary of Government. When they divorced in 2005 and she left her position, one thousand people were fired.

At the national level, mass firings are not common with changes in the administration. In general, all top- and some mid-level bureaucrats are replaced, together with "those more obviously linked to previous political authorities or clearly identified as activists," but the rest of the jobs are usually maintained (Scherlis 2013, 73).[21] The partisan change in the national administration in 2015 may have been an exception. After twelve years of Peronist governments (Néstor Kirchner, 2003–07, and Cristina Fernández de Kirchner, 2007–15), Mauricio Macri (2015–19) of the right-wing party Propuesta Republicana (PRO) took office in December 2015. During his first months in power, a significant number of national public sector employees lost their jobs. Depending on the sources, the estimated numbers range from 8,000 to 25,000 (Moscovich 2016). In April 2016, the administration announced that the number of employees dismissed was 10,921, which constituted 5 percent of the 217,000 employees working directly for the executive at the time. The Minister of Modernization explained that they had revisited all the short-term contracts in place when they took office, and they had decided not to renew those 10,921. Almost all (90 percent) of the contracts that were not renewed were short-term hires made by the previous administration during its last two years in office (2013–15).[22]

Often, employees hired by previous administrations are not fired but are ignored, demoted, or bypassed. Because employees are routinely hired at the discretion of the administration in power and then locked in their positions with permanent contracts, politicians do not trust employees hired by previous administrations (Bambaci, Spiller, and Tommasi 2007; Ferraro 2011; Iacoviello and Llano 2017; Scherlis 2013). The practice of bypassing the merit system and sidestepping the permanent bureaucracy has become standard in the

[21] This is also true for those hired under short-term contracts (*contratados*): "even though many of them got their positions through a political connection, the large majority of personnel are much more concerned with keeping their jobs than with any party loyalty" (Scherlis 2013, 73).

[22] "El Gobierno informó que los despidos en la administración pública llegaron a los 10.921 trabajadores" (*La Nación*, April 5, 2016). See also "En el gobierno admiten que hubo 10.000 despidos en el Estado" (*Clarín*, April 1, 2016), "El gobierno confirma que no renovó cerca de 11.000 contratos" (*Clarín*, April 5, 2016), and "En tren de justificar despidos" (*Página12*, April 6, 2016).

Argentine administration. Frequently, new and "more trustworthy" employees are hired by expanding the overall number of officials, by restructuring or eliminating existing organizations and creating new ones, or by creating new job titles and responsibilities (Grindle 2012; Iacoviello and Zuvanic 2006a; Iacoviello and Llano 2017).

Like the national administration, most local governments have some sort of civil service regulations that include open competition for hires and tenure rights. Just as in the national administration, these regulations are easily bypassed through the widespread use of flexible short-term contracts (Gil García 2017; Scherlis 2010). However, provincial and municipal governments are more politicized than the national administration (Calvo and Murillo 2019; Scherlis 2010; Zuvanic, Iacoviello, and Gusta 2010). The distribution of patronage jobs to maintain a network of activists is much more common at the local level, where jobs are used "to organize, run, and mobilize extended electoral machines on the ground" (Scherlis 2010, 220). In fact, in his analysis of patronage appointments in four Argentinean provinces, Scherlis (2010, 251) concludes that: "no party can develop electoral machines without first controlling the state agencies that can provide the necessary financial, organizational, and human resources to do so."

Given these characteristics of the public administration at all levels of government, it is not surprising that, in line with the theory of self-enforcing patronage, public sector employees in Argentina are indeed more involved in political activities than non-public employees. According to a survey from 1997, political activists constituted 4.2 percent of public sector employees compared to 1.36 percent of the total population (cited by Calvo and Murillo 2019, 164). In the same vein, data from the AmericasBarometer (2004–19) shows that, compared to salaried private sector employees, Argentinean public employees are more likely to attend meetings of political parties or political organizations (by 13 percentage points), identify with a political party (by 11 percentage points), participate in demonstrations or protests (by 11 percentage points), participate in electoral campaigns (by 9 percentage points), and turn out to vote (by 5 percentage points) (see Table 7.7 in the Chapter Appendix).[23]

7.2.2   Bolivia

Since the 1980s, Bolivia has been implementing institutional reforms and attempting to create a meritocratic system in its public administration. Those efforts, however, have so far translated into very limited changes, creating only a few "meritocratic enclaves" within a highly politicized public sector (Zuvanic,

---

[23] All differences are significant at the 99 percent level. See the Chapter Appendix for details on the data. Comparing public sector employees to a broader set of workers, including salaried private employees but also business owners or partners, the self-employed, and unpaid workers yields very similar results (Table 7.7 in the Chapter Appendix). Regression analysis including controls for age, gender, education, and year fixed effects yields very similar results (Table 7.8).

Iacoviello, and Gusta 2010). Political criteria continue to dominate the process of hiring and firing, even though the few institutions reached by the institutional reforms have hired personnel through open public competitions (Iacoviello and Zuvanic 2006b; Zuvanic, Iacoviello, and Gusta 2010).

The Bolivian public administration has been described as a "patronage bureaucracy" (Zuvanic, Iacoviello, and Gusta 2010), "approaching the neo-patrimonial ideal type" (Gingerich 2013a), and as plagued with "bureaucratic informality" and "patronage appointments" (World Bank 2000). As described by Gingerich (2013a, 514), entry into the Bolivian administration "is supposedly based largely on partisan affiliation, not merit, and the assiduous cultivation of political contacts is characterized as the principal means of rising up the ranks."[24] According to the IDB index described above, in 2004 Bolivia was among the Latin American countries with the weakest merit systems, and with very politicized decisions regarding public employee selection and dismissal (Iacoviello 2006; Iacoviello and Zuvanic 2006b). With 22 points (ranking 9th out of 18 countries), Bolivia was below Argentina (52 points) and below the Latin American average (33 points) in the index, but still far from the worst cases of El Salvador (9 points) and Panama (2 points). In 2014, with a regional average of 42 points and several countries showing improvement, Bolivia's score decreased to 7 points. Together with Honduras, it scored lowest among the 16 countries included in the study (Cortázar Velarde, Lafuente, and Sanginés 2014).

Two main factors appear to explain this significant decrease (Iacoviello and Strazza 2014, 26). First, the agency in charge of implementing Bolivia's civil service reforms, the Superintendency (*Superintendencia del Servicio Civil*), an autonomous agency with ministerial rank, was replaced in 2006 by a third-tier unit, the General Directorate of the Civil Service (*Dirección General del Servicio Civil*). With this change, "the system's leadership lost both authority and political, technical, and coordinating capacity." Second, the MAS (*Movimiento al Socialismo*) government's decision to increase the participation of historically marginalized groups through discretional hiring instead of through competitions weakened the merit criteria in the administration.[25]

Indeed, when MAS leader Evo Morales (2006–19) was elected as the first indigenous president in Bolivian history, significant social and political transformations took place. Importantly, "new patterns of political incorporation" have empowered the majority indigenous population, which was long marginalized from politics, with both "inside" and "outside" ways to influence politics (Anria 2016). A significant number of Bolivians of indigenous

[24] Gingerich (2013a, 2013b) shows, however, that there is significant variation within the Bolivian public administration.

[25] The 2006 IDB report explicitly noted the low number of indigenous public sector employees in the administration (Iacoviello and Zuvanic 2006b, 101).

heritage (mainly Quechua and Aymara) were elected to office or appointed to positions in the administration. This was particularly visible in the Legislative Assembly, where the social and demographic profile of representatives has changed drastically since 2006. The share of seats held by middle-class professionals went from 49 percent in 1993–97 to 18 percent in 2010–14, while the seat share of artisans, workers, and those employed in the primary sector increased from 4 percent to 26 percent in the same period (Anria 2016). Descriptive representation – an increase in the presence of previously underrepresented groups such as women, the indigenous, and workers in general – has also improved significantly at the local level and in the judiciary (Wolff 2018). In the bureaucracy, improvement was more pronounced in certain areas than others; it was particularly prominent where policies affect defined constituencies, such as miners or peasants (Anria 2018, 143–49). In the Ministry of Rural Development and Land, for instance: "peasant groups have gained control ... Its social composition reveals the diversity of peasant-based groups in Bolivia, and top ministerial positions (as well as positions of medium importance) are staffed by grassroots leaders who represent civil society groups" (Anria 2018, 146). As a consequence of this more inclusive political system, turnout and reported support for and satisfaction with democracy increased among indigenous populations (Madrid 2012).

In line with other leftist governments in the region and with rising commodity prices (Polga-Hecimovich 2019), the size of the administration grew significantly under Morales. The total number of public employees increased from 38,258 in 2001 to 297,039 in 2013. Most of this increase came from decentralized offices and state-owned companies (many of them newly nationalized), which went from having 5,524 employees in 2001 to 193,659 in 2013 (Sologuren 2014, based on official data). Official data on the Bolivian administration is extremely limited. Indeed, researchers at a center within the Bolivian Vice-president's Office (*Centro de Investigaciones Sociales (CIS) de la Vicepresidencia*) assert that there is no institution in charge of collecting data on the bureaucracy (Sologuren, Pinto, and Durán 2014). They opted to conduct a survey (not a census) to collect basic information about the composition of the public administration. Comparing data from this survey, collected in 2013, with data from the last census of the public administration in 2001, Sologuren (2014) shows that the Bolivian administration is younger and more gender balanced than it was in 2001 and has a significant indigenous presence (the 2001 census did not ask about ethnicity).[26] In the parts of the administration selected for interviews,

---

[26] The survey included interviews with 1,174 public employees from three different areas of the public administration: the municipality of La Guardia, the Chuquisaca administration, and the Ministry of Education in La Paz. The comparisons with the 2001 census of the public administration are with employees from those three areas (Sologuren, Pinto, and Durán 2014).

46 percent of the respondents identified themselves as indigenous (mainly Quechua and Aymara).

Political connections are crucial for personnel decisions. A 1999 World Bank survey of 738 public employees at different hierarchical levels in fifteen different agencies supports this claim. Respondents were asked to estimate the ratio of public employees perceived to have been hired for political reasons in the agency where they worked; the average was 43 percent (World Bank 2000). When hires are political, new incumbents have good reasons to distrust old employees and to want to hire new (more loyal) ones, which in turn politicizes firing decisions. In a 2003 survey conducted by Gingerich across fourteen different institutions in Bolivia, in which 1,038 public employees were interviewed, respondents were asked to rank the importance of the following factors for dismissal from their institutions: poor performance, unethical behavior, insubordination, and political factors. Political factors were deemed as the most important determinant of dismissals by 32 percent of respondents. In the same vein, 68 percent of respondents indicated that it was "highly probable" or "probable" that they would lose their posts in the near future (Gingerich 2013b).[27]

Lazar's (2004) ethnographic account of local elections in El Alto (the poorest city in Bolivia, close to La Paz) presents a similar picture of political bias in hiring and firing. Residents in El Alto participate in campaign events such as rallies and political meetings to show loyalty to the party with the expectation of getting a job in return. Choosing the correct side is crucial: "family livelihoods depend on making the correct calculations about party allegiance since future employment may be linked to party membership" (Lazar 2004, 229). Jobs are part of the expectations of citizens, who feel that "if you had worked for the party, you should be rewarded" (Lazar 2004, 232). In the end, both low-level public employees and those with the expectation of becoming public employees end up providing a range of political services. This results in high levels of participation at the lower levels of the administration (Lazar 2004, 232). At the core of these high levels of participation are employees who think they may lose their jobs if the opposition gains power. Doña Sofía, for instance, a known militant for Condepa (the local incumbent party) who had worked in the administration for many years, "knew that when Condepa lost the election she would lose her job" (Lazar 2004, 232). As local public employees in Argentina, perceived supporters are afraid of a change in the administration, making them work hard to try to keep the incumbent in office: "It is almost as if Doña Sofía and Angela [her daughter] were standing for election themselves" (Lazar 2004, 232).

Although the social and ethnic composition of the administration has changed, other things are not that different from what scholars described in the 2000s. There

---

[27] Data from the survey conducted by the World Bank also reflects very high rates of personnel turnover. Among the employees interviewed, 54 percent reported the possibility of losing their jobs as likely or very likely, and 74 percent believed that turnover was a "serious" or "very serious" problem in the administration (World Bank 2000).

is still no civil service career path in place, and hiring and firing is essentially discretionary (*cargos de libre remoción*) (Cortázar Velarde, Lafuente, and Sanginés 2014; Sologuren, Pinto, and Durán 2014). Yet, Sologuren, Pinto, and Durán (2014), based on their survey of three institutions, argue that there is indeed an increase in the number of positions that are filled through open competitions. According to their public employee survey, there is also an increase in the use of short-term contracts compared to more regular contracts (*personal de planta*) (Sologuren 2014). Unfortunately, official data on the types of contracts in the administration is not available. However, the precarious state of Bolivian public employment is clear in the fact that in 2012 only 77 percent of public employees had health insurance associated with their jobs and only 82 percent had retirement benefits (Arcidiácono et al. 2014, 68): two benefits that regular (*de planta*) public employees always enjoyed.[28]

Among the public employees interviewed by Sologuren, Pinto, and Durán (2014), 50 percent at the Ministry of Education, 41 percent at La Guardia Municipality, and 9 percent at the Governorship of Chuquisaca reported being politically active (*militar*) in the MAS party.[29] At the same time, 37 percent reported being affiliated with a social organization (union or other organization). According to data from the AmericasBarometer (2004–19), compared to salaried private sector employees, Bolivian public employees are 8 percentage points more likely to participate in protests, 4 percentage points more likely to work in electoral campaigns, 10 percentage points more likely to attend meetings of political organizations, 9 percentage points more likely to identify with a political party, and 14 percentage points more likely to turn out to vote (see Table 7.7 in the Chapter Appendix).[30]

In sum, the weak Bolivian civil service system provides ample opportunity for patronage appointments that Bolivian politicians can use for political gain. Although the evidence in this regard is more anecdotal and indicative than conclusive, jobs in the Bolivian administration were and still appear to be disproportionally distributed to supporters. As detailed for the Argentinean municipalities studied in this book, patronage appointments tend to make public employees "respond primarily to their patrons and perform functions

---

[28] In terms of public employees' health insurance coverage, Bolivia ranked tenth out of the twelve countries included in the study, only scoring better than Ecuador and Peru. In terms of retirement benefits, only Paraguay, Mexico and Honduras scored worse than Bolivia (out of fourteen countries) (Arcidiácono et al. 2014, 68).

[29] In the World Bank survey described above, 30 percent of the employees interviewed reported having made some contribution to a political party (World Bank 2000). In Gingerich's 2003 survey, he finds 14 percent of respondents to be affiliated with a political party (Gingerich 2013b, 196).

[30] All differences are significant at the 99 percent level. Comparing public employees to a broader group of workers (including salaried private employees, business owners or partners, self-employed workers, and unpaid workers) yields similar results (see Table 7.7). Regression analysis including controls for age, gender, education, and year fixed effects yields similar results, except in the case of working for campaigns that lack statistical significance once controls are included and turnout that, while still significant, yields a smaller coefficient (see Table 7.8 in the Chapter Appendix).

that may or may not be among their official duties" (World Bank 2000, 45). Bolivian parties rely on the bureaucracy for political support activities that go beyond the official duties of public sector jobs. Political connections seem to be still fundamental in hiring and firing decisions; connections with social movements, particularly with those that represent the historically marginalized indigenous population, are now also important (Anria 2018).

7.2.3   Chile

On the opposite end of the spectrum, the Chilean national public sector is considered to closely approximate a highly professional, Weberian ideal-type bureaucracy, displaying a "comparatively high level of capacity and autonomy" (Luna and Mardones 2016, 40). Indeed, Chilean "meritocratic bureaucracy" is characterized not only by a high degree of autonomy – isolation from political manipulation – but also by high levels of technical capacity (Zuvanic, Iacoviello, and Gusta 2010). Together with Brazil, Chile has one of the most developed civil service systems in the region (Cortázar Velarde, Lafuente, and Sanginés 2014), making it a hard case for testing the theory of self-enforcing patronage. According to the merit index described in Section 7.1, Chile – together with Brazil and Costa Rica – was classified in 2004 among the region's strongest merit systems, in which there is widespread acceptance of meritocratic principles for selection, promotion, and dismissal of public employees (Iacoviello 2006). Ranked second out of the eighteen countries in the study, Chile, with 62 points, was far above the Latin American average of 33 points and above Argentina's score of 52 points. By 2014, Chile had improved its score to 67, ranking fourth of sixteen countries on the merit index (after Brazil, Costa Rica, and Uruguay) and significantly above the average of 40 points for the region (Cortázar Velarde, Lafuente, and Sanginés 2014).

Since 1960, once appointed (generally through patronage), Chilean public sector employees have enjoyed tenure rights (Grindle 2012). Since 1989, the Administrative Statute (*Estatuto Administrativo*, Law 18,834) regulates the civil service, with clear rules about hiring and promotions as well as competition for entry into certain positions in the public administration. Moreover, following a corruption scandal involving the payment of additional salaries, in cash, to senior bureaucrats (*sobresueldos*) in the Ministry of Public Works, a new civil service reform was passed in 2003. The newly created *Sistema de Alta Dirección Pública* (Law 19,882) introduced merit criteria for senior executive positions in 100 public agencies (out of the 141 that existed at the time).[31] By December 2010,

---

[31] The new recruitment system (overseen by a political commission) put some limits on discretionary appointments but "left considerable room for discretion by hiring officials" (Grindle 2012, 224). Candidates for open positions are selected based on merit and included on lists of three or five candidates (depending on the position), but the final decision among those finalists is made by a politician at his or her own discretion. If none of the candidates is chosen, the position can remain open.

the system covered 915 senior positions. Indeed, the positions open to competition increased from 4 percent in 2003 to 80 percent in 2010. Turnover remained low: between 2006 and 2009, removals of senior bureaucrats amounted to only 4 to 8 percent, depending on rank (Cortázar Velarde, Lafuente, and Sanginés 2014). In part because of this system, Chile is considered a regional leader in terms of civil service professionalization and meritocracy (Cortázar Velarde, Lafuente, and Sanginés 2014).

However, as in Argentina, Bolivia, and other Latin American countries, the use of flexible short-term contracts allows hiring outside the system. Employees under short-term contracts in Chile not only do not enjoy job stability, but they are also not legally required to be hired through an open competition.[32] Nevertheless, even under these conditions, 50 percent of temporary positions are still filled with open, meritocratic recruitment (Llano 2014, 17). Since 2009, all positions, including temporary ones, can be advertised on an official portal (www.empleospublicos.cl), which makes information about vacancies of all types easily available to everyone.[33] In a large survey of national civil servants (*funcionarios*) conducted in 2019, 50 percent of those hired in the last five years reported having heard about their jobs through some sort of public advertisement (Schuster et al. 2020).[34]

The use of short-term contracts has significantly increased in recent years. Between 2006 and 2016, the central public administration went from having 201,857 to 296,080 employees, a 47 percent increase. During the same period, the administration shows a decrease in 6,313 permanent employees (*de planta*), while the number of temporary contracts increased for all categories: 82,406 more employees hired on annual contracts (*a contrata*), 16.593 more hired as freelance workers (*a honorarios*), and 1.537 more hired under *Código de Trabajo* regulations, which govern the rights of private sector employees (Chamorro and Rosende 2018). By 2018, the majority of employees in the national administration were *a contrata* (56 percent), followed by *de planta*

---

[32] There are two main types of temporary contracts in the Chilean administration: those subject to renewal on December 31 of each year (*a contrata*) and those that can be terminated at any time (*a honorarios*) and are, in theory, hired for specific tasks that are not part of the ordinary administration. In practice, many of these freelance workers perform regular tasks in the administration for long periods of time, without any of the rights and benefits of public employees, such as the right to unionize, maternity and paternity leave, paid vacations, or sick leave. There is a third category of temporary contracts (*Código de Trabajo*) that basically have the same rights as private employees; it's a small group in the administration, concentrated in specific agencies (Valdebenito Pedrero 2017).

[33] In 2009, the portal advertised thirty-five positions and 5,224 applications were received; in 2013, 2,778 positions were advertised, and 186,727 applications were received (Llano 2014).

[34] The survey was conducted online in 2019 in cooperation with the Chilean National Department of Civil Service. Around 21,400 bureaucrats across sixty-five different areas of the administration participated. Participants in the survey were disproportionally male, between thirty and forty-nine years old, and more educated than the average civil servant (Schuster et al. 2020).

(23 percent), and *a honorarios* (9 percent) (Dirección de Presupuestos del Ministerio de Hacienda 2019).[35]

Despite the proliferation of these temporary contracts, the level of stability in the national public sector has been quite high (Iacoviello 2009a; Llano 2014). The average time in the administration for an employee on an annual contract was ten years (Llano 2014).[36] The fact that the same center-left coalition won the presidency four times consecutively between 1990 and 2010 (Patricio Aylwin, Eduardo Frei, Ricardo Lagos, and Michelle Bachelet) is probably an important factor in maintaining this stability. When Sebastián Piñera became president in 2010 with the support of a right-wing coalition, the new administration "worked to reclaim positions that were filled through the new high-level appointment system so that they could be assigned to political appointees" (Grindle 2012, 226). Indeed, the number of employees on annual contracts which were not renewed increased around the time of the 2010 election, and the same happened in 2014 when Michelle Bachelet returned to the presidency (Llano 2014).[37] Turnover for senior positions rose from 4 percent for senior level I positions and 8 percent for level II positions between 2006 and 2009 to 64 percent and 24 percent, respectively, in 2010 (Cortázar Velarde, Lafuente, and Sanginés 2014).

Even with the implementation of civil service reforms and the relatively frequent use of open and competitive hiring processes, political ideology and personal and political connections still matter for appointments to the public administration. In the large survey of bureaucrats mentioned above, 36 percent of respondents reported that the help of family, friends, or other personal contact had at least some importance in their obtaining a job in the public sector; while 10 percent reported that the help of a politician or someone with political connections had at least some importance in their gaining a job (Schuster et al. 2020). Moreover, in a survey of voters, Calvo and Murillo (2013, 2019) show that the perceived likelihood of being offered a public sector job decreases with ideological distance from the five main Chilean parties of the period.[38] The greater the ideological distance between the party and the voter, the lower the expectation of receiving a public job from that party. For instance, a one-point increase in ideological distance (measured on a ten-point scale) from the Socialist Party results in a 4.24 percent decrease in the estimated likelihood of being offered a public sector job by that party. At the same time, knowing relatively more PS and PPD party activists (a way of

---

[35] The remaining contracts were *Código de Trabajo* (5 percent), substitutes (5 percent), and other types of contracts (1 percent) (Dirección de Presupuestos del Ministerio de Hacienda 2019).

[36] Note, however, that this number is based on interviews and not official data.

[37] In 2008, the number of personnel on annual contracts (*a contrata*) whose contracts were not renewed was 3,027, increasing to 4,338 in 2009, 5,176 in 2010, and 7,394 in 2011 (Llano 2014, 21).

[38] Partido Socialista (PS), Partido por la Democracia (PPD), Democracia Cristiana (DC), Unión Demócrata Independiente (UDI), and Renovación Nacional (RN).

measuring proximity to partisan networks) increases the perceived likelihood of being offered a job (Calvo and Murillo 2013). Unquestionably, political networks have a more crucial role in shaping the expectations of obtaining a public sector job in Argentina than in Chile, yet incumbency and the possibility of distributing public employment also matters in Chile for partisan network building (Calvo and Murillo 2019).[39]

In contrast to the characterization of the Chilean national administration as generally having high levels of stability, in the survey of public employees conducted by Gingerich (2013b) described above, 40 percent of respondents estimated that it was "highly probable" or "probable" that they would lose their jobs in the near future (compared to 68 percent in the Bolivian case).[40] The change in administration in 2010, after twenty years of presidents from the same coalition, showed that the fear was justified. Only three months after Piñera's inauguration in March 2010, 1,400 public employees were fired, and another 1,200 contracts that were subject to renewal were terminated. The president justified the mass layoffs by characterizing those fired as political activists (*operadores*).[41] The majority of senior executives in the administration when Piñera took office were fired (Garrido Silva 2013, 13). By August 2012, of the 529 senior bureaucrats hired through the High-Level Public Management System and still in office, 473 (89 percent) had been hired during Piñera's administration (Garrido Silva 2013, 10).[42] In the survey of Chilean bureaucrats conducted by Schuster et al. (2020), 49 percent of respondents reported that government transitions have an effect on their job stability.

Local administrations – as in other Latin American countries – are significantly more politicized than the national administration (Calvo and Murillo 2019; Fuenzalida, Inostroza, and Morales 2014; Leyton Navarro 2006). The 2003 national civil service reform left regional and municipal

---

[39] Partisan networks are also more ideological in Chile than in Argentina. Chilean left-wing voters are significantly more likely to know activists from the leftist parties while right-wing voters are more likely to know activists from the right-wing parties. Argentinean voters' ideology, in contrast, is not associated with their connections to Radical or Peronist activists. Regardless of ideology, and because the Peronist network is larger, all voters were more likely to know more Peronist than non-Peronist activists (Calvo and Murillo 2019).

[40] For Chile, the survey included 595 public employees across six national agencies (Gingerich 2013b). Note that the survey was conducted in 2004, before the 2003 civil service reform was fully implemented.

[41] "Piñera justificó despidos masivos en el sector público" (Emol, June 10, 2010). See also "Gobierno desvinculó a 1373 personas y no renovó 1255 contratos hasta el 31 de mayo" (*El Mercurio*, June 10, 2010); "PRSD y ANEF amenazan con acusación constitucional contra Lavín por despidos" (Emol, June 13, 2010); and "PS solidariza con paro de ANEF y denuncia hostigamiento a funcionarios públicos" (Emol, August 26, 2010).

[42] Based on information obtained from the High-Level Public Management System. Note that the president can legally fire all bureaucrats hired under this system, even before their contracts expire. The main difference is that employees receive severance pay if the contract is ended early (Garrido Silva 2013).

administrations in Chile largely untouched (Cortázar Velarde, Fuenzalida, and Lafuente 2016), so local bureaucracies exhibit lower levels of professionalization than the national bureaucracy and higher levels of public employee turnover (Fuenzalida, Inostroza, and Morales 2014). A city councilman from the Socialist Party explains it bluntly: "in the municipalities there is a strong party base for employment because there is no High Management System. Instead, they have a fiction about competition of the employees that are already there but in general many local [political] operators have taken refuge in the municipality" (cited by Calvo and Murillo 2019, 92). As in Argentina and Bolivia, with a new administration, negative changes in working conditions or even potential job losses seem very plausible to at least some Chilean employees. Another interview with a Chilean mayor talking about his retirement illustrates this point: "I have not retired from [current municipality of which he is mayor] because this is a very large municipality ... There is a very large team of people working with me here, they depend directly from me, and therefore I cannot make the decision on my own. If I leave, around 500 people fall [lose their jobs]" (cited by Calvo and Murillo 2019, 92).

The widespread use of temporary contracts gives full discretion in hiring and firing to the incumbent. As in the national public administration, the use of these contracts at the local and municipal level has increased in recent years. From 2008 to 2014, the number of municipal employees increased by about 44 percent, from 57,916 to 83,204 employees: 284 more permanent employees *(de planta)*, 1,807 more employees with annual contracts *(a contrata)*, and 23,179 employees on freelance contracts *(a honorarios)*. In 2014, the majority of public employees at the local level were on freelance contracts (50 percent), followed by permanent contracts (34 percent), and annual contracts (16 percent). That same year, ten municipalities employed more than 82 percent of their personnel under freelance contracts (Valdebenito Pedrero 2017, based on official data).[43]

Chilean mayors thus have full discretion to hire and fire as they please, which has allowed them to build a partisan network for voter mobilization within the local administration (Corvalan, Cox, and Osorio 2018; Toro 2017). Consistent with the use of municipal resources for electoral mobilization, a higher rate of municipal employment has been shown to be correlated with higher levels of local voter turnout (Mimica and Navia 2019). According to data from the Chilean National Institute of Statistics from 2003, 1.17 percent of public sector employees reported participation in political parties compared to 0.19 percent of the general population (cited by Calvo and Murillo 2019, 164). Similarly, data from the AmericasBarometer (2004–19) shows that, compared to salaried private employees, Chilean public employees are

---

[43] Valdebenito Pedrero (2017) contrasts this official information with information provided by the Tax Revenue System and finds that the number of *a honorarios* or freelance employees appeared to be even higher than what the government reports.

9 percentage points more likely to participate in protests, 6 percentage points more likely to help with campaigns, 5 percentage points more likely to attend political meetings, and 11 percentage points more likely to vote (see Table 7.7 in the Chapter Appendix).[44]

7.3 SUMMARY

This chapter shows that there are good reasons to expect that the theory of self-enforcing patronage developed in this book will carry strong explanatory power in other countries in Latin America. Most Latin American administrations have weak civil service systems with ample opportunities for partisan and personal bias in hiring and firing, which causes many public employees to be afraid of a change in administration. This alignment of interests makes them loyal supporters of the *status quo* and, as a consequence, more likely participants in political activities that could help the incumbent stay in power. Indeed, across Latin American countries, public sector employees are more likely to be involved in political activities such as attending political meetings and helping with electoral campaigns. Even in a country like Chile, with one of the most professionalized public administrations in the region, there is evidence consistent with the theory of self-enforcing patronage. The Chilean civil service system still allows for significant discretion in hiring and firing, especially at the local level but, as shown with the after effects of the election of Piñera in 2010, it also can take place at the national level. In Chile, as in the rest of Latin America, there are good reasons for supporters to fear a change in administration.

7.4 CHAPTER APPENDIX

LAPOP DATA: QUESTION WORDING AND CODING

Dataset: "2004–18 LAPOP AmericasBarometer Merge (v1.0 w)." Source: The AmericasBarometer by the Latin American Public Opinion Project (LAPOP), www.LapopSurveys.org. Downloaded from http://datasets.americasbarometer.org.eu1.proxy.openathens.net/database/index.php (last accessed January 1, 2020).

---

[44] All differences are significant at the 99 percent level. Unlike Argentina and Bolivia, and Latin American countries in general (when polling all countries together), the AmericasBarometer data do not show that Chilean public sector employees are more likely to identify with a political party than salaried private employees. Using an alternative coding for non-public employees that includes salaried private employees, business owners and partners, self-employed workers, and unpaid workers yield similar results (see Table 7.7). Results are also robust to regression analysis including controls for age, education, gender, and year fixed effects (see Table 7.8 in the Chapter Appendix).

Public Employee

Question (only to those who replied in the previous question that they were working): "In this job you are: 1) A salaried employee of the government or an independent state-owned enterprise? 2) A salaried employee in the private sector? 3) Owner or partner in a business? 4) Self-employed? or 5) Unpaid worker?"

Coding: Public Employee I is coded "1" if individuals responded with option 1 and "0" if individuals responded option 2; all other responses are coded as missing. Public Employee II is coded "1" if individuals responded with option 1 and "0" otherwise (response options 2, 3, 4, or 5).

Protests

Question: "In the last 12 months, have you participated in a demonstration or protest march?"

Coding: "1" if individuals responded yes, and "0" otherwise.

Campaigns

Question: "There are people who work for parties or candidates during electoral campaigns. Did you work for any candidate or party in the last presidential elections?"

Coding: "1" if individuals responded yes, and "0" otherwise.

Meetings

Question: "I am going to read you a list of groups and organizations. Please tell me if you attend meetings of these organizations **at least** once a week, once or twice a month, once or twice a year, or never (. . .) Meetings of a political party or political organization? Do you attend them . . . ?"

Coding: "1" if individuals responded once a week, once or twice a month, or once or twice a year, and "0" if they responded never.

Party ID

Question: "Do you currently identify with a political party?"

Coding: "1" if individuals responded yes, and "0" otherwise.

Turnout

Question: "Did you vote in the last presidential elections of (year)?"

Coding: "1" if individuals responded yes, and "0" otherwise.

TABLE 7.1 *LAPOP data (2004–19) – Descriptive statistics*

Variable	N	Mean	Std. Dev.	Min	Max
Public Employee I	51,668	.278	.448	0	1
Public Employee II	110,525	.130	.336	0	1
Protests	144,663	.090	.286	0	1
Campaigns	129,531	.104	.305	0	1
Meetings	207,336	.149	.356	0	1
Party ID	193,317	.314	.464	0	1
Turnout	217,066	.756	.430	0	1
Education	223,400	9.24	4.54	0	18
Female	226,439	.513	.50	0	1
Age	226,021	39.41	16.05	16	112
Country	226,454			1	18
Year	226,454			2004	2019

TABLE 7.2 *LAPOP data (2004–19) – Observations by country and wave (year)*

Variable	N	2004	2006/7	2008	2010	2012	2014	2016/7	2018/9
Argentina	8,976			✓	✓	✓	✓	✓	✓
Bolivia	21,569	✓	✓	✓	✓	✓	✓	✓	✓
Brazil	11,222		✓	✓	✓	✓	✓	✓	✓
Chile	11,414		✓	✓	✓	✓	✓	✓	✓
Colombia	12,213	✓	✓	✓	✓	✓	✓	✓	✓
C. Rica	12,046	✓	✓	✓	✓	✓	✓	✓	✓
DR	15,047	✓	✓	✓	✓	✓	✓	✓	✓
Ecuador	17,991	✓	✓	✓	✓	✓	✓	✓	✓
El Salvador	12,488	✓	✓	✓	✓	✓	✓	✓	✓
Guatemala	12,395	✓	✓	✓	✓	✓	✓	✓	✓
Honduras	12,612	✓	✓	✓	✓	✓	✓	✓	✓
Mexico	12,476	✓	✓	✓	✓	✓	✓	✓	✓
Nicaragua	12,607	✓	✓	✓	✓	✓	✓	✓	✓
Panama	12,455	✓	✓	✓	✓	✓	✓	✓	✓
Paraguay	9,888		✓	✓	✓	✓	✓	✓	✓
Peru	11,668		✓	✓	✓	✓	✓	✓	✓
Uruguay	10,319		✓	✓	✓	✓	✓	✓	✓
Venezuela	9,068		✓	✓	✓	✓	✓	✓	

TABLE 7.3 *Political services by public and salaried private sector employees (t-tests)*

	Protests	Campaigns	Meetings	Party ID	Turnout
Public Employees	0.18	0.21	0.23	0.40	0.88
	(0.004)	(0.004)	(0.004)	(0.004)	(0.003)
	N=10,149	N=8,557	N=13,364	N=13,243	N=14,026
Salaried Private Employees	0.09	0.10	0.12	0.31	0.76
	(0.002)	(0.002)	(0.002)	(0.002)	(0.002)
	N=25,236	N= 22,849	N=34,720	N=34,195	N=36,230
Difference in means	0.09***	0.10***	0.11***	0.10***	0.12***
	(0.004)	(0.005)	(0.004)	(0.005)	(0.004)
	N=35,385	N=31,406	N=48,084	N=47,438	N=50,256
Years	2010–19	2004–12	2004–19	2006–19	2004–19
# of countries	18	18	18	18	18

Note: Unweighted sample. Public employees are those employed at any level of the state government or a state company. Salaried private employees are those employed in the private sector with a regular salary (*asalariados*). Two-sample *t*-test with unequal variance. Standard errors in parentheses. *** $p < 0.01$, ** $p < 0.05$, * $p < 0.1$.

TABLE 7.4 *Political services by public and non-public sector employees (t-tests)*

	Protests	Campaigns	Meetings	Party ID	Turnout
Public Employees	0.18	0.21	0.23	0.40	0.88
	(0.004)	(0.004)	(0.004)	(0.004)	(0.003)
	N=10,149	N=8,557	N=13,364	N=13,243	N=14,026
Non-Public Employees	0.09	0.11	0.15	0.32	0.78
	(0.001)	(0.001)	(0.001)	(0.002)	(0.001)
	N=65,550	N=58,318	N=90,059	N=86,636	N=92,929
Difference in means	0.09***	0.09***	0.08***	0.09***	0.10***
	(0.004)	(0.005)	(0.004)	(0.005)	(0.003)
	N=75,699	N=66,875	N=103,423	N=99,879	N=106,955
Years	2010–19	2004–12	2004–19	2006–19	2004–19
# of countries	18	18	18	18	18

Note: Unweighted sample. Public employees are those employed at any level of the state government or a state company. Non-public employees are those holding any type of employment (salaried private sector, self-employed, business owners or partners, and unpaid workers). Two-sample *t*-test with unequal variance. Standard errors in parentheses. *** $p < 0.01$, ** $p < 0.05$, * $p < 0.1$.

TABLE 7.5 *Political services in Latin America – OLS regressions*

	Protests	Campaigns	Meetings	Party ID	Turnout
Public Employee	0.07***	0.09***	0.10***	0.08***	0.04***
(0–1)	(0.00)	(0.01)	(0.00)	(0.01)	(0.00)
Education	0.01***	0.00***	0.00	0.00***	0.01***
(in years)	(0.00)	(0.00)	(0.00)	(0.00)	(0.00)
Female	−0.00	−0.02***	−0.02***	−0.04***	0.02***
(0–1)	(0.00)	(0.00)	(0.00)	(0.00)	(0.00)
Age	−0.00	0.00***	0.00***	0.00***	0.01***
(in years)	(0.00)	(0.00)	(0.00)	(0.00)	(0.00)
Constant	−0.03***	−0.01	0.10***	0.17***	0.33***
	(0.01)	(0.01)	(0.01)	(0.02)	(0.01)
Country FE	YES	YES	YES	YES	YES
Year FE	YES	YES	YES	YES	YES
Observations	35,132	31,157	47,701	47,119	49,856
R-squared	0.04	0.04	0.07	0.10	0.13

Note: OLS regressions with political services as dependent variables. Public employee coded "1" for public employees, and "0" for salaried private employees. All regressions include controls for age, gender, education, and country and year fixed effects. Weighted data (so each country has an N=1,500). Standard errors in parentheses were calculated using the STATA svyset command to account for design effects, due to clustering, weighting, and stratification. *** $p < 0.01$, ** $p < 0.05$, * $p < 0.1$.

TABLE 7.6 *Political services in Latin America – Logistic regressions*

	Protests	Campaigns	Meetings	Party ID	Turnout
Public Employees	0.65***	0.73***	0.74***	0.37***	0.34***
(0–1)	(0.04)	(0.04)	(0.03)	(0.03)	(0.03)
Education	0.09***	0.04***	0.00	0.02***	0.10***
(in years)	(0.01)	(0.00)	(0.00)	(0.00)	(0.00)
Female	−0.06*	−0.15***	−0.21***	−0.18***	0.10***
(0–1)	(0.04)	(0.04)	(0.03)	(0.02)	(0.03)
Age	−0.00**	0.01***	0.01***	0.02***	0.07***
(in years)	(0.00)	(0.00)	(0.00)	(0.00)	(0.00)
Constant	−3.80***	−3.21***	−2.16***	−1.52***	−2.06***
	(0.14)	(0.13)	(0.11)	(0.09)	(0.09)
Country FE	YES	YES	YES	YES	YES
Year FE	YES	YES	YES	YES	YES
Observations	35,132	31,157	47,701	47,119	49,856

Note: Logistic regressions with political services as dependent variables. Public employee coded "1" for public employees, and "0" for salaried private employees. All regressions include controls for age, gender, education, and country and year fixed effects. Weighted data (so each country has an N=1,500). Standard errors in parentheses were calculated using the STATA svyset command to account for design effects, due to clustering, weighting, and stratification. *** $p < 0.01$, ** $p < 0.05$, * $p < 0.1$.

TABLE 7.7 *Political services by public and non-public sector employees (t-tests) in Argentina, Bolivia, and Chile*

		Protests	Campaigns	Meetings	Party ID	Turnout
Compared to Salaried Private Employees	Argentina	0.11***	0.09***	0.13***	0.11***	0.05***
		(0.017)	(0.018)	(0.015)	(0.018)	(0.011)
		N=2,306	N=1,571	N=2,475	N=2,872	N=2,915
	Bolivia	0.08***	0.04***	0.10***	0.09***	0.14***
		(0.017)	(0.016)	(0.014)	(0.016)	(0.012)
		N=2,461	N=1,791	N=2,773	N=3,079	N=3,124
	Chile	0.09***	0.06***	0.05***	0.03	0.11***
		(0.020)	(0.019)	(0.014)	(0.018)	(0.020)
		N=2,699	N=2,013	N=3,026	N=3,596	N=3,475
Compared to all other workers	Argentina	0.12***	0.09***	0.11***	0.10***	0.07***
		(0.016)	(0.017)	(0.015)	(0.016)	(0.010)
		N=4,201	N=2,620	N=4,289	N=5,026	N=5,101
	Bolivia	0.08***	0.06***	0.09***	0.06***	0.08***
		(0.014)	(0.014)	(0.013)	(0.014)	(0.078)
		N=7,658	N=5344	N=8,250	N=9,268	N=9,400
	Chile	0.10***	0.06***	0.05***	0.03	0.09***
		(0.019)	(0.019)	(0.013)	(0.018)	(0.020)
		N=4,049	N=2,958	N=4,495	N=5,305	N=5,127
	Years	2010–19	2004–12	2004–19	2006–19	2004–19

Note: Unweighted sample. Difference in means between public sector employees and a) salaried private sector employees (rows 1–3), and b) all other workers (rows 4–6) who participate in each of the political activities. Public employees are those employed at any level of the state government or a state company. Salaried private employees are those employed in the private sector (*asalariados*); other workers include salaried private employees, business owners and partners, self-employed and unpaid workers. Two-sample *t*-test with unequal variance. Standard errors in parentheses. *** $p < 0.01$, ** $p < 0.05$, * $p < 0.1$.

TABLE 7.8 *Political services in Argentina, Bolivia, and Chile – OLS regressions*

	Argentina					Bolivia					Chile				
	Protests	Campaigns	Meetings	Party ID	Turnout	Protests	Campaigns	Meetings	Party ID	Turnout	Protests	Campaigns	Meetings	Party ID	Turnout
Public Employee	0.09***	0.10***	0.14***	0.10***	0.03**	0.07***	0.03	0.12***	0.10***	0.05***	0.07***	0.06***	0.04***	0.01	0.07***
	(0.02)	(0.02)	(0.02)	(0.02)	(0.01)	(0.02)	(0.02)	(0.02)	(0.02)	(0.01)	(0.02)	(0.02)	(0.01)	(0.02)	(0.02)
Education	0.01***	-0.00	0.00	0.00	0.00***	0.00	0.00	-0.01***	-0.01***	0.01***	0.01***	0.00***	0.00***	0.01***	0.02***
	(0.00)	(0.00)	(0.00)	(0.00)	(0.00)	(0.00)	(0.00)	(0.00)	(0.00)	(0.00)	(0.00)	(0.00)	(0.00)	(0.00)	(0.00)
Female	0.01	-0.02	-0.07***	-0.06***	0.01	-0.04*	-0.06***	-0.03*	-0.08***	0.03*	-0.02	-0.01	-0.02***	-0.02*	0.01
	(0.01)	(0.01)	(0.01)	(0.02)	(0.01)	(0.02)	(0.02)	(0.01)	(0.02)	(0.02)	(0.01)	(0.01)	(0.01)	(0.01)	(0.02)
Age	-0.00	0.00	-0.00	0.00***	0.00***	0.00	0.00***	0.00	0.00*	0.01***	-0.00***	0.00	0.00*	0.00***	0.01***
	(0.00)	(0.00)	(0.00)	(0.00)	(0.00)	(0.00)	(0.00)	(0.00)	(0.00)	(0.00)	(0.00)	(0.00)	(0.00)	(0.00)	(0.00)
Constant	-0.00	0.12***	0.16***	0.11**	0.63***	0.09*	0.01	0.13***	0.34***	0.24***	0.02	-0.01	-0.01	-0.05	-0.07
	(0.05)	(0.04)	(0.03)	(0.04)	(0.03)	(0.05)	(0.04)	(0.03)	(0.05)	(0.04)	(0.04)	(0.03)	(0.02)	(0.05)	(0.06)
Year FE	Yes	Yes	Yes	Yes	Yes	Yes	Yes	Yes	Yes	Yes	Yes	Yes	Yes	Yes	Yes
Obs.	2,288	1,561	2,455	2,851	2,893	2,453	1,787	2,766	3,072	3,115	2,685	1,998	3,009	3,579	3,459
R-squared	0.05	0.03	0.06	0.03	0.05	0.02	0.03	0.04	0.05	0.17	0.06	0.02	0.02	0.05	0.18

Note: OLS regressions with political services as dependent variables. Public employee coded "1" for public employees, and "0" for salaried private employees. All regressions include controls for age, gender, education, and year fixed effects. Standard errors in parentheses were calculated using the STATA svyset command to account for design effects, due to clustering, weighting, and stratification. *** $p < 0.01$, ** $p < 0.05$, * $p < 0.1$.

8

Conclusions and Broader Implications

This final chapter revisits the book's main argument and discusses the main findings and implications. It begins by summarizing its theory about the sustainability of patronage contracts that exchange public sector jobs for political services without a need for punishment or reciprocity and the main empirical findings that support the theory. It then discusses the theory's implications for our understanding of patronage employees' motives and behavior, as well as of clientelistic exchanges more broadly. Following this, the chapter discusses the likelihood of curbing clientelism if the theory of self-enforcing patronage advanced here is correct. The chapter concludes with a discussion of the particularly damaging effects of patronage for the quality of democracy and equal access to the state.

8.1 REVISITING THE ARGUMENT

In this book, I set out to answer two main questions: *what* do public sector employees do in exchange for their jobs and *why* do they do it? In the preceding chapters, I showed that public employees under patronage contracts provide political services to the patron who hires them. These services – attending rallies, helping with campaigns, monitoring elections, and granting favors – are essential for obtaining and maintaining electoral support. Incumbents' ability to distribute public sector jobs to people who will provide political services gives politicians a powerful electoral tool. In fact, political services are the key mechanism that explains the connection between patronage appointments and electoral competition. Importantly, the patronage employees involved in these services are not just the political brokers who have been the main focus of the literature so far. Numerous other more anonymous and less influential but still important public employees are also involved in the provision of political services.

Patronage contracts, however, are risky. Since the exchange of the job for political support is sequenced and the law cannot be used to enforce such agreements, defection and betrayal are always a possibility. In this book, I have focused on the commitment problems that arise from the sequenced nature of the exchange in one particular case: when the politician distributes public sector jobs with the expectation of obtaining future political support from the client. Citizens who receive public sector jobs with the implicit or explicit understanding that they will provide political services in return can easily renege on their side of the agreement *after* getting the job. Why would patronage employees comply with their side of the agreement?

This book develops a novel explanation for why public sector employees (the clients) comply with their side of the patronage contract even after obtaining the job from the politician (the patron). Departing from existing explanations, the theory of self-enforcing patronage posits that patronage employees stick to the agreement because they believe that their fates are tied to the political fate of their patron. Patrons do not need to monitor clients and threaten to punish non-compliers. To make patronage work, politicians only need to be able to distribute patronage contracts to those closely connected to the political network – that is, perceived supporters. When patronage jobs are distributed to perceived or "branded" supporters, patronage contracts are self-sustaining. Only perceived supporters – whose fates are tied to the political fate of the politician who hired them – can credibly commit to provide political support in the future. Supporters believe that their patronage jobs and working conditions will be maintained by the incumbent politician (their patron) but not by a competing politician. Once perceived or branded as incumbent supporters, patronage employees have low expectations of keeping their jobs and working conditions if the opposition were to win.

The *actual* firing or demotion of public employees may happen only rarely, in certain specific places, or for certain types of employees. Nonetheless, employees' belief in this possibility is enough to incentivize them to support their patron. When something as valuable as one's livelihood is at stake, clients are less willing to take the risk of defecting. When jobs are distributed by proximity to the politician's network, patronage contracts are incentive-compatible, and the commitment problem associated with the sequenced nature of the exchange disappears. Supporters with patronage jobs believe that it is in their best interest to provide political services to help the incumbent remain in power. This alignment of interests between patrons and clients makes patronage contracts self-sustaining over time.

Indeed, what makes patronage such a persistent informal institution is the fact that, given the other actors' strategies, no one can see a way out.[1] As it has been argued for the case of corruption (e.g., Andvig and Moene 1990; Fisman

---

[1] Informal institutions are "socially shared rules, usually unwritten, that are created, communicated, and enforced outside of officially sanctioned channels" (Helmke and Levitsky 2004, 727).

and Golden 2017), patronage can be conceptualized as an equilibrium – a result of interactions among actors in which, given the behavior of others, no individual actor can see a way to make themselves better off by choosing a different strategy. A politician who opts out of hiring public sector employees as political workers may find themselves at a disadvantage at campaign time and may even lose the election.[2] A citizen who decides not to get close to a political network to get a patronage job may find themselves without a job. Patronage is so persistent because politicians want to win elections and citizens want to keep their jobs and working conditions, which – they believe – are tied to the politician staying in office. The theory of self-enforcing patronage helps to understand the ubiquity and persistence of patronage – patronage is a self-sustaining equilibrium because the incentives of clients and patrons are aligned.

The empirical evidence provided in Chapters 3 to 6 supports this theory. The list and survey experiment results, as well as the interviews with public employees, brokers, and politicians, show that supporters are indeed more likely than non-supporters to be involved in the provision of political services and that they are also more afraid of losing their jobs or suffering negative changes in working conditions with a change in administration. Once we take into account the incentive alignment predicted by the theory of self-enforcing patronage, the need for monitoring and threats of punishment is limited to certain types of employees and certain types of services. Employees hired by previous administrations, often from a different party than the incumbent, have no fear of losing their jobs or experiencing changes for the worse if the opposition gets into power. These employees lack the incentive alignment upon which the self-enforcing theory of patronage is constructed.

The theory developed in this book is not merely a theory to explain how patronage works in Argentina. It carries explanatory power in other contexts as well. Chapter 7 showed that many of the patterns expected by the theory of self-enforcing patronage are present elsewhere in Latin America. Many countries – even those such as Chile and Brazil, considered to have well-functioning professional bureaucracies – tend to have civil service systems that leave ample opportunity for political bias in hiring and firing, giving public employees good reasons to fear a change in the administration and an incentive to engage in political services that help to keep the incumbent in power.

By providing a direct assessment of the specific mechanisms behind the electoral returns to patronage politics, this book makes two key contributions. First, it presents the first systematic attempt to measure and describe the types and extent of the political services that patronage

---

[2] Chauchard (2018) makes a similar argument about the distribution of handouts in Indian elections. In his account, politicians in Mumbai know that distributing handouts is an inefficient way of getting votes, but they keep on doing it because the other politicians do it – they are afraid of being the only ones not distributing handouts and getting punished by voters for it.

employees provide for the patron who hires them. Second, the theory of self-enforcing patronage developed and tested in this book provides a novel explanation of the enforcement of these patronage contracts: an explanation that is key to understanding the ubiquity and persistence of patronage arrangements and that also has important implications for understanding the functioning of clientelistic exchanges more broadly.

8.2 TAKING CLIENTS SERIOUSLY

Most of the political science literature on clientelism focuses on elite-level strategies.[3] It often portrays clients as passive, myopic, nonstrategic, or mainly driven by short-term reactions to the actions of politicians.[4] For instance, as Nichter (2009) points out, in the elite-centered debate about whether clientelistic benefits are targeted at swing or core voters, voters' own strategies are completely ignored. In most of this debate, voters are treated as passive actors whose only role is to accept or reject the non-negotiable clientelistic offer that parties make.[5] Voters are also assumed to be sincere in their political preferences, which are exogenous and stable over time. The preferences of swing voters may be more or less conditional on what the parties do, but core voters, from this perspective, are assumed to have an ideological commitment to their party that is exogenous to past or future material redistribution.[6] Even though most theories of voting behavior portray voters as primarily concerned with their own well-being, core clients in the clientelism literature are often assumed to be non-instrumental voters, only motivated by their unconditional loyalty to the party.

In fact, the political science literature on clientelism is plagued with arguments that imply some sort of asymmetry between the rationality of the

---

[3] This is not true for the sociological literature. Besides the previously mentioned seminal work of Auyero, the sociological literature has often paid more attention to the clients' perspective than the political science literature (for the Argentinean case see, e.g., Quirós 2008; Rocca Rivarola 2019; Vommaro 2007; Vommaro and Combes 2019; Vommaro and Quirós 2011).

[4] In a recent paper, Auerbach and Thachil (2018) make a similar argument and show that, in the case of the selection of brokers in India, clients have "nontrivial agency." Similarly, and in line with Chapter 5 in this book and Oliveros (2016), Nichter and Peress (2017) focus on non-passive clients who make requests from brokers. Muñoz's (2014, 2018) analysis of clientelism in Peru and Lazar's (2004) analysis of clientelism in Bolivia are also important exceptions.

[5] This is particularly evident in the formal literature, which often depicts clients as price takers whose only choice is to take or refuse the offer (e.g., Nichter 2008; Stokes 2005). See Zarazaga (2015) for an exception.

[6] An important exception to this general approach is Díaz-Cayeros, Estévez, and Magaloni (2016), who argue that political parties invest in core supporters to maintain their loyalty. They do not take the preferences of core voters as static and independent from the redistribution of welfare; rather, they argue that voter commitments to a party are "constructed through reciprocal material and symbolic exchanges, past, present, and future" (Díaz-Cayeros, Estévez, and Magaloni 2016, 10). For a similar perspective, see also Calvo and Murillo (2019) and Zarazaga (2016).

client and the rationality of the other actors (non-clients, the patron, and/or the broker). Take, for instance, the theories of reciprocity discussed in Chapter 2 (e.g., Finan and Schechter 2012; Lawson and Greene 2014). According to these theories, clients comply with their side of the agreement by providing political support because they want to help the person who helped them (with a handout, a favor, a public sector job, or some other benefit). To the extent that these theories are about clientelism, the goal of patrons and brokers is clear – they want to extract political support from their clients. While patrons and their brokers are self-interested strategic actors with clear instrumental goals, clients are assumed to be noble and altruistic individuals who care about "doing the right thing."

According to the theories of monitoring and punishment also discussed in Chapter 2, clients comply with their side of the clientelistic agreement because they are afraid that the patron will punish them if they fail to do so.[7] This perspective also suggests a different rationality for the behavior of clients *vis-à-vis* other voters. In general, the starting point of any rational theory of voting is that voters choose parties and politicians that make them better off. When the empirical evidence does not match this assumption, scholars have tried to provide explanations for the "anomaly." For instance, according to a vast literature on the political economy of elections, in unequal societies the poor should vote for the left because it favors higher taxes and redistribution (e.g., Acemoglu and Robinson 2006; Boix 2003). When this is not the case, and poor voters support right-wing parties instead – which are typically opposed to redistribution – it is assumed that something is happening that makes citizens vote against their interests.[8] Under "normal circumstances," it is assumed that it is rational for voters to reward or punish candidates according to what they have done or could do in the future to make them better off. Thus, if rational poor voters are supposed to support Left parties that favor redistribution, rational clients should support those who provide them with benefits such as handouts, favors, or public sector jobs.

Yet, from the perspective of the theories of monitoring and punishment, the fact that clients receive something from a patron that makes them better off is not enough to secure their support. The assumption is that clients would collect the benefit but then withhold support from the politician who provided the benefit, either supporting another politician or not supporting anyone (Zucco 2010). While rational voters in most voting theories are assumed to support politicians who would make them better off, this is not enough – from this perspective – to explain the political behavior of clients. Like core voters in the core/swing literature, the assumption is that clients' preferences are somehow

---

[7] See, among others, Brusco et al. (2004), Nichter (2008), Stokes (2005, 2007), and Stokes et al. (2013). Chapter 2 discusses this literature at length.

[8] See, for instance, De la O and Rodden (2008) and Huber and Stanig (2011) on how religion undermines the expected negative relationship between income and left voting.

exogenous, orthogonal, or unaffected by the distribution of benefits. Clients in this literature need some enforcement mechanism (beyond the benefit itself) to guarantee the provision of clients' political support and the success of the clientelistic exchange.

In contrast, the argument put forward in this book suggests that clients do not act qualitatively differently from other voters.[9] Clients, like any other voter, care about their own well-being. They are not necessarily more noble and altruistic than others, and they do not need to be "forced into" supporting a politician who makes them better off. Like any other voter, clients choose to support the politician who makes them better off. They choose to support the politician who guarantees the continuity of the benefit because they understand it is in their best interest to do so. To the extent that clients believe that the continuation of the benefit is conditional on the patron remaining in a position of power, clients have an incentive to help the patron achieve this goal. In the specific type of clientelistic exchange discussed in this book, patronage employees have an incentive to help the politician who hired them to stay in power, which is why they comply with the agreement and provide the services needed to facilitate the politician's electoral success. When the clientelistic exchange is incentive-compatible, neither feelings of reciprocity nor monitoring and the threat of punishment are *necessary* to sustain the exchange. To the extent that patrons and clients share the same interests, there is no need for any exogenous enforcement mechanism.

8.3   IMPLICATIONS FOR CURBING CLIENTELISM

The theory of self-enforcing patronage advanced in this book has implications for our understanding of clientelistic exchanges and their persistence more generally. A direct implication of the theory is that neither monitoring nor reciprocity is necessary for a clientelistic exchange to take place. Whether the benefit exchanged is a public sector job, cash, food, or a favor, clientelistic exchanges are possible and sustainable in the absence of monitoring and feelings of reciprocity.

---

[9] There is evidence that voters are less myopic, more rational, and better judges of their own interests than the literature on clientelistic exchanges often assumes. For instance, Zucco (2010, 2013) shows that a non-clientelistic conditional cash transfer (CCT) program in Brazil is associated with more votes for the incumbent party, suggesting that voter responses to CCTs are similar to retrospective economic voting. De la O (2013, 2015) in turn shows that the programmatic Mexican CCT program fostered support for the incumbent. These two examples are particularly significant because the types of voters who are targeted by CCT programs (the poor) are often the same as those who are targeted by clientelism. Without discretion, monitoring, and punishment, policies that make voters better off are rewarded at the polls, suggesting that the poor react in the same way as theories of economic retrospective voting argue for other voters. See also Baldwin (2013, 2015) for an argument that emphasizes the sophisticated decision-making process by which poor rural voters in Africa decide their votes.

Departing from existing theories, I argue that clients can make an active and strategic decision to support their patron because they think it is in their best interest to do so. Clients provide political services to their patrons, not as a short-term reaction to the patron's actions or because they are thankful, but because they understand that the continuation of the benefit is conditional on the patron remaining in the position of power that grants access to these benefits. Whether it is a public sector job, some material benefit, or a favor, when clients believe that the continuation of the benefit is tied to the success of the patron, clientelistic agreements become self-sustaining. If clients believe that the continuation of the benefit is contingent on the patron or broker maintaining the position of power, they have a strong incentive to support them and help them stay in that position, either by providing electoral support or through the political services studied in this book. As shown by Auyero's (2001, 123) research, patrons and brokers seem to be fully aware of the importance of generating and maintaining this belief among clients:

> With each problem that they solve for a client, brokers are continually better positioning themselves so that, at election time, they will essentially be able to blackmail their clients, the implied threat being that, if the broker and his or her patron are forced from office, the broker's clients will no longer receive the benefits of the social programs established by the patron and run by the broker.

With the important exceptions of Auyero (2001), Zarazaga (2014, 2015), and research on the distribution of land (e.g., Albertus et al. 2016; Boone 2011), the literature on clientelism has mainly ignored this alternative mechanism that sustains clientelistic exchanges. Instead, most of the literature on clientelism often adopts a definition of clientelism that implies the existence of monitoring and punishment.[10] The alternative mechanism for the sustainability of clientelistic exchanges that I develop in this book brings attention to the importance of taking the interests and actions of clients more seriously. In doing so, it makes clear that clients might simply want to ensure that the broker or the politician behind the broker gets the support needed to maintain the position that allows the flow of benefits to continue.

Note that I am not arguing that fear of punishment (or feelings of reciprocity) are never present in clientelistic exchanges or that they are not possible, but rather that neither of these two factors are *necessary* characteristics of such arrangements. Certainly, the absence of coercion might be interpreted in a positive light. As Stokes et al. (2013, 249) argue, "the voter who faces no

---

[10] Chapter 1 discusses these definitions. See also Van de Walle (2007, 63–64) on Benin and Nigeria and Kramon (2016a) on Kenya for cases in which clientelistic exchanges are also sustained with no "instrumentality." Both Muñoz (2014, 2018) in Peru and Chauchard (2018) in India show that clientelism also happens in contexts with weak parties, where monitoring and the threat of punishment are not feasible. The type of clientelism they focus on, however, is what has been called "electoral clientelism" (Nichter 2011), which happens just around elections and does not imply a long-term relationship between clients and brokers.

conditionality has greater autonomy than the voter who faces possible sanctions if he defects." If clientelistic arrangements can be self-sustaining without punishment, however, clientelism becomes less costly, more difficult to detect, and even more difficult to curb.

If the patron (or broker) does not need to invest resources to identify non-compliers and credibly commit to punish them, the cost of clientelism is significantly reduced.[11] For a patron to be able to monitor clients and punish those who fail to fulfill their promises, resources need to be invested in costly political machines. While the cost of clientelism does not disappear in the absence of monitoring and punishment, clientelistic agreements can be self-enforcing if clients believe that the continuation of the benefit is conditional on the patron or broker maintaining their position of power. In the specific case of patronage agreements, the relationship between being in power and the ability to distribute jobs is straightforward, so patrons might not need to invest expensive resources in convincing patronage employees that their jobs are tied to the reelection of the incumbent. As shown in Chapter 5, this may also be the case for the provision of favors by state employees, in which the link between the favor and the administration is immediate and clear. In other cases, however, patrons and brokers might need to invest more in personally claiming credit for the benefits distributed and in "creating the appearance that were they not there, the benefits would not be delivered" (Auyero, Lapegna, and Poma 2009, 5). While this continuous effort to link the benefit to the patron remaining in the position of power is not completely free, it is substantially cheaper than the alternative of monitoring to identify and punish non-compliers.

In the absence of coercion and threats of punishment, clientelism becomes more difficult to detect and curb. Convincing clients that the benefit is contingent on the patron's success is a significantly more subtle and less visible mechanism than punishing – or threatening to punish – non-compliers. Crucially, it is perfectly legal. Threatening citizens to make them vote in a certain way, abstain from voting, or provide any type of political support is clearly against the law. Often, such threats are either implicit or only made explicit in private settings, so clientelistic arrangements may still be difficult to detect. However, when clientelistic exchanges are self-enforcing and patrons only need to make clients believe (or remember) that the continuation of the benefit might be at risk if the election is lost, the arrangement becomes legal. In fact, this way of "campaigning" is almost indistinguishable from the type of campaign that any programmatic politician might conduct. Campaigning on

---

[11] It could be argued that this reduction in cost would be even more significant if the theories of reciprocity were correct. Lawson and Greene (2014, 73) make this point, arguing that if reciprocity works, clientelism "might not require highly organized and deeply rooted political machines." However, Finan and Schechter (2012) argue that brokers target reciprocal individuals, which means that brokers are still needed in order to identify reciprocal clients. Nevertheless, this section focuses on theories of monitoring and punishment, which are the most accepted in the literature on clientelism.

the fact that the opposition might fail to maintain certain policies – fiscal austerity, support for education, a conditional cash-transfer program, or any other policy subject to change – is a perfectly legal and common electoral campaign strategy. There is nothing substantively different in these types of promises. Both types of politicians – clientelistic and programmatic – try to tie the continuation of a certain policy or benefit to their continuation in power.

In this way, clientelism becomes less visible, more difficult to detect, and even more difficult to limit. In the end, curbing clientelism is reduced to limiting the discretion that politicians and their brokers enjoy in distributing benefits. In the case studied in this book, patronage contracts are sustained by the ability of the politician to distribute jobs to those closely connected to the political network (perceived supporters), who believe that their jobs are contingent on the success of their patron. This belief is based on the fact that a new incumbent will have the same discretion as the old one to hire supporters, so "disloyal" supporters of the previous administration will suffer the consequences. Only limiting discretion in hiring decisions can prevent politicians from choosing perceived supporters over non-supporters, which would change the clients' belief that their jobs are tied to the success of the patron. More generally, clientelistic exchanges depend on the discretionary power of patrons and brokers to distribute benefits. When benefits are distributed discretionally, clients tend to think that their continuation is tied to the patron who distributes them. Only by limiting the original discretion in the distribution is it possible to curb clientelistic exchanges that are not sustained by an illegal enforcement mechanism.

All in all, the theory of self-enforcing patronage provides yet another example of the need to pay serious attention to informal institutions. As described in Chapter 7, formal civil service systems across the world coexist with informal rules around political criteria for hiring and firing (e.g., Cortázar Velarde, Lafuente, and Sanginés 2014; Grindle 2012; Schuster 2017). While formal rules stipulate the use of meritocratic criteria for hiring and firing decisions, the informal incentives of patronage politics described in this book trump the formal rules in many countries around the world. As pointed out by Helmke and Levitsky (2004), informal institutional change can happen as a consequence of changes in formal institutional strength or effectiveness. Only strengthening the formal rules about discretional hiring would change the informal incentives highlighted by the theory of self-enforcing patronage.[12]

---

[12] Of course, the impact of formal rules changes should not be overstated: "many informal institutions have proved resilient even in the face of large-scale legal or administrative reform" (Helmke and Levitsky 2004, 732). Many studies of the origins of effective reform aimed at the depoliticization of the state point to electoral competition as the main driver of these types of reforms (e.g., Geddes 1994; Grzymala-Busse 2003, 2007; Ting et al. 2013). See Schuster (2016) for a recent review of this literature.

8.4   WHAT'S SO WRONG WITH PATRONAGE?

Most non-normative conceptualizations of democracy – including minimalistic ones – contain two distinct elements. First, they always explicitly include the element of competitive elections for the most important governmental positions. Second, sometimes less explicitly, they add some "surrounding conditions," external to the electoral process itself, that are necessary and/or sufficient for the existence of *truly* fair and competitive elections (G. O'Donnell 2010, 13–18). In other words, democracies can be thought of as containing elements that regulate, in a particular way, the "access to power" as well as the "exercise of power" (Mazzuca 2010). A key distinction in the exercise of power dimension is "whether goods and services are provided according to universal/general standards, like merit and need, or particularistic decisions based on personal connections and the ruler's discretion" (Mazzuca 2010, 343). An important characteristic of patronage – one shared with other misuses of state resources like pork-barrel politics and the manipulation of targeted public programs – is that it can affect both the access to power and the exercise of power dimensions of democracy.

Concerning the electoral component (access to power), when clients believe that it is in their best interest to help their patron stay in power – as in the theory developed in this book – distributing patronage jobs provides a self-sustaining incumbency advantage with potentially important effects on electoral outcomes. Elections might still be competitive, but with the use of state resources by the incumbent party to finance political workers, elections are less fair for the opposition. Patronage, moreover, has a potentially stronger effect on electoral competition than other forms of clientelism because of its multiplier effect. Indeed, the political services provided by patronage employees are aimed at getting votes outside the public administration itself. Patronage exchanges are in this regard quite unique – the beneficiaries of the benefit (the job) are of course expected to vote for the incumbent, but crucially the services provided by patronage employees are expected to get the vote of others as well. In general, the literature on clientelism has mainly related the problems with clientelistic exchanges to electoral outcomes. Most authors focus on discussing the negative effects of clientelism in relation to political competition and the way clientelistic exchanges affect representation, vertical accountability, and the choice of leaders (Stokes et al. 2013).

Undeniably, patronage shares these damaging effects on the quality of democratic competition with other forms of clientelism. First, when there is fair competition, elections provide information about the distribution of citizens' preferences, which makes it easier for these preferences to be represented and translated into public policies (Stokes 2007, 2009). If incumbents have an unfair advantage, elections tend to be less informative about the distribution of citizens' preferences, which damages the quality of representation and the accountability of the system. Second, fair competition makes politicians more "responsive," in the sense that it provides an incentive for politicians to act in ways that will obtain or maintain citizens' support at the ballot box. When competition is less fair, politicians can more easily ignore voters' preferences. Finally, when elections are less informative about citizens' preferences and performance in office is not the main driver of reelection success or failure, the choice of leaders is affected (Stokes et al. 2013).[13]

However, the distribution of patronage jobs also implies the manipulation of state resources for political gain. The fact that, by definition, the resources used are public resources marks a fundamental distinction from other types of clientelism. While other forms of clientelistic exchanges can be implemented using state resources, non-incumbent politicians using private or partisan funds can also deploy them. Being in power is always an advantage when it comes to implementing clientelistic agreements, but when the type of benefit exchanged is a public sector job, it is a necessary condition.

In this sense, patronage has much in common with the manipulation of targeted public programs (such as scholarships, food distribution programs, and conditional cash transfer programs) and pork-barrel politics. Any non-programmatic strategy designed to win votes will, if successful, affect electoral competition and, consequently, the choice of leaders, the accountability of the system, and the quality of representation (Stokes et al. 2013). However, when these strategies are implemented by the state with state resources, they affect both the exercise of power and the access to power dimensions of democracy (Mazzuca 2010). Patronage contracts are designed to finance political workers; when successful, they will have an effect on political competition, generating the same negative consequences as other types of clientelistic exchanges. But the fact that state resources are used makes patronage contracts fundamentally different from other types of clientelistic arrangements.

The existence of political bias in the distribution of public sector jobs affects the independence of the public administration and raises serious concerns about the possibility of equal treatment by the state. When jobs are distributed discretionally and according to political criteria, employees owe their jobs to the politician who hired them. This lack of independence could in turn generate a lack of impartiality *vis à vis* citizens. As the evidence presented in Chapter 5 shows, knowing the right person in the public administration can make an important difference in getting things done. More generally, in patronage democracies, knowing a state official increases voters' likelihood of obtaining valuable services and resources from the state (Chandra 2004, 2007). Need and

---

[13] See Stokes et al. (2013, 245–54) for a longer discussion of the effects of different types of non-programmatic distribution and their consequences for the quality of democracy.

proximity to a state official, however, do not necessarily go together, which generates serious questions about equal access *to,* and equal treatment *by* the state. Even if voters are in crucial need of help, they may not be connected to a patronage employee or politician who is in a position to help. Moreover, those with access to state officials have a strong incentive to keep on supporting the politician in power to make sure that their connection to the state remains safe. This situation, in turn, fosters the incumbency advantage and helps to reproduce the unequal access to the state.

Whether or not clientelistic exchanges involve the use of public offices and public money has important political consequences that make these kinds of exchanges particularly damaging for democracy. Abuses in the exercise of power, such as the distribution of patronage jobs, the manipulation of targeted public programs, or pork-barrel politics, are all non-programmatic forms of distributive politics that have an effect on both the access to power and the exercise of power. Once in office, the use of public resources for political gain provides an unfair advantage to incumbent parties. The abuses in the exercise of power dimension reinforce the unfairness in the access to power dimension, guaranteeing that the electoral playing field will remain skewed in favor of the incumbent party.

This discussion suggests that building a democratic society is not just about getting the political regime right, but also about getting the state right. Unequal access to the state, of which patronage is an important cause, plagues many democracies with areas of low intensity citizenship (G. O'Donnell 1993). In the extreme, as G. O'Donnell (1993) points out, when citizens are unable to get fair treatment from the state or to obtain the public benefits and services from state agencies to which they are entitled, the liberal component of democracy suffers.

Appendix

Interviews with political activists and brokers in Greater Buenos Aires

1. Gerónimo. Peronist broker and councilman in Malvinas Argentinas. Malvinas Argentinas, August 20, 2009.
2. José. Peronist broker in a Peronist municipality in Greater Buenos Aires and provincial public employee. La Plata, August 5, 2009.
3. Lucas. President of the local branch of the Peronist party in an opposition municipality in Greater Buenos Aires, political appointee in a high-level position in the provincial government of Buenos Aires, and important Peronist political operative (*operador político*) in the province. La Plata, August 5, 2009.
4. Martín. Peronist. High-ranking official in the provincial government of Buenos Aires. La Plata. August 5, 2009.
5. Pablo. Peronist broker in an opposition municipality in Greater Buenos Aires and provincial public employee. La Plata, August 5, 2009.
6. Ramiro. Peronist broker in San Isidro, Greater Buenos Aires. San Isidro, April 30, 2010.
7. Sergio. Peronist broker and municipal public employee in La Matanza. La Matanza, August 10, 2009.
8. Telma. Peronist broker in Ituzaingó, Greater Buenos Aires. Runs a health center with support from the municipality. Ituzaingó, August 3, 2009.

Interviews with high-level officials and politicians in Salta, Santa Fe, and Tigre

1. Salta. Deputy Secretary of Human Resources, November 17, 2010 and May 30, 2011.
2. Salta. Deputy Secretary of Information Technology, November 17, 2010.
3. Salta. Director of the Office of Institutional Strengthening, November 17, 2010.
4. Salta. Employee in the Office of Institutional Strengthening, June 14, 2011.

5. Salta. Director General of Personnel, June 1, 2011.
6. Salta. City Council Director of Personnel (since 1993), career civil servant, June 14, 2011.
7. Salta. City councilman from the opposition Radical party, August 1, 2011.
8. Santa Fe. Provincial public employee in charge of municipality relations, June 7, 2010.
9. Santa Fe. Secretary of Government, June 10, 2010.
10. Santa Fe. Deputy Secretary of the Civil Service Office, June 10, 2010.
11. Santa Fe. Employee in charge of training, Civil Service Office, Santa Fe, June 15, 2010.
12. Tigre. City councilman from the Peronist party (close to the mayor), July 13, 2010,
13. Tigre. Director General of Personnel and two high-ranking career public employees at the Office of Personnel, July 15, 2010.

Cited interviews with public sector employees

1. Ana, F, 31, Salta (since 2005), administrative employee, high school degree, tenured, June 15, 2011.
2. Beatriz, F, 48, Tigre (since 2008), territorial agent (*agente territorial*), some high school, untenured, August 17, 2010.
3. Daniela, F, 27, Salta (since 2009), administrative employee in the Office of Human Resources, some college, untenured, August 5, 2011.
4. Fernando, M, 61, Salta (since 1982), Head of Maintenance (in charge of 30/40 people), high school degree, tenured, August 5, 2011.
5. Francisco, M, 51, Tigre (since 2002), administrative employee, some tertiary education, untenured, September 22, 2010.
6. Jaime, M, 28, Salta (since 2008), legal advisor (lawyer), postgraduate degree, untenured, June 15, 2011.
7. Joaquín, M, 38, Tigre (since 2007), psychologist, college degree, untenured, August 26, 2010.
8. Jorge, M, 50, Santa Fe (since 1983), Director of Photography, Municipal Art Center, some college, tenured, July 22, 2010.
9. Josefina, F, 36, Salta (since 2002), telephone operator, some high school, untenured, June 15, 2011.
10. Laura, F, 44, Tigre (since 1988), administrative employee, high school degree, tenured, January 6, 2011.
11. María, F, 47, Salta (since 1997), administrative employee, high school degree, tenured, August 8, 2011.

12. Mariano, M, 27, Salta (since 2006), administrative employee and Peronist political broker, high school degree, tenured, August 1, 2011.

13. Mariela, F, 38, Tigre (since 2009), administrative employee, some college, untenured, August 27, 2010.

14. Marisa, F, 44, Salta (since 2008), legal advisor (lawyer), postgraduate degree, untenured, June 8, 2011.

15. Mauricio, M, 63, Salta (since 1971), director in the Public Works Department (in charge of 250 people), high school degree, tenured, June 13, 2011.

16. Micaela, F, 43, Salta (since 1989), private secretary to a high-ranking official (in charge of 2 people), some college, tenured, August 10, 2011.

17. Natalia, F, 53, Tigre (since 2009), street sweeper, did not complete elementary school, untenured, August 25, 2010.

18. Paulina, F, 31, Salta (since 2005), system analyst, college degree, untenured, June 8, 2011.

19. Sabrina, F, 50, Santa Fe (since 1985), director of the Oversight Office (*Sindicatura*) (in charge of 6 people), postgraduate degree, tenured, August 16, 2011.

20. Sofía, F, 37, Salta (since 2007), administrative employee, some college, tenured, June 8, 2011.

21. Soledad, F, 36, Salta (since 2007), architect, college degree, untenured, August 3, 2011.

22. Valeria, F, 45, Tigre (since 2001), high-ranking employee in the Personnel Office (in charge of 9 people), postgraduate degree, tenured, August 23, 2010.

23. Viviana, F, 61, Salta (since 1979), administrative employee, high school degree, tenured, August 3, 2011.

A.2 SURVEY METHODOLOGY

The survey consisted of face-to-face interviews of 1,184 low- and mid-level local public sector employees in the Argentinean municipalities of Salta (Salta Province), Santa Fe (Santa Fe Province), and Tigre (Buenos Aires Province).[1] Together with a team of research assistants, we interviewed 389 employees in Salta, 395 in Santa Fe, and 400 in Tigre. The survey was administered between August 10 and December 30, 2010 in Santa Fe, between August 11 and November 26, 2010 in Tigre, and from June 6 to August 11, 2011 in Salta.[2] It was preceded by a pilot

[1] The survey methodology and the survey instrument were approved under Columbia University IRB protocol IRB-AAAE9968.

[2] The survey in Salta was scheduled to start in November 2010 but changes in the electoral calendar generated by the death of the likely Peronist presidential candidate, Néstor Kirchner, made the authorities in Salta reluctant to allow me to conduct the survey on the scheduled dates. They were

administered in Santa Fe between July 22 and July 29, 2010, consisting of forty cases. The goal of the pilot was to test the survey instrument – particularly the list experiments – and elicit feedback from interviewers and respondents about question wording and clarity. On average, survey interviews lasted twenty-four minutes.

Interviewers were recruited from Humanities and Social Science departments of universities in Santa Fe, Salta, and Buenos Aires, and were either advanced undergraduates or recent graduates.[3] Extensive training was conducted for interviewers on the survey instrument (particularly the survey and list experiments), on how to explain and properly administrate the second (sensitive) part of the survey, and on IRB-related issues of respondent protection. For the purpose of survey verification, basic information about the employees (age, years in the position, and type of contract) was obtained from each of the municipalities and was not distributed to the enumerators. If this information did not match that reported in the survey instrument beyond the reasonable expected mistakes, I conducted further verification of the interviews administered by the same interviewer by meeting in person with each respondent.[4]

The contact rate for the survey was 59 percent, the response rate was 56 percent, and the refusal rate 3 percent. The margin of error was 2.7 percent.[5] To obtain the 1,184 surveys, a random sample of 2,173 public employees was selected from the payroll lists provided by the local authorities (excluding elected officials, high-level positions, and teachers). Table A1 presents the contact, response, and refusals rates across municipalities, as well as the details for failed contacts (also see Tables A2-A6).

both worried about sharing the list of employees with me and about the survey itself. The time was particularly problematic for them, they argued, because provincial elections were called earlier than usual (April 2011) – rumor at the time was that the reason behind the early elections was the governor being considered as a candidate for the vice presidency – and 2000 employees were being considered for tenure. The local authorities only agreed to give me the information and authorization necessary to conduct the survey after the local elections. As a result, the survey in Salta was administered after the April 2011 local elections (in which both the governor and the mayor were reelected), but before the October 2011 national elections.

3 The enumerators were: Anastasia Peralta Ramos, Ignacio César, Ignacio Puente, and Nicolás Schujman in Tigre; Leilen Lua Bouchet, Nahuel Avalos Theules, Alejandro Núñez Avendaño, and Leonardo Pez in Santa Fe; and Sofía Checa, Marcela Godoy, Mariana Godoy, Mariana Macazaga, Gonzalo Rodríguez, and Ludovica Pian in Salta. I conducted 160 interviews myself. I thank the enumerators for their invaluable help and persistence in getting the interviews done as well as for their feedback on the general project. Their sense of humor made the fieldwork for this project fun and enjoyable.

4 With this methodology, one enumerator was identified as fabricating the responses. The full set of interviews she had conducted was replaced by a new set conducted by a different interviewer. There was no need to replace the names of employees selected because the *entire* set of interviews was fabricated so the new enumerator used the originally selected names.

5 Rates calculated according to the American Association of Public Opinion Research.

TABLE A 1 *Sample and contact, refusal, and response rates*

	Salta	Santa Fe	Tigre	Total	As % of sample
Total N in payroll	4,619	5,070	2,569		
Sample frame	4,263	4,528	2,406	11,197	
Random sample	764	696	713	2,173	
Complete interviews	389	395	400	1,184	54%
Refusals	17	20	32	69	3%
Non-Contact					
Sick, holidays, or leave	44	24	28	96	4%
Doesn't work there anymore	26	11	19	56	3%
Just not there (random reasons)	127	39	125	291	13%
Wrong workplace	36	31	39	106	5%
No one knows the employee	101	59	8	168	8%
No attempt to contact	24	117	62	203	9%
Contact Rate	55%	61%	62%	59%	
Refusal Rate	2%	3%	5%	3%	
Response Rate	53%	58%	58%	56%	

Note: Sample frame excludes elected officials, high-level positions, and teachers. The margin of error was 2.7 percent. Rates calculated according to the methodology of the American Association of Public Opinion Research.

TABLE A 2 *Survey sample representativeness (Salta)*

	Survey		Sample frame	
	N=389	%	N=4,263	%
Gender				
Male	228	58.61	2,701	63.35
Female	161	41.39	1,562	36.65
Hired under current mayor	211*	54.24	1,491**	46.75
Older than 40 years old	230	59.13	2,121***	70.04
Tenure				
With tenure	242	62.21	2,992****	77.11
No tenure	146	37.53	888****	22.89
Secretariat				
Finance	106	27.25	732	17.17
Public Works	68	17.48	788	18.48
Government	40	10.28	522	12.24
Chief of Cabinet	38	9.77	514	12.06

(continued)

TABLE A 2 *(continued)*

	Survey		Sample frame	
	N=389	%	N=4,263	%
Commerce and Participation	25	6.43	175	4.11
Social Assistance	19	4.88	318	7.46
Planning and Development	19	4.88	124	2.91
General Secretary	16	4.11	185	4.34
Environment	12	3.08	266	6.24
Others and Missing	47	12.08	639	14.99

* 1 missing observation
** 1,074 missing observations
*** 1,235 missing observations
**** 383 missing observations

TABLE A 3 *Survey sample representativeness (Santa Fe)*

	Survey		Sample frame	
	N=395	%	N=4,528	%
Gender				
Male	235	59.49	2,917	64.42
Female	160	40.51	1,611	35.58
Hired under current mayor	141	35.70	1,949**	44.87
Older than 40 years old	270*	67.94	2,765***	63.34
Tenure				
With tenure	256	64.81	2,484	54.86
No tenure	139	35.19	2,044	45.14
Secretariat				
Social Development	143	36.20	1,579	34.87
Public Works	52	13.16	718	15.86
Finance and Economy	50	12.66	370	8.17
Security	38	9.62	550	12.15
Government	25	6.33	415	9.17
Urban Planning	21	5.32	190	4.20
Culture	20	5.06	307	6.78
Production	15	3.80	100	2.21
Others and Missing	31	7.85	299	6.60

* 2 observations missing
** 184 observations missing
*** 163 observations missing

TABLE A 4 *Survey sample representativeness (Tigre)*

	Survey		Sample frame	
	N=400	%	N=2,406	%
Gender				
Male	193	48.25	1,323	54.99
Female	207	51.75	1,083	45.01
Hired under current mayor	184*	46.00	1,034***	45.37
Older than 40 years old	192**	48.61	1,201***	52.70
Tenure				
With tenure	88	22.00	475	19.74
No tenure	312	78.00	1,931	80.26
Secretariat				
Sanitary Policy and HR	127	31.99	896	37.24
Public Services	105	26.45	590	24.52
Community Promotion	51	12.85	317	13.18
Citizen Protection	37	9.32	160	6.65
Finance and Administration	23	5.79	87	3.62
Institutional Relations	12	3.02	83	3.45
Public Investment	11	2.77	55	2.29
Public Revenue	9	2.27	63	2.62
Urban Control	9	2.27	32	1.33
Others	16	4.03	123	5.11

* 2 missing observations
** 5 missing observations
*** 127 missing observations

TABLE A 5 *Covariate balance across type of questionnaires, by municipality*

Variable	Tigre		Santa Fe		Salta		Whole sample	
	Type 1	Type 2	Type 1	Type 2	Type 1	Type 2	Type 1	Type 2
Observations	199	201	196	199	196	193	591	593
Female	0.55	0.48	0.41	0.40	0.40	0.42	0.46	0.44
Age	39.33	39.65	44.63	44.80	43.86	43.11	42.61	42.51
Education	6.37	6.11	5.30	5.11	5.56	5.63	5.74	5.62

Note: The balanced distribution of the variables across the two conditions suggests that the groups are fairly equivalent on observable characteristics. None of the differences between the control and treatment groups are statistically significant (at the 95 percent confidence level).

TABLE A 6 *Covariate balance across type of questionnaires, by enumerator*

	Type 1	Type 2	Total N	Total %
Alejandro	42	43	85	7%
Anastasia	41	39	80	7%
Gonzalo	28	29	57	5%
Ignacio C.	39	39	78	7%
Ignacio P.	43	44	87	7%
Leilen	23	23	46	4%
Leonardo	23	22	45	4%
Ludovica	16	15	31	3%
Marcela	41	41	82	7%
Mariana G.	7	6	13	1%
Mariana M.	29	29	58	5%
Nahuel	100	103	203	17%
Nicolás	44	46	90	8%
Sofía	36	33	69	6%
Virginia (me)	79	81	160	14%
Total	591	593	1,184	

A.3 WORDING, OPERATIONALIZATION, AND DESCRIPTIVE STATISTICS

A.3.1 Descriptive Statistics (Table A7)

TABLE A 7 *Descriptive statistics (main variables)*

Variable	N	Mean	Std. Dev.	Min	Max
List experiments					
Favors	1,181	1.36	1.24	0	5
Campaigns	1,169	1.30	0.83	0	5
Rallies	1,170	1.50	0.97	0	5
Monitoring	1,172	0.99	0.74	0	4
Survey experiments					
Stability	1,131	7.95	2.74	0	10
Change	1,027	0.25	0.55	−1	1
Other variables					
Mayor supporter*	1,184	0.33	0.47	0	1

(*continued*)

TABLE A 7 *(continued)*

Variable	N	Mean	Std. Dev.	Min	Max
Mayor voter*	1,113	0.61	0.49	0	1
Primary education	1,181	0.31	0.46	0	1
Secondary education	1,181	0.46	0.50	0	1
College	1,181	0.23	0.42	0	1
Age	1,184	3.20	1.21	1	5
Female	1,184	0.45	0.50	0	1
Tenure	1,183	0.50	0.50	0	1
Current mayor	1,181	0.45	0.50	0	1
Reciprocal	1,176	0.86	0.34	0	1

Note: * denotes questions asked in the protected part of the questionnaire (Part B).

A.3.2 Direct Questions Wording

Mayor Supporter

Do you identify yourself with any party? Which party do you identify yourself with?

¿Se identifica Ud. con algún partido político?¿Con cuál partido se identifica Ud.?

Respondents who mentioned the mayor's party in each municipality were coded as Supporters; all the rest were coded as zero.

Supporter (1)
Non-supporter (0)

Mayor Voter

Which party did you vote for in the last municipal elections for mayor (2007/2011)?

¿A qué partido/candidato votó en las últimas elecciones municipales para intendente (2007/2011)?

Respondents who reported the party of the incumbent mayor in each municipality were coded as Mayor Voters; all the rest were coded as zero. Respondents who were not registered to vote in the municipality where they worked were coded as missing.

Mayor Voter (1)
Mayor Non-voter (0)

College

Which is your maximum level of education?

¿Cuál es el máximo nivel educativo alcanzado por Ud.?

Recoded into two categories:

College (1)
No College (0)

Education

An alternative coding for education was used in some cases as a robustness test:

Completed primary school (1)
Secondary school (2)
University or tertiary education (3)

Age

Could you tell me your age?

¿Podría decirme su edad?

Recoded into five age categories:

18–25 (1)
26–35 (2)
36–45 (3)
46–55 (4)
More than 55 (5)

Female

Note the sex of the respondent

Registrar el sexo del entrevistado

Female (1)
Male (0)

Tenure

What type of contract do you have in the municipality?

¿Qué tipo de contrato tiene Ud. con la municipalidad?

Tenure (1) (*permanente*)
No Tenure (0) (*temporario/contratado*)

Current Mayor

Respondents were first asked about their first year in the job and then if they could recall who was the mayor at the time (survey instrument contained a list of all former mayors and their terms):

Do you remember who the mayor was?

¿Recuerda quién era el intendente?

Responses were coded "1" if hired by the current/incumbent mayor and "0" otherwise.

Current Mayor (1)
Non-current Mayor (0)

Reciprocal

How much do you agree or disagree with the following statement: "We always have to return the favors that people have done for us" Would you say you ...

- Strongly agree
- Agree more than disagree
- Disagree more than agree
- Strongly disagree

¿Qué tan de acuerdo o en desacuerdo está Ud. con la siguiente afirmación: "Siempre hay que regresar los favores que alguien nos hace". Diría Ud. que está ...

- *Muy de acuerdo*
- *Más de acuerdo que en desacuerdo*
- *Más en desacuerdo que de acuerdo*
- *Muy en desacuerdo*

Reciprocal (1): Strongly agree + Agree more than disagree
Nonreciprocal (0): Strongly disagree + Disagree more than agree

Mayor Party Parents (Chapter 3)

When you were younger, do you remember if your father (mother) identified himself (herself) with any political party? With which party did your father (mother) identify himself (herself)?

¿Cuándo usted era más joven, ¿recuerda si su padre(madre) se identificaba con algún partido político? ¿Con cuál partido se identificaba su padre(madre)?

Responses with both of the respondent's parents having the same partisanship as the incumbent mayor when the respondent was young were coded "1" and "0" otherwise.

Importance of Different Criteria for Hiring Decisions (Chapter 3)

I am going to read you a list of criteria that can be used when hiring employees. Please tell me which of the following you believe are important when hiring someone in the area you work in. Please tell me if you believe they matter a lot, they matter, they don't matter much, or they don't matter at all.

The question was followed by a table that listed the criteria: (1) work experience; (2) education; (3) partisan affiliation; (4) political ideology; and (5) personal connections.

A continuación le voy a leer una lista de criterios que se pueden utilizar a la hora de contratar empleados. Dígame, por favor, cuáles de ellos cree Ud. que son criterios importantes a la hora de contratar un empleado nuevo <u>en el área que Ud. trabaja</u>. Dígame, por favor, si Ud. cree que importan mucho, importan, importan poco o no importan nada.

(1) experiencia laboral/antecedentes laborales; (2) estudios; (3) afiliación partidaria; (4) ideología política; (5) conexiones personales.

Frequency of Favors (Chapter 5)

Working for the state, surely a lot of people come to you to ask for help with some errand or task in the municipality, right? How frequently do people come to you to ask you for favors related to your work here at the municipality?

- Never
- A couple of times a year or less
- A couple of times a month
- A couple of times a week. Specify:
- Every day

Trabajando en el Estado seguramente mucha gente se le acerca para pedirle ayuda con algún trámite o gestión en la municipalidad ¿Verdad? ¿Con qué frecuencia diría Ud. que se le acerca gente a pedirle favores relacionados con su trabajo en la municipalidad?

- Nunca
- Algunas veces al año o menos
- Algunas veces al mes
- Algunas veces por semana. Especificar:
- Todos los días

Personal Connections (Chapter 5)

How likely is it that the person who is asking you for a favor is: (a) a friend or acquaintance, (b) a relative, (c) a stranger sent by someone you know, and (d) a complete stranger?

- Very likely
- Likely
- Not very likely
- Unlikely

¿Podría decirme cuál es la probabilidad de que la persona que le pide el favor sea ... (a) un amigo o conocido, (b) un familiar, (c) un desconocido mandado por alguien que usted conoce, (d) un completo desconocido?

- *Muy probable*
- *Probable*
- *Poco probable*
- *Nada probable*

Helpfulness (Chapter 5)

Now I am going to ask about a hypothetical situation. Imagine that someone comes to you and asks you for a favor, but the thing they are asking for is actually handled by another office or person; you would: (a) tell them that you are not the person in charge of that, (b) tell them which office they should go to, or (c) tell them which office they should go to and give them the name of someone you know at that office to make sure that the problem gets solved.

Ahora le planteo una situación hipotética. Supóngase que alguien se le acerca para pedirle un favor pero lo que le están pidiendo, en realidad, depende de otra oficina o persona, entonces Ud.: (a) le dice que eso no depende de Ud., (b) le indica a cuál oficina tiene que dirigirse, o (c) le indica a cuál oficina tiene que dirigirse y le dá el nombre de alguna persona que Ud. conoce en esa oficina para asegurarse de que el problema se solucione.

A.3.3 List Experiments (Chapters 4 and 5)

I am going to hand you a card that mentions a number of activities. I would like for you to tell me HOW MANY of those you did <u>during last year's elections (2009/2011)</u>. Please do not tell me which ones, just HOW MANY.

Le voy a entregar una tarjeta donde figuran una serie de actividades, quisiera que me señale cuántas de ellas realizó Ud. <u>en las elecciones del último año (2009/2011)</u>. Por favor, no me diga cuáles, sino solamente cuántas.

Note: 2009 for Santa Fe and Tigre; 2011 for Salta.

(A) Electoral Campaigns

- Be a candidate
- Get informed about the different candidates
- **Work/help in the electoral campaign**
- Get disenfranchised
- Cast a straight-ticket vote for any of the parties

- *Ser candidato*
- *Informarse sobre los distintos candidatos*
- **_Trabajar/ ayudar en la campaña electoral_**

- *Impugnar el voto*
- *Votar la lista completa de algún partido*

(B) Political Rallies

- Participate in political meetings
- Vote in any party's primary
- **Attend political rallies**
- Abstain from voting
- Get informed about the election on the news

- *Participar de reuniones políticas*
- *Votar en las internas de algún partido*
- ***Concurrir a movilizaciones o actos electorales***
- *Abstenerse de votar*
- *Informarse acerca de la elección en las noticias*

(C) Monitoring Elections

- Decide your vote at the last minute
- Split the ticket
- **Be an election monitor**
- Abstain
- Cast a null vote

- *Decidir el voto a último momento*
- *Cortar boleta*
- ***Ser fiscal de mesa***
- *No votar*
- *Anular el voto*

(D) Favors

I am going to hand you a card that mentions a number of activities. I would like for you to tell me HOW MANY of them you did <u>in the last week</u>. Please do not tell me which ones, just HOW MANY.

Le voy a entregar una tarjeta donde figuran una serie de actividades, quisiera que me señale cuántas de ellas realizó Ud. <u>en la última semana</u>. Por favor, no me diga cuáles, sino solamente cuántas.

- Talk about politics with someone
- Try to convince someone of the strengths and weaknesses of a politician
- **Help someone with an errand or task at City Hall**
- Try to convince someone about the strengths and weaknesses of a policy
- Have a serious fight with someone due to political differences

- *Hablar de política con alguien*
- *Tratar de convencer a alguien sobre las fortalezas y debilidades de algún político*
- **Ayudar a alguien con algún trámite o gestión en la municipalidad**
- *Tratar de convencer a alguien sobre las fortalezas y debilidades de alguna política pública*
- *Tener una pelea seria con alguien a raíz de diferencias políticas*

A.3.4 Survey Experiments (Chapter 6)

Perception of Job Stability (Tigre and Santa Fe)

On a scale from 0 to 10, where 0 means "Not at all likely," and 10 means "Very likely," how likely is it that you will continue working for the municipality next year, after the 2011 mayoral elections (if the incumbent mayor is not re-elected and the opposition wins)?

To facilitate the response, respondents were handed a card with the following figure:

Not at all likely					Likely					Very likely	DK
0	1	2	3	4	5	6	7	8	9	10	99

En una escala de 0 a 10, donde 0 es Nada probable, y 10 es Muy probable, ¿Cuán probable es que Ud. siga trabajando en la municipalidad el año que viene, luego de las elecciones para intendente de 2011(si el actual intendente no fuese reelecto y ganara la oposición)?

Perception of Job Stability (Salta)[6]

Now imagine that the next mayoral elections, instead of being in 2015, are next year. On this same scale (0 to 10), how likely is it that you keep on working for the municipality next year, after these hypothetical elections (if the incumbent mayor is not re-elected and the opposition wins)?

Ahora imagínese que las próximas elecciones para intendente, en lugar de ser en 2015, fueran el año que viene. En esta misma escala, ¿Cuan probable es que Ud. siga trabajando en la municipalidad el año que viene, luego de estas supuestas elecciones, (si el actual intendente no fuese reelecto y ganara la oposición)?

---

[6] I used a slightly different question in Salta because of the timing of the upcoming mayoral election. The surveys in Santa Fe and Tigre were conducted about a year before the next provincial and mayoral elections, whereas the survey in Salta was conducted right after local elections and almost four years before the next ones. The main issue with this was that many employees in Salta who did not have tenure at the time of the survey were expecting to get tenure in the next four years, and this expectation would affect their responses to the question about job stability.

Perception of Change (Tigre and Santa Fe)

On a scale from 0 to 10, where 0 means "Not at all likely," and 10 means "Very likely," how likely do you think it is that your level of satisfaction with your job will change next year, after the 2011 mayoral elections (**if the incumbent mayor is not re-elected and the opposition wins**)?

*En una escala de 0 a 10, donde 0 es Nada Probable, y 10 es Muy probable ¿Cuán probable cree Ud. que es que ese nivel de conformidad con su trabajo cambie el año que viene, luego de las elecciones para intendente de 2011 (**si el actual intendente no fuese reelecto y ganara la oposición**)?*

Perception of Change (Salta)

On a scale from 0 to 10, where 0 means "Not at all likely," and 10 means "Very likely," how likely do you think it is that your level of satisfaction with your job will change in 4 years, after the 2015 mayoral elections (**if the incumbent mayor is not re-elected and the opposition wins**)?

En una escala de 0 a 10, donde 0 es NADA Probable, y 10 es MUY Probable ¿Cuan probable cree Ud. que es que ese nivel de conformidad con su trabajo cambie en 4 años, luego de las próximas elecciones para intendente de 2015 si el actual intendente no fuese reelecto y ganara la oposición?

Direction of Change

Do you think that your situation will be better, the same, or worse?

¿Ud. cree que su situación será mejor, igual o peor?

References

Acemoglu, Daron and James A. Robinson. 2006. *Economic Origins of Dictatorship and Democracy*. New York: Cambridge University Press.

Ahart, Allison M. and Paul R. Sackett. 2004. "A New Method of Examining Relationships between Individual Difference Measures and Sensitive Behavior Criteria: Evaluating the Unmatched Count Technique." *Organizational Research Methods* 7 (1): 101–14.

Akhtari, Mitra, Diana Moreira, and Laura Trucco. 2017. "Political Turnover, Bureaucratic Turnover, and the Quality of Public Services." *Proceedings. Annual Conference on Taxation and Minutes of the Annual Meeting of the National Tax Association* 110: 1–84.

Albertus, Michael. 2015. "The Role of Subnational Politicians in Distributive Politics: Political Bias in Venezuela's Land Reform under Chávez." *Comparative Political Studies* 48 (13): 1667–710.

Albertus, Michael, Alberto Díaz-Cayeros, Beatriz Magaloni, and Barry R. Weingast. 2016. "Authoritarian Survival and Poverty Traps: Land Reform in Mexico." *World Development* 77: 154–70.

Aldrich, John H. 1993. "Rational Choice and Turnout." *American Journal of Political Science* 37 (1): 246–78.

Alesina, Alberto, Reza Baqir, and William Easterly. 2000. "Redistributive Public Employment." *Journal of Urban Economics* 48 (2): 219–41.

Alesina, Alberto, Stephan Danninger, and Massimo Rostagno. 2001. "Redistribution through Public Employment: The Case of Italy." *IMF Staff Papers* 48 (3): 447–73.

Anderson, Christopher J. and Yuliya V. Tverdova. 2003. "Corruption, Political Allegiances, and Attitudes toward Government in Contemporary Democracies." *American Journal of Political Science* 47 (1): 91–109.

Andvig, Jens Chr and Karl Ove Moene. 1990. "How Corruption May Corrupt." *Journal of Economic Behavior & Organization* 13 (1): 63–76.

Anria, Santiago. 2016. "More Inclusion, Less Liberalism in Bolivia." *Journal of Democracy* 27 (3): 99–108.

   2018. *When Movements Become Parties: The Bolivian Mas in Comparative Perspective*. New York: Cambridge University Press.

Arcidiácono, Malena, Laura Carella, Leonardo Gasparini, Pablo Gluzmann, and Jorge Puig. 2014. "El Empleo Público En América Latina. Evidencia de Las Encuestas de Hogares." *CAF Banco de Desarrollo de América Latina* CAF Documento de Trabajo 2014/05. https://scioteca.caf.com/handle/123456789/711

Ascencio, Sergio and Miguel R. Rueda. 2019. "Partisan Poll Watchers and Electoral Manipulation." *American Political Science Review* 113 (3): 727–42.

Auerbach, Adam M. and Tariq Thachil. 2018. "How Clients Select Brokers: Competition and Choice in India's Slums." *American Political Science Review* 112 (4): 775–91.

Auyero, Javier. 2000. "The Logic of Clientelism in Argentina: An Ethnographic Account." *Latin American Research Review* 35 (3): 55–81.

2001. *Poor People's Politics: Peronist Survival Networks and the Legacy of Evita.* Durham: Duke University Press.

2007. *Routine Politics and Violence in Argentina: The Gray Zone of State Power.* New York: Cambridge University Press.

Auyero, Javier, Pablo Lapegna, and Fernanda Page Poma. 2009. "Patronage Politics and Contentious Collective Action: A Recursive Relationship." *Latin American Politics and Society* 51 (3): 1–31.

Aytaç, S. Erdem. 2014. "Distributive Politics in a Multiparty System: The Conditional Cash Transfer Program in Turkey." *Comparative Political Studies* 47 (9): 1211–37.

Aytaç, S. Erdem and Susan C. Stokes. 2019. *Why Bother?: Rethinking Participation in Elections and Protests.* New York: Cambridge University Press.

Baker, Andy and Dalton Dorr. 2019. "Dynamics of Mass Partisanship in Three Latin American Democracies." In *Campaigns and Voters in Developing Democracies: Argentina in Comparative Perspective*, edited by Noam Lupu, Virginia Oliveros, and Luis Schiumerini, 89–113. Ann Arbor: University of Michigan Press.

Baldwin, Kate. 2013. "Why Vote with the Chief? Political Connections and Public Goods Provision in Zambia." *American Journal of Political Science* 57 (4): 794–809.

2015. *The Paradox of Traditional Chiefs in Democratic Africa.* New York: Cambridge University Press.

Bambaci, Juliana, Pablo T. Spiller, and Mariano Tommasi. 2007. "The Bureaucracy." In *The Institutional Foundations of Public Policy: A Transactions Theory and an Application to Argentina*, edited by Pablo T. Spiller and Mariano Tommasi, 156–81. Cambridge: Cambridge University Press.

Banfield, Edward C. and James Q. Wilson. 1963. *City Politics.* Cambridge: Harvard University Press.

Behrend, Jacqueline. 2011. "The Unevenness of Democracy at the Subnational Level: Provincial Closed Games in Argentina." *Latin American Research Review* 46 (1): 150–76.

Bersch, Katherine, Sérgio Praça, and Matthew M. Taylor. 2017. "State Capacity, Bureaucratic Politicization, and Corruption in the Brazilian State." *Governance* 30 (1): 105–24.

Besley, Timothy, Torsten Persson, and Daniel M. Sturm. 2010. "Political Competition, Policy and Growth: Theory and Evidence from the US." *The Review of Economic Studies* 77 (4): 1329–52.

Blair, Graeme and Kosuke Imai. 2012. "Statistical Analysis of List Experiments." *Political Analysis* 20 (1): 47–77.

Boix, Carles. 2003. *Democracy and Redistribution*. New York: Cambridge University Press.

Boone, Catherine. 2011. "Politically Allocated Land Rights and the Geography of Electoral Violence: The Case of Kenya in the 1990s." *Comparative Political Studies* 44 (10): 1311–42.

Boräng, Frida, Agnes Cornell, Marcia Grimes, and Christian Schuster. 2018. "Cooking the Books: Bureaucratic Politicization and Policy Knowledge." *Governance* 31 (1): 7–26.

Bozçağa, Tuğba and Alisha C. Holland. 2018. "Enforcement Process Tracing: Forbearance and Dilution in Urban Colombia and Turkey." *Studies in Comparative International Development* 53 (3): 300–23.

Brassiolo, Pablo, Ricardo Estrada, and Gustavo Fajardo. 2020. "My (Running) Mate, the Mayor: Political Ties and Access to Public Sector Jobs in Ecuador." *Journal of Public Economics* 191: 104286.

Brierley, Sarah. 2021. "Combining Patronage and Merit in Public Sector Recruitment." *Journal of Politics* 83 (1): 182–97.

Brierley, Sarah and Noah L. Nathan. 2019. "The Connections of Party Brokers." *Working Paper*. www.sarahbrierley.com/publication/connections/connections.pdf

Brollo, Fernanda, Pedro Forquesato, and Juan Gozzi. 2017. "To the Victor Belongs the Spoils? Party Membership and Public Sector Employment in Brazil." *Working Paper*. http://dx.doi.org/10.2139/ssrn.3028937.

Brollo, Fernanda, Katja Kaufmann, and Eliana La Ferrara. 2020. "The Political Economy of Program Enforcement: Evidence from Brazil." *Journal of the European Economic Association* 18 (2): 750–91.

Brollo, Fernanda and Ugo Troiano. 2016. "What Happens When a Woman Wins an Election? Evidence from Close Races in Brazil." *Journal of Development Economics* 122: 28–45.

Brown, Vonda. 2011. "How Governments Abuse Advertisement in Latin America." *Open Society Foundations*. www.opensocietyfoundations.org/voices/how-governments-abuse-advertising-latin-america

Brusco, Valeria, Marcelo Nazareno, and Susan C. Stokes. 2004. "Vote Buying in Argentina." *Latin American Research Review* 39 (2): 66–88.

Callen, Michael, Saad Gulzar, Syed Ali Hasanain, and Muhammad Yasir Khan. 2016. "The Political Economy of Public Employee Absence: Experimental Evidence from Pakistan." *NBER Working Paper No. 22340.*

Callen, Michael, Saad Gulzar, and Arman Rezaee. 2020. "Can Political Alignment Be Costly?" *The Journal of Politics* 82 (2): 612–26.

Calvo, Ernesto and Juan Pablo Micozzi. 2005. "The Governor's Backyard: A Seat-Vote Model of Electoral Reform for Subnational Multiparty Races." *Journal of Politics* 67 (4): 1050–74.

Calvo, Ernesto and María Victoria Murillo. 2004. "Who Delivers? Partisan Clients in the Argentine Electoral Market." *American Journal of Political Science* 48 (4): 742–57.

2013. "When Parties Meet Voters Assessing Political Linkages Through Partisan Networks and Distributive Expectations in Argentina and Chile." *Comparative Political Studies* 46 (7): 851–82.

2019. *Non-Policy Politics: Richer Voter, Poorer Voter, and the Diversification of Parties' Electoral Offers*. New York: Cambridge University Press.

Calvo, Ernesto and Gergely Ujhelyi. 2012. "Political Screening: Theory and Evidence from the Argentine Public Sector." *Working Paper*. https://ideas.repec.org/p/hou/wpaper/201303201.html

Camp, Edwin. 2017. "Cultivating Effective Brokers: A Party Leader's Dilemma." *British Journal of Political Science* 47 (3): 521–43.

Cantú, Francisco. 2019. "Groceries for Votes: The Electoral Returns of Vote Buying." *The Journal of Politics* 81 (3): 790–804.

Casas, Agustín, Guillermo Díaz, and André Trindade. 2017. "Who Monitors the Monitor? Effect of Party Observers on Electoral Outcomes." *Journal of Public Economics* 145: 136–49.

Chambers-Ju, Christopher. 2017. "Protest or Politics? Varieties of Teacher Representation in Latin America." PhD dissertation, UC Berkeley.

  2021. "Adjustment Policies, Union Structures, and Strategies of Mobilization: Teacher Politics in Mexico and Argentina." *Comparative Politics* 53 (2): 185–207.

Chamorro, Catalina and Patricio Rosende. 2018. "Empleo Público en Chile: Nudos críticos, desafíos y líneas de desarrollo para una agenda 2030." *Ministerio de Hacienda, Gobierno de Chile.* http://biblioteca.digital.gob.cl/handle/123456789/3659.

Chandra, Kanchan. 2004. *Why Ethnic Parties Succeed: Patronage and Ethnic Head Counts in India.* New York: Cambridge University Press.

  2007. "Counting Heads: A Theory of Voter and Elite Behavior in Patronage Democracies." In *Patrons, Clients, and Policies: Patterns of Democratic Accountability and Political Competition*, edited by Herbert Kitschelt and Steven I. Wilkinson, 84–109. New York: Cambridge University Press.

Charron, Nicholas, Carl Dahlström, Mihály Fazekas, and Victor Lapuente. 2017. "Careers, Connections, and Corruption Risks: Investigating the Impact of Bureaucratic Meritocracy on Public Procurement Processes." *The Journal of Politics* 79 (1): 89–104.

Chattharakul, Anyarat. 2010. "Thai Electoral Campaigning: Vote-Canvassing Networks and Hybrid Voting." *Journal of Current Southeast Asian Affairs* 29 (4): 67–95.

Chauchard, Simon. 2018. "Electoral Handouts in Mumbai Elections." *Asian Survey* 58 (2): 341.

Chávez, Rebecca Bill. 2003. "The Construction of the Rule of Law in Argentina: A Tale of Two Provinces." *Comparative Politics* 35 (4): 417–37.

  2007. "The Appointment and Removal Process for Judges in Argentina: The Role of Judicial Councils and Impeachment Juries in Promoting Judicial Independence." *Latin American Politics and Society* 49 (2): 33–58.

Chong, Dennis. 1991. *Collective Action and the Civil Rights Movement.* Chicago: University of Chicago Press.

Chubb, Judith. 1981. "The Social Bases of an Urban Political Machine: The Case of Palermo." *Political Science Quarterly* 96 (1): 107–25.

  1982. *Patronage, Power and Poverty in Southern Italy: A Tale of Two Cities.* New York: Cambridge University Press.

Cingolani, Luciana, Kaj Thomsson, and Denis de Crombrugghe. 2015. "Minding Weber More Than Ever? The Impacts of State Capacity and Bureaucratic Autonomy on Development Goals." *World Development* 72: 191–207.

Cohen, Mollie J. 2018. "Protesting via the Null Ballot: An Assessment of the Decision to Cast an Invalid Vote in Latin America." *Political Behavior* 40 (2): 395–414.

Colonnelli, Emanuele, Mounu Prem, and Edoardo Teso. 2018. "Patronage and Selection in Public Sector Organizations." *Working Paper.* https://doi.org/10.2139/ssrn.2942495.

Cooperman, Alicia Dailey. 2019. "Trading Favors: Local Politics and Development in Brazil." PhD Dissertation. Columbia University.

Corbacho, Ana, Daniel W. Gingerich, Virginia Oliveros, and Mauricio Ruiz-Vega. 2016. "Corruption as a Self-Fulfilling Prophecy: Evidence from a Survey Experiment in Costa Rica." *American Journal of Political Science* 60 (4): 1077–92.

Cornell, Agnes. 2014. "Why Bureaucratic Stability Matters for the Implementation of Democratic Governance Programs." *Governance* 27 (2): 191–214.

Cornell, Agnes and Marcia Grimes. 2015. "Institutions as Incentives for Civic Action: Bureaucratic Structures, Civil Society, and Disruptive Protests." *The Journal of Politics* 77 (3): 664–78.

Corstange, Daniel. 2009. "Sensitive Questions, Truthful Answers? Modeling the List Experiment with LISTIT." *Political Analysis* 17 (1): 45–63.

Cortázar Velarde, Juan Carlos, Javier Fuenzalida, and Mariano Lafuente. 2016. "Merit-Based Selection of Public Managers: Better Public Sector Performance." *Inter-American Development Bank.* https://publications.iadb.org/en/merit-based-selection-public-managers-better-public-sector-performance-exploratory-study

Cortázar Velarde, Juan Carlos, Mariano Lafuente, and Mario Sanginés, eds. 2014. *A Decade of Civil Service Civil Reforms in Latin America (2004–13).* Washington, DC: Inter-American Development Bank.

Corvalan, Alejandro, Paulo Cox, and Rodrigo Osorio. 2018. "Indirect Political Budget Cycles: Evidence from Chilean Municipalities." *Journal of Development Economics* 133: 1–14.

Coutts, Elisabeth and Ben Jann. 2011. "Sensitive Questions in Online Surveys: Experimental Results for the Randomized Response Technique (RRT) and the Unmatched Count Technique (UCT)." *Sociological Methods & Research* 40 (1): 169–93.

Cox, Gary W. and Mathew D. McCubbins. 1986. "Electoral Politics as a Redistributive Game." *The Journal of Politics* 48 (2): 370–89.

Cruz, Cesi. 2015. "Vote Secrecy and Democracy in the Philippines." In *Building Inclusive Democracies In ASEAN,* edited by Ronald U. Mendoza, Edsel L. Beja Jr, Julio C. Teehankee, Antonio G. M. La Viña, and Maria Fe Villamejor-Mendoza, 39–52. Manila, Philippines: Anvil Publishing.

2019. "Social Networks and the Targeting of Vote Buying." *Comparative Political Studies* 52 (3): 382–411.

Cruz, Cesi and Philip Keefer. 2015. "Political Parties, Clientelism, and Bureaucratic Reform." *Comparative Political Studies* 48 (14): 1942–73.

Dahlberg, Stefan, Carl Dahlström, Petrus Sundin, and J. Teorell. 2013. "The Quality of Government Expert Survey 2008–2011: A Report." QoG Working Paper Series 15.

Dahlström, Carl and Victor Lapuente. 2017. *Organizing Leviathan: Politicians, Bureaucrats, and the Making of Good Government.* Cambridge: Cambridge University Press.

Dahlström, Carl, Victor Lapuente, and Jan Teorell. 2012. "The Merit of Meritocratization: Politics, Bureaucracy, and the Institutional Deterrents of Corruption." *Political Research Quarterly* 65 (3): 656–68.

Dalton, Dan R., James C. Wimbush, and Catherine M. Daily. 1994. "Using the Unmatched Count Technique (UCT) to Estimate Base Rates for Sensitive Behavior." *Personnel Psychology* 47 (4): 817–29.

De La O. and Ana L. 2013. "Do Conditional Cash Transfers Affect Electoral Behavior? Evidence from a Randomized Experiment in Mexico." *American Journal of Political Science* 57 (1): 1–14.

  2015. *Crafting Policies to End Poverty in Latin America*. New York: Cambridge University Press.

De La O., Ana L., and Jonathan A. Rodden. 2008. "Does Religion Distract the Poor? Income and Issue Voting around the World." *Comparative Political Studies* 41 (4–5): 437–76.

De la Torre, Carlos and Catherine Conaghan. 2009. "The Hybrid Campaign: Tradition and Modernity in Ecuador's 2006 Presidential Election." *The International Journal of Press/Politics* 14 (3): 335–52.

De Luca, Miguel, Mark P. Jones, and María Inés Tula. 2002. "Back Rooms or Ballot Boxes? Candidate Nomination in Argentina." *Comparative Political Studies* 35 (4): 413–36.

De Luca, Miguel, Mark Jones, and María Inés Tula. 2006. "Machine Politics and Party Primaries: The Uses and Consequences of Primaries within a Clientelist Political System." *Paper Prepared for Conference of the Mobilizing Democracy Group of the American Political Science Association*, New York.

Desposato, Scott W. 2007. "How Does Vote Buying Shape the Legislative Arena?" In *Elections for Sale: The Causes and Consequences of Vote Buying*, edited by Frederic Charles Schaffer, 101–22. Boulder, CO: Lynne Rienner Publishers.

Díaz-Cayeros, Alberto, Federico Estévez, and Beatriz Magaloni. 2016. *The Political Logic of Poverty Relief: Electoral Strategies and Social Policy in Mexico*. New York: Cambridge University Press.

Dirección de Presupuestos del Ministerio de Hacienda (Chile). 2019. "Informe Anual Del Empleo Público 2018." www.dipres.cl/598/articles-198056_doc_pdf.pdf

Domínguez, Lucila. 2017. "Primarias Obligatorias Subnacionales En Argentina (2003–2015)." Thesis UTDT. Buenos Aires. https://repositorio.utdt.edu/bitstream/handle/utdt/6526/LCP_2017_Dom%C3%ADnguez.pdf?sequence=1&isAllowed=y

Driscoll, Barry. 2018. "Why Political Competition Can Increase Patronage." *Studies in Comparative International Development* 53 (4): 404–27.

Druckman, James N., Donald P. Green, James H. Kuklinski, and Arthur Lupia. 2006. "The Growth and Development of Experimental Research in Political Science." *American Political Science Review* 100 (4): 627–35.

Eaton, Kent and Christopher Chambers-Ju. 2014. "Teachers, Mayors, and the Transformation of Clientelism in Colombia." In *Clientelism, Social Policy, and the Quality of Democracy*, edited by Diego Abente Brun and Larry Diamond, 88–113. Baltimore: John Hopkins University Press.

Echebarría, Koldo, ed. 2006. *Informe Sobre La Situación Del Servicio Civil En América Latina*. Washington: Inter-American Development Bank.

Evans, Peter and James E. Rauch. 1999. "Bureaucracy and Growth: A Cross-National Analysis of the Effects of "Weberian" State Structures on Economic Growth." *American Sociological Review* 64 (5): 748–65.

Ferejohn, John A. and Morris P. Fiorina. 1974. "The Paradox of Not Voting: A Decision Theoretic Analysis." *American Political Science Review* 68 (2): 525–36.

Ferraro, Agustín. 2006. "Una Idea Muy Precaria: El Nuevo Servicio Civil y Los Viejos Designados Políticos En Argentina." *Latin American Research Review* 41 (2): 165–82.

2011. "A Splendid Ruined Reform: The Creation and Destruction of a Civil Service in Argentina." In *International Handbook on Civil Service Systems*, edited by Andrew Massey, 152–77. Cheltenham: Edward Elgar.

Figueroa, Valentín. 2021. "Political Corruption Cycles: High-Frequency Evidence from Argentina's Notebooks Scandal." *Comparative Political Studies*, 54 (3).

Finan, Frederico and Laura Schechter. 2012. "Vote-Buying and Reciprocity." *Econometrica* 80 (2): 863–81.

Fisman, Ray and Miriam A. Golden. 2017. *Corruption: What Everyone Needs to Know.* Oxford: Oxford University Press.

Folke, Olle, Shigeo Hirano, and James M. Snyder. 2011. "Patronage and Elections in US States." *American Political Science Review* 105 (3): 567–85.

Frye, Timothy, Ora John Reuter, and David Szakonyi. 2014. "Political Machines at Work: Voter Mobilization and Electoral Subversion in the Workplace." *World Politics* 66 (2): 195–228.

2019. "Hitting Them With Carrots: Voter Intimidation and Vote Buying in Russia." *British Journal of Political Science* 49 (3): 857–81.

Fuenzalida, Javier, José Inostroza, and Marjorie Morales. 2014. "Alta Dirección Pública Municipal: Un Primer Paso Para Resolver Los Nudos Críticos de La Descentralización Chilena." *Revista Del CLAD Reforma y Democracia* 59: 119–50.

Gailmard, Sean and John W. Patty. 2012. "Formal Models of Bureaucracy." *Annual Review of Political Science* 15: 353–77.

Gaines, Brian J., James H. Kuklinski, and Paul J. Quirk. 2007. "The Logic of the Survey Experiment Reexamined." *Political Analysis* 15 (1): 1–20.

Garrido Silva, Carolina. 2013. "The Civil Service System and the Professionalization of Public Sector in Chile: Assessing the Stability of Bureaucrats." Working Paper, Columbia University.

Geddes, Barbara. 1994. *Politician's Dilemma: Building State Capacity in Latin America.* Berkeley: University of California Press.

Gervasoni, Carlos. 2010. "A Rentier Theory of Subnational Regimes: Fiscal Federalism, Democracy, and Authoritarianism in the Argentine Provinces." *World Politics* 62 (2): 302–40.

Gibson, Edward L. 2005. "Boundary Control: Subnational Authoritarianism in Democratic Countries." *World Politics* 58 (1): 101–32.

2013. *Boundary Control: Subnational Authoritarianism in Federal Democracies.* New York: Cambridge University Press.

Gibson, Edward L. and Ernesto Calvo. 2000. "Federalism and Low-Maintenance Constituencies: Territorial Dimensions of Economic Reform in Argentina." *Studies in Comparative International Development* 35 (3): 32–55.

Gil García, Magdalena. 2017. "Políticas de Empleo Público En La Provincia de Buenos Aires (1991-2016)." *Revista Perspectivas de Políticas Públicas* 7 (13): 139–60.

Gingerich, Daniel W. 2010. "Understanding Off-the-Books Politics: Conducting Inference on the Determinants of Sensitive Behavior with Randomized Response Surveys." *Political Analysis* 18 (3): 349–80.

2013a. "Governance Indicators and the Level of Analysis Problem: Empirical Findings from South America." *British Journal of Political Science* 43 (3): 505–40.

2013b. *Political Institutions and Party-Directed Corruption in South America: Stealing for the Team.* New York: Cambridge University Press.

Gingerich, Daniel W. and Luis Fernando Medina. 2013. "The Endurance and Eclipse of the Controlled Vote: A Formal Model of Vote Brokerage under the Secret Ballot." *Economics & Politics* 25 (3): 453–80.

Gingerich, Daniel W., Virginia Oliveros, Ana Corbacho, and Mauricio Ruiz-Vega. 2016. "When to Protect? Using the Crosswise Model to Integrate Protected and Direct Responses in Surveys of Sensitive Behavior." *Political Analysis* 24 (2): 132–56.

Giraudy, Agustina. 2007. "The Distributive Politics of Emergency Employment Programs in Argentina (1993-2002)." *Latin American Research Review* 42 (2): 33–55.

2010. "The Politics of Subnational Undemocratic Regime Reproduction in Argentina and Mexico." *Journal of Politics in Latin America* 2 (2): 53–84.

2013. "Varieties of Subnational Undemocratic Regimes: Evidence from Argentina and Mexico." *Studies in Comparative International Development* 48 (1): 51–80.

2015. *Democrats and Autocrats: Pathways of Subnational Undemocratic Regime Continuity within Democratic Countries.* Oxford: Oxford University Press.

Giraudy, Agustina, Eduardo Moncada, and Richard Snyder. 2019. "Subnational Research in Comparative Politics: Substantive, Theoretical, and Methodological Contributions." In *Inside Countries: Subnational Research in Comparative Politics*, edited by Agustina Giraudy, Eduardo Moncada, and Richard Snyder, 3–54. New York: Cambridge University Press.

Glynn, Adam N. 2013. "What Can We Learn with Statistical Truth Serum? Design and Analysis of the List Experiment." *Public Opinion Quarterly* 77 (S1): 159–72.

Golden, Miriam A. 2003. "Electoral Connections: The Effects of the Personal Vote on Political Patronage, Bureaucracy and Legislation in Postwar Italy." *British Journal of Political Science* 33 (2): 189–212.

Golden, Miriam, and Brian Min. 2013. "Distributive politics around the world." *Annual Review of Political Science* 16: 73–99.

González-Ocantos, Ezequiel, Chad Kiewiet de Jonge, Carlos Meléndez, Javier Osorio, and David W. Nickerson. 2012. "Vote Buying and Social Desirability Bias: Experimental Evidence from Nicaragua." *American Journal of Political Science* 56 (1): 202–17.

González-Ocantos, Ezequiel, Chad Kiewiet de Jonge, and Covadonga Meseguer. 2018. "Remittances and Vote Buying." *Latin American Research Review* 53 (4): 689–707.

González-Ocantos, Ezequiel, Chad Kiewiet de Jonge, and David W. Nickerson. 2014. "The Conditionality of Vote-Buying Norms: Experimental Evidence from Latin America." *American Journal of Political Science* 58 (1): 197–211.

2015. "Legitimacy Buying: The Dynamics of Clientelism in the Face of Legitimacy Challenges." *Comparative Political Studies* 48 (9): 1127–58.

González-Ocantos, Ezequiel and Paula Muñoz. 2018. "Clientelism." In *The SAGE Handbook of Political Sociology*, edited by William Outhwaite and Stephen Turner, 750–766. Thousand Oaks, CA: Sage Publications Ltd.

González-Ocantos, Ezequiel and Virginia Oliveros. 2019. "Clientelism in Latin American Politics." In *The Encyclopedia of Latin American Politics*, edited by Gary Prevost and Harry Vanden. Oxford: Oxford University Press. https://doi.org /10.1093/acrefore/9780190228637.013.1677

Gordin, Jorge P. 2002. "The Political and Partisan Determinants of Patronage in Latin America 1960-1994: A Comparative Perspective." *European Journal of Political Research* 41 (4): 513–49.

Gottlieb, Jessica. 2017. "Explaining Variation in Broker Strategies: A Lab-in-the-Field Experiment in Senegal." *Comparative Political Studies* 50 (11): 1556–92.

Graziano, Luigi. 1976. "A Conceptual Framework for the Study of Clientelistic Behavior." *European Journal of Political Research* 4 (2): 149–74.

Greene, Kenneth F. 2010. "The Political Economy of Authoritarian Single-Party Dominance." *Comparative Political Studies* 43 (7): 807–34.

2019. "Dealigning Campaign Effects in Argentina in Comparative Perspective." In *Campaigns and Voters in Developing Democracies: Argentina in Comparative Perspective*, edited by Noam Lupu, Virginia Oliveros, and Luis Schiumerini, 162–86. Ann Arbor: University of Michigan Press.

Grindle, Merilee S. 2012. *Jobs for the Boys: Patronage and the State in Comparative Perspective*. Cambridge, Mass: Harvard University Press.

Grzymala-Busse, Anna. 2003. "Political Competition and the Politicization of the State in East Central Europe." *Comparative Political Studies* 36 (10): 1123–47.

2007. *Rebuilding Leviathan: Party Competition and State Exploitation in Post-Communist Democracies*. New York: Cambridge University Press.

2008. "Beyond Clientelism Incumbent State Capture and State Formation." *Comparative Political Studies* 41 (4–5): 638–73.

Hafner-Burton, Emilie M., Susan D. Hyde, and Ryan S. Jablonski. 2014. "When Do Governments Resort to Election Violence?" *British Journal of Political Science* 44 (1): 149–79.

Hassan, Mai. 2017. "The Strategic Shuffle: Ethnic Geography, the Internal Security Apparatus, and Elections in Kenya." *American Journal of Political Science* 61 (2): 382–95.

Hecock, R. Douglas. 2006. "Electoral Competition, Globalization, and Subnational Education Spending in Mexico, 1999–2004." *American Journal of Political Science* 50 (4): 950–61.

Helmke, Gretchen and Steven Levitsky. 2004. "Informal Institutions and Comparative Politics: A Research Agenda." *Perspectives on Politics* 2 (4): 725–40.

Henderson, Jeffrey, David Hulme, Hossein Jalilian, and Richard Phillips. 2007. "Bureaucratic Effects: 'Weberian' State Agencies and Poverty Reduction." *Sociology* 41 (3): 515–32.

Herrera, Veronica. 2017. *Water and Politics: Clientelism and Reform in Urban Mexico*. Ann Arbor: University of Michigan Press.

Hicken, Allen. 2011. "Clientelism." *Annual Review of Political Science* 14: 289–310.

Hiskey, Jonathan T. 2003. "Demand-Based Development and Local Electoral Environments in Mexico." *Comparative Politics* 36 (1): 41–59. https://doi.org/10 .2307/4150159.

Holland, Alisha C. 2016. "Forbearance." *American Political Science Review* 110 (2): 232–46.

2017. *Forbearance as Redistribution: The Politics of Informal Welfare in Latin America.* New York: Cambridge University Press.

Holland, Alisha C. and Brian Palmer-Rubin. 2015. "Beyond the Machine Clientelist Brokers and Interest Organizations in Latin America." *Comparative Political Studies* 48 (9): 1186–1223.

Holzner, Claudio A. 2010. *Poverty of Democracy: The Institutional Roots of Political Participation in Mexico.* Pittsburgh: University of Pittsburgh Press.

Hopkin, Jonathan. 2004. "The Problem with Party Finance: Theoretical Perspectives on the Funding of Party Politics." *Party Politics* 10 (6): 627–51.

Huber, John D. and Piero Stanig. 2011. "Church-State Separation and Redistribution." *Journal of Public Economics* 95 (7–8): 828–36.

Huntington, Samuel P. 1991. "Democracy's Third Wave." *Journal of Democracy* 2 (2): 12–34.

Iacoviello, Mercedes. 2006. "Análisis Comparativo Por Subsistemas."*Informe Sobre La Situación Del Servicio Civil En América Latina*, edited by Koldo Echebarría, 533–72. Washington, DC: Inter-American Development Bank.

2009a. "Diagnóstico Institucional Del Sistema de Servicio Civil de Chile." In *Evaluación Final Del Programa de Fortalecimiento de La Dirección Nacional de Servicio Civil.* BID – Gobierno de Chile.

2009b. "Informe de República Dominicana." In *Barómetro de la Profesionalización de los Servicios Civiles de Centroamérica y República Dominicana*, edited by Francisco Longo, 30–81. Santo Domingo: AECID, FLACSO, and SICA.

Iacoviello, Mercedes and Mariana Chudnovsky. 2015. "La Importancia Del Servicio Civil En El Desarrollo de Capacidades Estatales En América Latina." *CAF Banco de Desarrollo de América Latina* Working Paper 2015/02.

Iacoviello, Mercedes and Mercedes Llano. 2017. "Confianza Mata Mérito: El Impacto de La Concentración de Poder Presidencial En La Gestión de Recursos Humanos En El Estado Argentino." *Temas y Debates* 33: 91–105.

Iacoviello, Mercedes and Luciano Strazza. 2014. "Diagnostic of the Civil Service in Latin America." In *A Decade of Civil Service Civil Reforms in Latin America (2004–13)*, edited by Juan Carlos Cortázar Velarde, Mariano Lafuente, and Mario Sanginés, 13–57. Washington, DC: Inter-American Development Bank.

Iacoviello, Mercedes and Laura Zuvanic. 2006a. "Síntesis Del Diagnóstico: Caso Argentina." In *Informe Sobre La Situación Del Servicio Civil En América Latina*, edited by Koldo Echebarría, 73–96. Washington, DC: Inter-American Development Bank.

2006b. "Síntesis Del Diagnóstico: Caso Bolivia." In *Informe Sobre La Situación Del Servicio Civil En América Latina*, edited by Koldo Echebarría, 97–118. Washington, DC: Inter-American Development Bank.

Iaryczower, Matias, Garrett Lewis, and Matthew Shum. 2013. "To Elect or to Appoint? Bias, Information, and Responsiveness of Bureaucrats and Politicians." *Journal of Public Economics* 97: 230–44.

Imai, Kosuke. 2011. "Multivariate Regression Analysis for the Item Count Technique." *Journal of the American Statistical Association* 106 (494): 407–16.

Iturburu, Mónica. 2012a. "Informe El Salvador." In *Segundo Informe Barómetro de la Profesionalización del Empleo Público en Centroamérica y República Dominicana*, edited by Eduardo Rolando Castillo Quintana. Agencia Española de Cooperación Internacional (AECID) and Secretaría General del Sistema de la Integración Centroamericana (SG-SICA).

2012b. "Informe Guatemala." In *Segundo Informe Barómetro de la Profesionalización del Empleo Público En Centroamérica y República Dominicana*, edited by Eduardo Rolando Castillo Quintana. Agencia Española de Cooperación Internacional (AECID) and Secretaría General del Sistema de la Integración Centroamericana (SG-SICA).

Iyer, Lakshmi and Anandi Mani. 2012. "Traveling Agents: Political Change and Bureaucratic Turnover in India." *Review of Economics and Statistics* 94 (3): 723–39.

James, Scott C. 2006. "Patronage Regimes and American Party Development from 'The Age of Jackson' to the Progressive Era." *British Journal of Political Science* 36 (1): 39–60.

Johnston, Michael. 1979. "Patrons and Clients, Jobs and Machines: A Case Study of the Uses of Patronage." *American Political Science Review* 73 (2): 385–98.

Jones, Mark P. and Wonjae Hwang. 2005. "Party Government in Presidential Democracies: Extending Cartel Theory beyond the US Congress." *American Journal of Political Science* 49 (2): 267–82.

Jones, Mark P., Sebastián Saiegh, Pablo T. Spiller, and Mariano Tommasi. 2002. "Amateur Legislators–Professional Politicians: The Consequences of Party-Centered Electoral Rules in a Federal System." *American Journal of Political Science* 46 (3): 656–69.

Kemahlioğlu, Özge. 2012. *Agents or Bosses?: Patronage and Intra-Party Politics in Argentina and Turkey*. Colchester: ECPR Press.

Kemahlioğlu, Özge and Reşat Bayer. 2020. "Favoring Co-Partisan Controlled Areas in Central Government Distributive Programs: The Role of Local Party Organizations." *Public Choice*, 1–19. https://doi.org/10.1007/s11127-019-00774-5

Key, V. O. 1956. *Politics, Parties, and Pressure Groups*. 4th ed. New York: Thomas Y. Crowell Company.

Kiewiet de Jonge, Chad and David W. Nickerson. 2014. "Artificial Inflation or Deflation? Assessing the Item Count Technique in Comparative Surveys." *Political Behavior* 36 (3): 659–82.

Kitschelt, Herbert. 2007. "The Demise of Clientelism in Affluent Capitalist Democracies." In *Patrons, Clients, and Policies. Patterns of Democratic Accountability and Political Competition*, edited by Herbert Kitschelt and Steven I. Wilkinson, 298–321. New York: Cambridge University Press.

Kitschelt, Herbert and Melina Altamirano. 2015. "Clientelism in Latin America: Effort and Effectiveness." In *The Latin American Voter: Pursuing Representation and Accountability in Challenging Contexts*, edited by Ryan E. Carlin, Matthew M. Singer and Elizabeth J. Zechmeister, 246–74. Ann Arbor: University of Michigan Press.

Kitschelt, Herbert, Juan Pablo Luna, and Elizabeth J. Zechmeister. 2010. "Programmatic Structuration and Democratic Performance." In *Latin American*

Party Systems, edited by Herbert Kitschelt, Kirk A. Hawkins, Juan Pablo Luna, Guillermo Rosas, and Elizabeth J. Zechmeister, 279–305. Cambridge: Cambridge University Press.

Kitschelt, Herbert and Steven I. Wilkinson. 2007a. "A Research Agenda for the Study of Citizen-Politician Linkages and Democratic Accountability." In *Patrons, Clients, and Policies: Patterns of Democratic Accountability and Political Competition*, edited by Herbert Kitschelt and Steven I. Wilkinson, 322–43. New York: Cambridge University Press.

2007b. "Citizen-Politician Linkages: An Introduction." In *Patrons, Clients, and Policies: Patterns of Democratic Accountability and Political Competition*, edited by Herbert Kitschelt and Steven I. Wilkinson, 1–49. New York: Cambridge University Press.

eds. 2007c. *Patrons, Clients and Policies: Patterns of Democratic Accountability and Political Competition*. 1st ed. New York: Cambridge University Press.

Kopecký, Petr. 2011. "Political Competition and Party Patronage: Public Appointments in Ghana and South Africa." *Political Studies* 59 (3): 713–32.

Kopecký, Petr and Peter Mair. 2006. "Political Parties and Patronage in Contemporary Democracies: An Introduction." *Paper prepared for the ECPR Joint Sessions of Workshops, Nicosia, Cyprus*, 25–30 April.

2012. "Party Patronage as an Organizational Resource." In *Party Patronage and Party Government in European Democracies*, edited by Petr Kopecký, Peter Mair, and Maria Spirova, 3–16. Oxford: Oxford University Press.

Kopecký, Petr, Peter Mair, and Maria Spirova, eds. 2012. *Party Patronage and Party Government in European Democracies*. Oxford: Oxford University Press.

Kopecký, Petr, Jan-Hinrik Meyer Sahling, Francisco Panizza, Gerardo Scherlis, Christian Schuster, and Maria Spirova. 2016. "Party Patronage in Contemporary Democracies: Results from an Expert Survey in 22 Countries from Five Regions." *European Journal of Political Research* 55 (2): 416–31.

Kopecký, Petr, Gerardo Scherlis, and Maria Spirova. 2008. "Conceptualizing and Measuring Party Patronage." *Political Concepts, Committee on Concepts and Methods Working Paper Series* 25: 1–18.

Kramon, Eric. 2016a. "Electoral Handouts as Information: Explaining Unmonitored Vote Buying." *World Politics* 68 (3): 454–98.

2016b. "Where Is Vote Buying Effective? Evidence from a List Experiment in Kenya." *Electoral Studies* 44: 397–408.

Kuklinski, James H., Paul M. Sniderman, Kathleen Knight, Thomas Piazza, Philip E. Tetlock, Gordon R. Lawrence, and Barbara Mellers. 1997. "Racial Prejudice and Attitudes toward Affirmative Action." *American Journal of Political Science* 41 (2): 402–19.

Larreguy, Horacio, John Marshall, and Pablo Querubín. 2016. "Parties, Brokers, and Voter Mobilization: How Turnout Buying Depends upon the Party's Capacity to Monitor Brokers." *American Political Science Review* 110 (1): 160–79.

Larreguy, Horacio, César E. Montiel Olea, and Pablo Querubín. 2017. "Political Brokers: Partisans or Agents? Evidence from the Mexican Teachers' Union." *American Journal of Political Science* 61 (4): 877–91.

Lawson, Chappell and Kenneth F. Greene. 2014. "Making Clientelism Work: How Norms of Reciprocity Increase Voter Compliance." *Comparative Politics* 47 (1): 61–85.

Lazar, Sian. 2004. "Personalist Politics, Clientelism and Citizenship: Local Elections in El Alto, Bolivia." *Bulletin of Latin American Research* 23 (2): 228–43.

Lehoucq, Fabrice. 2007. "When Does a Market for Votes Emerge? Historical and Theoretical Perspectives." In *Elections for Sale: The Causes and Consequences of Vote Buying*, edited by Frederic Charles Schaffer, 33–45. Boulder, CO: Lynne Rienner Publishers.

Leiras, Marcelo, María Page, Soledad Zárate, and Josefina Mignone. 2016. "Votar En El Conurbano: La Experiencia de Administrar Una Mesa y Fiscalizar La Elección 2015." *Documento de Políticas Públicas* 177, CIPPEC: 1–10.

Levitsky, Steven. 2003. *Transforming Labor-Based Parties in Latin America: Argentine Peronism in Comparative Perspective*. Cambridge: Cambridge University Press.

Levitsky, Steven and María Victoria Murillo, eds. 2005. *Argentine Democracy: The Politics of Institutional Weakness*. University Park, Pennsylvania: Pennsylvania State University Press.

2009. "Variation in Institutional Strength." *Annual Review of Political Science* 12: 115–33.

Leyton Navarro, Cristian Marcelo. 2006. "Balance Del Proceso de Descentralización En Chile 1990–2005. Una Mirada Regional y Municipal." Magister Thesis, Universidad de Chile. http://repositorio.conicyt.cl/handle/10533/178886?show=full

Lipsky, Michael. 1980. *Street-Level Bureaucracy: Dilemmas of the Individual in Public Service*. New York: Russell Sage Foundation.

Lizzeri, Alessandro and Nicola Persico. 2001. "The Provision of Public Goods under Alternative Electoral Incentives." *American Economic Review* 91 (1): 225–39.

2004. "Why Did the Elites Extend the Suffrage? Democracy and the Scope of Government, with an Application to Britain's 'Age of Reform.'" *The Quarterly Journal of Economics* 119 (2): 707–65.

Llano, Mercedes. 2014. *Diagnóstico Institucional Del Servicio Civil En América Latina: Chile*. Washington, DC: Inter-American Development Bank.

Lodola, Germán. 2005. "Protesta Popular y Redes Clientelares En La Argentina: El Reparto Federal Del Plan Trabajar (1996-2001)." *Desarrollo Económico* 44 (176): 515–36.

Longo, Francisco. 2006a. "Análisis Comparativo Por Índices." In *Informe Sobre La Situación Del Servicio Civil En América Latina*, edited by Koldo Echebarría, 573–92. Washington, DC: Inter-American Development Bank.

2006b. "Una Lectura Transversal de Los Resultados." In *Informe Sobre La Situación Del Servicio Civil En América Latina*, edited by Koldo Echebarría, 593–610. Washington, DC: Inter-American Development Bank.

Luna, Juan Pablo and Rodrigo Mardones. 2016. "Targeted Social Policy Allocations by 'Clean' State Bureaucracies: Chile 2000–2009." *Journal of International and Comparative Social Policy* 32 (1): 36–56.

Lupu, Noam. 2015. "Partisanship in Latin America." In *The Latin American Voter: Pursuing Representation and Accountability in Challenging Contexts*, edited by Ryan E. Carlin, Matthew M. Singer, and Elizabeth J. Zechmeister, 226–45. Ann Arbor: University of Michigan Press.

Lupu, Noam, Carlos Gervasoni, Virginia Oliveros, and Luis Schiumerini. 2015. "Argentine Panel Election Study." www.noamlupu.com/data.html

Lupu, Noam, Virginia Oliveros, and Luis Schiumerini. 2019. "Toward a Theory of Campaigns and Voters in Developing Democracies." In *Campaigns and Voters in Developing Democracies: Argentina in Comparative Perspective*, edited by Noam Lupu, Virginia Oliveros, and Luis Schiumerini, 1–27. Ann Arbor: University of Michigan Press.

Madrid, Raúl L. 2012. "Indigenous Parties and Democracy in the Andes." In *The Rise of Ethnic Politics in Latin America*, 162–84. New York: Cambridge University Press.

Magaloni, Beatriz. 2006. *Voting for Autocracy: Hegemonic Party Survival and Its Demise in Mexico*. Cambridge: Cambridge University Press.

Magaloni, Beatriz, Alberto Díaz-Cayeros, and Federico Estévez. 2007. "Clientelism and Portfolio Diversification: A Model of Electoral Investment with Applications to Mexico." In *Patrons, Clients, and Policies: Patterns of Democratic Accountability and Political Competition*, edited by Herbert Kitschelt and Steven I. Wilkinson, 182–205. New York: Cambridge University Press.

Mares, Isabela, Aurelian Muntean, and Tsveta Petrova. 2017. "Pressure, Favours, and Vote-Buying: Experimental Evidence from Romania and Bulgaria." *Europe-Asia Studies* 69 (6): 940–60.

Mares, Isabela and Lauren E. Young. 2016. "Buying, Expropriating, and Stealing Votes." *Annual Review of Political Science* 19: 267–88.

2018. "The Core Voter's Curse: Clientelistic Threats and Promises in Hungarian Elections." *Comparative Political Studies* 51 (11): 1141–71.

2019a. *Conditionality & Coercion: Electoral Clientelism in Eastern Europe*. Oxford: Oxford University Press.

2019b. "Varieties of Clientelism in Hungarian Elections." *Comparative Politics* 51 (3): 449–80.

Mayhew, David R. 1974. *Congress: The Electoral Connection*. New Haven: Yale University Press.

Mazzuca, Sebastián L. 2010. "Access to Power versus Exercise of Power Reconceptualizing the Quality of Democracy in Latin America." *Studies in Comparative International Development* 45 (3): 334–57.

McMann, Kelly M. 2006. *Economic Autonomy and Democracy: Hybrid Regimes in Russia and Kyrgyzstan*. Cambridge: Cambridge University Press.

Medina, Luis Fernando and Susan C. Stokes. 2002. "Clientelism as Political Monopoly." Paper presented at the 2002 Annual Meetings of the American Political Science Association Conference. Boston.

2007. "Monopoly and Monitoring: An Approach to Political Clientelism." In *Patrons, Clients, and Policies. Patterns of Democratic Accountability and Political Competition*, edited by Herbert Kitschelt and Steven I. Wilkinson, 68–83. Cambridge: Cambridge University Press.

Meyer-Sahling, Jan-Hinrik. 2006. "The Rise of the Partisan State? Parties, Patronage and the Ministerial Bureaucracy in Hungary." *Journal of Communist Studies and Transition Politics* 22 (3): 274–97.

Meyer-Sahling, Jan-Hinrik and Kim Sass Mikkelsen. 2016. "Civil Service Laws, Merit, Politicization, and Corruption: The Perspective of Public Officials from Five East European Countries." *Public Administration* 94 (4): 1105–23.

Meyer-Sahling, Jan-Hinrik, Christian Schuster, and Kim Sass Mikkelsen. 2020. "Civil Service Management in Developing Countries: What Works?: Evidence from a Survey with 23,000 Civil Servants in Africa, Asia, Eastern Europe and Latin

America." Report for the UK Department for International Development (DFID). https://nottingham-repository.worktribe.com/output/1649287.

Micozzi, Juan Pablo. 2009. "The Electoral Connection in Multi-Level Systems with Non-Static Ambition: Linking Political Careers and Legislative Performance in Argentina." PhD Dissertation, Rice University. https://scholarship.rice.edu/handle/1911/61922

Mimica, Nicolás and Patricio Navia. 2019. "Causas y Efectos Del Patronazgo En Municipios de Chile, 2008-2012." *Perfiles Latinoamericanos* 27 (54): 83–109.

Moscovich, Lorena. 2016. "El Doble Estatus de Los Cuerpos Burocráticos Subnacionales: El Balance Entre Gestión Pública y Acumulación Política. Propuesta de Análisis Con Evidencia de Un País Federal." *Revista SAAP* 10 (1): 1–9.

Müller, Wolfgang C. 2006. "Party Patronage and Party Colonization of the State." In *Handbook of Party Politics*, edited by Richard S. Katz and William Crotty, 189–95. London: Sage Publications.

2007. "Political Institutions and Linkage Strategies." In *Patrons, Clients, and Policies. Patterns of Democratic Accountability and Political Competition*, edited by Herbert Kitschelt and Steven I. Wilkinson, 251–75. New York: Cambridge University Press.

Muñoz, Paula. 2014. "An Informational Theory of Campaign Clientelism: The Case of Peru." *Comparative Politics* 47 (1): 79–98.

2018. *Buying Audiences: Clientelism and Electoral Campaigns When Parties Are Weak*. New York: Cambridge University Press.

Murillo, María Victoria, Virginia Oliveros, and Rodrigo Zarazaga. 2021. "The Most Vulnerable Poor: Clientelism among Slum Dwellers." *Studies in Comparative International Development*. https://link.springer.com/article/10.1007/s12116-021-09324-x

Murillo, María Victoria and Lucas Ronconi. 2004. "Teachers' Strikes in Argentina: Partisan Alignments and Public-Sector Labor Relations." *Studies in Comparative International Development* 39 (1): 77–98.

Nazareno, Marcelo, Susan C. Stokes, and Valeria Brusco. 2006. "Réditos y Peligros Electorales Del Gasto Público En La Argentina." *Desarrollo Económico* 46 (181): 63–88.

Nichter, Simeon. 2008. "Vote Buying or Turnout Buying? Machine Politics and the Secret Ballot." *American Political Science Review* 102 (1): 19–31.

2009. "Declared Choice: Citizen Strategies and Dual Commitment Problems in Clientelism." In *APSA 2009 Toronto Meeting Paper*.

2011. "Electoral Clientelism or Relational Clientelism? Healthcare and Sterilization in Brazil." Paper Presented at the American Political Science Conference Meeting, Seattle Washington.

2014. "Conceptualizing Vote Buying." *Electoral Studies* 35: 315–27.

Nichter, Simeon and Michael Peress. 2017. "Request Fulfilling: When Citizens Demand Clientelist Benefits." *Comparative Political Studies* 50 (8): 1086–1117.

O'Donnell, Guillermo. 1993. "On the State, Democratization and Some Conceptual Problems: A Latin American View with Glances at Some Post-Communist Countries." *World Development* 21 (8): 1355–69.

1996. "Illusions about Consolidation." *Journal of Democracy* 7 (2): 34–51.

2010. *Democracy, Agency, and the State: Theory with Comparative Intent*. Oxford: Oxford University Press.

O'Donnell, María. 2005. *El Aparato: Los Intendentes Del Conurbano y Las Cajas Negras de La Política*. Buenos Aires: Aguilar.

O'Dwyer, Conor. 2004. "Runaway State Building: How Political Parties Shape States in Postcommunist Eastern Europe." *World Politics* 56 (4): 520–53.

Oliveros, Virginia. 2016. "Making It Personal: Clientelism, Favors, and the Personalization of Public Administration in Argentina." *Comparative Politics* 48 (3): 373–91.

   2019. "Perceptions of Ballot Integrity and Clientelism." In *Campaigns and Voters in Developing Democracies: Argentina in Comparative Perspective*, edited by Noam Lupu, Virginia Oliveros, and Luis Schiumerini, 213–38. Ann Arbor: University of Michigan Press.

Oliveros, Virginia and Gerardo Scherlis. 2004. "¿Elecciones Concurrentes o Elecciones Desdobladas?: La Manipulación de los Calendarios Electorales en la Argentina, 1983-2003." In *¿Qué Cambió en la Política Argentina? Elecciones, Instituciones y Ciudadanía en Perspectiva Comparada*, edited by Isidoro Cheresky and Jean-Michel Blanquer, 179–211. Buenos Aires: Homo Sapiens.

Oliveros, Virginia and Christian Schuster. 2018. "Merit, Tenure, and Bureaucratic Behavior: Evidence from a Conjoint Experiment in the Dominican Republic." *Comparative Political Studies* 51 (6): 759–92.

Olson, Mancur. 1965. *Logic of Collective Action: Public Goods and the Theory of Groups (Harvard Economic Studies. v. 124)*. Cambridge: Harvard University Press.

Ortiz de Rozas, Victoria. 2017. "Clientelismo, Territorio y Política Subnacional En Argentina. Aportes a Partir Del Caso de Santiago Del Estero." *Colombia Internacional* 90: 127–56.

Ostrom, Elinor. 2000. "Collective Action and the Evolution of Social Norms." *Journal of Economic Perspectives* 14 (3): 137–58.

Ostrom, Elinor and James Walker. 1997. "Neither Markets Nor States: Linking Transformation Processes in Collective Action Arenas." In *Perspectives on Public Choice: A Handbook*, edited by Dennis C. Mueller, 35–72. Cambridge: Cambridge University Press.

   2003. *Trust and Reciprocity: Interdisciplinary Lessons for Experimental Research*. Russell Sage Foundation.

Palmer-Rubin, Brian. 2016. "Interest Organizations and Distributive Politics: Small-Business Subsidies in Mexico." *World Development* 84: 97–117.

Panizza, Francisco, Conrado Ricardo Ramos Larraburu, and Gerardo Scherlis. 2018. "Unpacking Patronage: The Politics of Patronage Appointments in Argentina's and Uruguay's Central Public Administrations." *Journal of Politics in Latin America* 10 (3): 59–98.

Pasotti, Eleonora. 2010. *Political Branding in Cities: The Decline of Machine Politics in Bogotá, Naples, and Chicago*. New York: Cambridge University Press.

Pempel, T. John. 1990. "Introduction." In *Uncommon Democracies: The One-Party Dominant Regimes*, edited by T. John Pempel, 1–32. Ithaca: Cornell University Press.

Pepinsky, Thomas B., Jan H. Pierskalla, and Audrey Sacks. 2017. "Bureaucracy and Service Delivery." *Annual Review of Political Science* 20: 249–68.

Persson, Torsten and Guido Tabellini. 1999. "The Size and Scope of Government: Comparative Politics with Rational Politicians." *European Economic Review* 43 (4): 699–735.

2000. *Political Economics: Explaining Economic Policy*. Cambridge, Mass: MIT press.

Piattoni, Simona. 2001. "Clientelism in Historical and Comparative Perspective." In *Clientelism, Interests, and Democratic Representation*, edited by Simona Piattoni, 1–29. Cambridge: Cambridge University Press.

Pierskalla, Jan H. and Audrey Sacks. 2020. "Personnel Politics: Elections, Clientelistic Competition and Teacher Hiring in Indonesia." *British Journal of Political Science* 50 (4): 1283–305.

Polga-Hecimovich, John. 2019. "Bureaucracy in Latin America." In *The Encyclopedia of Latin American Politics*, edited by Gary Prevost and Harry Vanden. Oxford: Oxford University Press. https://oxfordre.com/politics/view/10.1093/acrefore/9780190228637.001.0001/acrefore-9780190228637-e-1675

Pollock, James Kerr. 1937. "The Cost of the Patronage System." *The Annals of the American Academy of Political and Social Science* 189 (1): 29–34.

Pomares, Julia, José Gasparin, and Diego Deleersnyder. 2013. "Evolución y Distribución Del Empleo Público En El Sector Público Nacional Argentino. Una Primera Aproximación." *Documento de Políticas Públicas N°117*. Buenos Aires: CIPPEC.

Pomares, Julia, María Page, and Gerardo Scherlis. 2011. "La Primera Vez de Las Primarias: Logros y Desafíos." *Documento de Políticas Públicas N°97*. Buenos Aires: CIPPEC.

Pradhanawati, Ari, George Towar Ikbal Tawakkal, and Andrew D. Garner. 2019. "Voting Their Conscience: Poverty, Education, Social Pressure and Vote Buying in Indonesia." *Journal of East Asian Studies* 19 (1): 19–38.

Quirós, Julieta. 2006. "Movimientos Piqueteros, Formas de Trabajo y Circulación de Valor En El Sur Del Gran Buenos Aires." *Anuario de Estudios En Antropología Social*, 151–60.

2008. "Piqueteros y Peronistas En La Lucha Del Gran Buenos Aires. Por Una Visión No Instrumental de La Política Popular." *Cuadernos de Antropología Social* 27: 113–31.

Rauch, James E. 1995. "Bureaucracy, Infrastructure, and Economic Growth: Evidence from US Cities during the Progressive Era." *The American Economic Review* 85 (4): 968–79.

Rauch, James E. and Peter B. Evans. 2000. "Bureaucratic Structure and Bureaucratic Performance in Less Developed Countries." *Journal of Public Economics* 75 (1): 49–71.

Remmer, Karen L. 2007. "The Political Economy of Patronage: Expenditure Patterns in the Argentine Provinces, 1983–2003." *Journal of Politics* 69 (2): 363–77.

Robinson, James A. and Thierry Verdier. 2013. "The Political Economy of Clientelism." *Scandinavian Journal of Economics* 115 (2): 260–91.

Rocca Rivarola, Dolores. 2019. "Militancia y Estado: Concepciones y Prácticas En Organizaciones Afines al Gobierno En Brasil (2003-2016) y Argentina (2003-2015)." *Perfiles Latinoamericanos* 27 (54): 51–81.

Ronconi, Lucas and Rodrigo Zarazaga. 2019. "Household-Based Clientelism: Brokers' Allocation of Temporary Public Works Programs in Argentina." *Studies in Comparative International Development Volume* 54: 365–80.

Roniger, Luis. 2004. "Political Clientelism, Democracy, and Market Economy." *Comparative Politics* 36 (3): 353–75.

Rose-Ackerman, Susan. 1999. *Corruption and Government: Causes, Consequences, and Reform*. Cambridge, UK: Cambridge University Press.

Rosenzweig, Steven C. 2015. "Does Electoral Competition Affect Public Goods Provision in Dominant-Party Regimes? Evidence from Tanzania." *Electoral Studies* 39: 72–84.

Rothstein, Bo, Marcus Samanni, and Jan Teorell. 2012. "Explaining the Welfare State: Power Resources vs. the Quality of Government." *European Political Science Review* 4 (1): 1–28.

Rueda, Miguel R. 2015. "Buying Votes with Imperfect Local Knowledge and a Secret Ballot." *Journal of Theoretical Politics* 27 (3): 428–56.

2017. "Small Aggregates, Big Manipulation: Vote Buying Enforcement and Collective Monitoring." *American Journal of Political Science* 61 (1): 163–77.

Scacco, Alexandra. 2010. "Who Riots? Explaining Individual Participation in Ethnic Violence." PhD Dissertation, Columbia University.

Schady, Norbert R. 2000. "The Political Economy of Expenditures by the Peruvian Social Fund (FONCODES), 1991–95." *American Political Science Review* 94 (2): 289–304.

Schaffer, Frederic Charles. 2007. "Why Study Vote Buying." In *Elections for Sale: The Causes and Consequences of Vote Buying*, edited by Frederic Charles Schaffer, 1–16. Boulder, CO: Lynne Rienner Publishers.

Schaffer, Frederic Charles and Andres Schedler. 2007. "What Is Vote Buying?" In *Elections for Sale: The Causes and Consequences of Vote Buying*, edited by Frederic Charles Schaffer, 17–30. Boulder, CO: Lynne Rienner Publishers.

Scherlis, Gerardo. 2005. "Provincial Partisan Patronage and National Party System Stability in Argentina, 1983–2005." Paper prepared for the Workshop *"Political Parties and Patronage," European Consortium for Political Research (ECPR) Joint Sessions, Nicosia, Cyprus, April*.

2010. "Patronage and Party Organization in Argentina: The Emergence of the Patronage Based Network Party." PhD Dissertation, Leiden University.

2013. "The Contours of Party Patronage in Argentina." *Latin American Research Review* 48 (3): 63–84.

Schiumerini, Luis. 2018. "Blessing and Curse: Incumbency and Democratic Accountability in Latin America." Book manuscript.

Schneider, Mark. 2019. "Do Local Leaders Know Their Voters? A Test of Guessability in India." *Electoral Studies* 61: 1–12.

Schuster, Christian. 2016. "What Causes Patronage Reform? It Depends on the Type of Civil Service Reform." *Public Administration* 94 (4): 1094–104.

2017. "Legal Reform Need Not Come First: Merit-based Civil Service Management in Law and Practice." *Public Administration* 95 (3): 571–88.

Schuster, Christian, Javier Fuenzalida, Jan Meyer-Sahling, Kim Sass Mikkelsen, and Noam Titelman. 2020. "Encuesta Nacional de Funcionarios En Chile: Evidencia Para Un Servicio Público Más Motivado, Satisfecho, Comprometido y Ético." Informe preparado para la Dirección Nacional del Servicio Civil, Santiago, Chile. www .serviciocivil.cl/wp-content/uploads/2020/01/Encuesta-Nacional-de-Funcionarios-Informe-General-FINAL-15ene2020-1.pdf

Scott, James C. 1972. "Patron-Client Politics and Political Change in Southeast Asia." *American Political Science Review* 66 (1): 91–113.

Seligson, Mitchell A. 2002. "The Impact of Corruption on Regime Legitimacy: A Comparative Study of Four Latin American Countries." *The Journal of Politics* 64 (2): 408–33.

Sells, Cameron. 2020. "Building Parties From City Hall: Party Membership and Municipal Government in Brazil." *The Journal of Politics* 82 (4): 1576–89.

Shefter, Martin. 1977. "Party and Patronage: Germany, England, and Italy." *Politics & Society* 7 (4): 403–51.

Snyder, Richard. 2001. "Scaling Down: The Subnational Comparative Method." *Studies in Comparative International Development* 36 (1): 93–110.

Sologuren, Ximena Soruco. 2014. "Burocracia Plurinacional." In *Composición Social Del Estado Plurinacional: Hacia La Descolonización de La Burocracia*, edited by Ximena Soruco Sologuren, Daniela Franco Pinto, and Mariela Durán, 19–92. La Paz: Centro de Investigaciones Sociales.

Sologuren, Ximena Soruco, Daniela Franco Pinto, and Mariela Durán, eds. 2014. *Composición Social Del Estado Plurinacional: Hacia La Descolonización de La Burocracia*. La Paz: Centro de Investigaciones Sociales.

Stasavage, David. 2005. "Democracy and Education Spending in Africa." *American Journal of Political Science* 49 (2): 343–58.

Stokes, Susan C. 2005. "Perverse Accountability: A Formal Model of Machine Politics with Evidence from Argentina." *American Political Science Review* 99 (3): 315–25.

2007. "Political Clientelism." In *The Oxford Handbook of Comparative Politics*, edited by Carles Boix and Susan C. Stokes, 648–674. Oxford: Oxford University Press.

2009. "Pork, by Any Other Name … Building a Conceptual Scheme of Distributive Politics." Paper Presented at the American Political Science Association Conference Meeting, Toronto, Canada.

Stokes, Susan C., Thad Dunning, Marcelo Nazareno, and Valeria Brusco. 2013. *Brokers, Voters, and Clientelism: The Puzzle of Distributive Politics*. New York: Cambridge University Press.

Strazza, Luciano 2012. "República Dominicana." In *Informe Barometro de La Profesionalización Del Empleo Público En Centroamérica y República Dominicana No. 2*, edited by Francisco Longo, 25–64. Santo Domingo: AECID, FLACSO and SICA.

Szwarcberg, Mariela. 2009. *Making Local Democracy: Political Machines, Clientelism, and Social Networks in Argentina*. PhD Dissertation, The University of Chicago.

2012. "Uncertainty, Political Clientelism, and Voter Turnout in Latin America: Why Parties Conduct Rallies in Argentina." *Comparative Politics* 45 (1): 88–106.

2015. *Mobilizing Poor Voters: Machine Politics, Clientelism, and Social Networks in Argentina*. New York: Cambridge University Press.

Ting, Michael M., James M. Snyder Jr, Shigeo Hirano, and Olle Folke. 2013. "Elections and Reform: The Adoption of Civil Service Systems in the US States." *Journal of Theoretical Politics* 25 (3): 363–87.

Toral, Guillermo. 2019. "The Benefits of Patronage: How the Political Appointment of Bureaucrats Can Enhance Their Accountability and Effectiveness." *Working Paper*. https://doi.org/10.2139/ssrn.3462459.

2020. "Turnover: How Electoral Accountability Disrupts the Bureaucracy and Service Delivery." *Working Paper*. www.guillermotoral.com/turnover.pdf

Toro, Sergio. 2017. "El Vínculo Distrital de Los Parlamentarios: Continuidad y Cambio de La Estructura de Intermediación Local En Chile." In *La Columna Vertebral Fracturada: Revisitando Intermediarios Políticos En Chile*, edited by Juan Pablo Luna and Rodrigo Mardones, 177–200. Santiago de Chile: RIL Editores.

Valdebenito Pedrero, Sebastián. 2017. "¿Cuántos Trabajadores Emplea El Estado de Chile? Problematización y Orden de Magnitud de La Contratación a Honorarios." In *Empleo Público En Chile: ¿Trabajo Decente En El Estado? Apuntes Para El Debate*, edited by Sonia Yáñez and Irene Rojas, 35–54. Santiago de Chile: Serie Libros Flacso – Chile.

Van de Walle, Nicolas. 2007. "Meet the New Boss, Same as the Old Boss? The Evolution of Political Clientelism in Africa." In *Patrons, Clients and Policies: Patterns of Democratic Accountability and Political Competition*, edited by Herbert Kitschelt and Steven I. Wilkinson, 50–67. New York: Cambridge University Press.

Vommaro, Gabriel. 2007. "'Acá No Conseguís Nada Si No Estás En Política'. Los Sectores Populares y La Participación En Espacios Barriales de Sociabilidad Política." *Anuario de Estudios En Antropología Social* 2006: 161–78.

Vommaro, Gabriel and Hélène Combes. 2019. *El clientelismo político: Desde 1950 hasta nuestros días*. Buenos Aires: Siglo XXI Editores.

Vommaro, Gabriel and Julieta Quirós. 2011. "'Usted Vino Por Su Propia Decisión': Repensar El Clientelismo En Clave Etnográfica." *Desacatos* 36: 65–84.

Waisbord, Silvio. 1996. "Secular Politics: The Modernization of Argentine Electioneering." In *Politics, Media, and Modern Democracy: An International Study of Innovations in Electoral Campaigning and Their Consequences*, edited by David L. Swanson and Paolo Mancini, 207–25. Westport, CT: Praeger.

Wang, Chin-Shou and Charles Kurzman. 2007. "The Logistics: How to Buy Votes." In *Elections for Sale: The Causes and Consequences of Vote Buying*, edited by Frederic Charles Schaffer, 61–78. Boulder, CO: Lynne Rienner Pub.

Weber, Max. 1978. *Economy and Society: An Outline of Interpretive Sociology*. Vol. 1. Berkeley: University of California Press.

Weitz-Shapiro, Rebecca. 2006. "Partisanship and Protest: The Politics of Workfare Distribution in Argentina." *Latin American Research Review* 41 (3): 122–47.

  2008. "The Local Connection: Local Government Performance and Satisfaction with Democracy in Argentina." *Comparative Political Studies* 41 (3): 285–308.

  2012. "What Wins Votes: Why Some Politicians Opt out of Clientelism." *American Journal of Political Science* 56 (3): 568–83.

  2014. *Curbing Clientelism in Argentina: Politics, Poverty, and Social Policy*. New York: Cambridge University Press.

Wilson, James Q. 1961. "The Economy of Patronage." *The Journal of Political Economy* 69 (4): 369–80.

Wolff, Jonas. 2018. "Political Incorporation in Measures of Democracy: A Missing Dimension (and the Case of Bolivia)." *Democratization* 25 (4): 692–708.

Wolfinger, Raymond E. 1972. "Why Political Machines Have Not Withered Away and Other Revisionist Thoughts." *The Journal of Politics* 34 (2): 365–98.

World Bank. 2000. "Bolivia: From Patronage to a Professional State." Report No. 20115–BO.

Xu, Guo. 2018. "The Costs of Patronage: Evidence from the British Empire." *American Economic Review* 108 (11): 3170–98.

Zarazaga, Rodrigo. 2014. "Brokers beyond Clientelism: A New Perspective through the Argentine Case." *Latin American Politics and Society* 56 (3): 23–45.

2015. "Plugged in Brokers: A Model of Vote-Buying and Access to Resources." *Journal of Applied Economics* 18 (2): 369–90.

2016. "Party Machines and Voter-Customized Rewards Strategies." *Journal of Theoretical Politics* 28 (4): 678–701.

Zarazaga, Rodrigo and Lucas Ronconi. 2018. *Conurbano Infinito: Actores Políticos y Sociales, Entre La Presencia Estatal y La Ilegalidad.* Buenos Aires: Siglo Veintiuno Editores.

Zucco, Cesar. 2010. "Conditional Cash Transfers and Voting Behavior: Redistribution and Clientelism in Developing Democracies." Princeton University. Unpublished Manuscript.

2013. "When Payouts Pay off: Conditional Cash Transfers and Voting Behavior in Brazil 2002–10." *American Journal of Political Science* 57 (4): 810–22.

Zuvanic, Laura, Mercedes Iacoviello, and Ana Laura Rodríguez Gusta. 2010. "The Weakest Link: The Bureaucracy and Civil Service Systems in Latin America." In *How Democracy Works: Political Institutions, Actors, and Arenas in Latin American Policymaking*, edited by Carlos Scartascini, Ernesto Stein, and Mariano Tommasi, 147–76. Washington, DC: Inter-American Development Bank.

Index